THE MAYS

TWENTY THREE

Varsity Publications Ltd
Old Examination Hall
Free School Lane
Cambridge CB2 3RF

First published 2015 by Varsity Publications Ltd

ISBN 978-0-902240-46-9

Designed and typeset
in Kalinga and Georgia
by Adam Thelwall

Printed and bound
by Y Lolfa Cyf. in Talybont, Wales

Original concept by
Peter Ho Davies, Adrian Woolfson, Ron Dimant

British Library Cataloguing in Publication Data
A CIP catalogue record of this book
is available from the British Library

Further copies of this book and other titles in the series can be bought through most booksellers or direct from Varsity Publications at the address above or at:

www.varsity.co.uk/themays

THE MAYS TWENTY THREE

GUEST EDITED BY

ALISON TURNBULL

QUENTIN BLAKE

VARSITY PUBLICATIONS

We need to learn to see surfaces.

We need to learn to see.

We need to learn to see finally an absence of meaning in all things.

Meaninglessness here is not a state we try to escape, but an achievement,

the achievement of the ordinary, transfigured through fiction.

We need to welcome the void, embrace the void.

Simon Critchley

EDITORIALS

Emily Fitzell ii

Quentin Blake iv

Alison Turnbull vi

CONTENT

HELEN IS OTHER PEOPLE
Dòmhnall Iain Dòmhnallach 1

SCHRÖDINGER'S PISTACHIO
Steve Wright 9

KINAESTHESIA I
Matt Broomfield 11

SONNET FROM THE INFERNO
Harry Cochrane 15

FIRE EATERS
Barney Couch 17

19 MORNING ABSTRACT AND MORNING STUDY #12
Dominic Hand

23 AMERICAN SHORT STORY
Mathilde Sergent

27 TN22
Ruth O'Connell Brown

29 EXODUS DRAMATICULE TAKEN FROM THE PLAY 'NEW EDEN'
Rebekah-Miron Clayton

35 WHAT IF EVERYTHING IN THE WORLD WERE A MISUNDERSTANDING?
Isaac Nowell

37 FROM DARWIN'S BURDEN (1)
Emily Everest-Phillips

41 OUR BODY
David Miller

47 HOUSE PARTY (FROM SIM CITY)
Alex Paseltiner

PERCUSSIVE INTERVENTION
First Year Architecture Students 49

CHEESE-BRANDING
Emma Levin 51

KAMAU BRATHWAITE DOES SOME FACEBOOK STALKING, CIRCA 1950
Ruth O'Connell Brown 55

FROM DARWIN'S BURDEN (2)
Emily Everest-Phillips 57

KINAESTHESIA III
Matt Broomfield 59

DADDY SHOT THE DOG
Jim Hilton 65

AFTERMATH I AND III
Sophie Sparkes 67

69 ALL IN THE FAMILY
Jonathan Crossley

77 FICCIONES TYPOGRAFIKA (614-616)
Dani Ismailov

79 PARTICULAR CONTROVERSIES INCLUDE...
Henry St Leger

ACKNOWLEDGEMENTS

85 Editorial Team

86 Sponsors

89 Contributors

segregation of poetry, prose and visual arts will be removed

in an attempt to move 'form' forward by spurning the tired standard divisions and returning to a blank & receptive canvas

attention will be turned back to the medium itself

in order to reengage with the multiplicitous ways in which we (& our work) speak, perform, reside (etc.) within the pages of a book

the anthology will be presented as fractious and living

call for submissions 2015

EMILY FITZELL

anthologies can be dusty places

(unsurprising for a legacy of the Georgian poets)

and so, like anything trying to build from within the bounds of tradition, here lies a project vulnerable to complacency, cliché and conservatism.

the mays has always structured itself around form. for ten years, poetry and prose appeared in separate volumes. both have shared a spine with visual art since 2003, though their separation has withstood.

: - sections - building - structures - from - formal silhouettes - :

in this anthology, we have avoided complacent, unambiguous work that is too preoccupied with its own self-containment and pristine form to deal hard and straight with the reader.

we have a new curatorial structure - one open to heterogeneity.

it acknowledges reading as a form of visual creativity.

it is structured by the interrelations of the works themselves.

it was with this in mind that alison and quentin were approached to be guest editors.
as part of that process, they were asked to create a response to the submissions.
their contributions announce the anthology's aim to encourage
exchange between mixed sources of narrative.

as you move around inside these covers, navigating your way through page, ink, acrylic, wax, pixel, cloth and skin, you will form a poetry of your own.
you will translate lines into text and textures, building your own architecture out of these works and their subtle interactions.

as you let these works unravel, you may notice some fraying round their edges.
for in their fierce commitment to emotion and intellect, these artists were unafraid of getting things wrong. all demonstrate great courage in their readiness to engage in the dialogue where criticism might happen.

in their occasional misprisions lie promise and personality.

QUENTIN BLAKE

the works that appear in these pages are certainly varied and distinctive, and know very well what they are about.

what I had not quite expected was the confidence displayed by so many of the contributions.

where one might have perhaps expected introspection we are presented with something acted out.

i wonder if these writers and artists can do it again.

v

ALISON TURNBULL

her tights all brown
big white hat makes me look like a baker
a single purple tear
too pink for the grey flesh
with her scoured pink knuckles
only the white is pickled
into the other green of the surroundings
roses flew from the papered wall
our soul's rotten black
raindrops tinged electric red
tarmac black
solid black kick start
somewhere in a saloon bar the gold fruit liquor
periods bleed blue
wear a lot of black
black article somewhere random
purple fake fur coats
leapt from his purple sheets knocking
heat rose he had read
white bread turning them
slid his thin white feet
two grey and one green
emblazoned with stencilled white
rust to autumn pink
twirled his hair brown
giving downtown a pink backdrop
employee uniforms black
with a red chili above the left breast
the green glow of the exit
leaving the sea of blue for the edge of black
and light

HELEN IS OTHER PEOPLE

Dòmhnall Iain Dòmhnallach

1 mam shat herself again the day.

a smelt her before a seen her. a woss just in the door, throwin my pinny off something desperate, an it woss pure hoofin like. a walked down the hall, past all the wee pastel an sugar paper drawins me an bobby had made when we were wee, an pushed open the door. it had trickled down her tights, all brown an that. a just sort of stared for a second. mam didn't say fuk all.

--- bobby woss posed to be looking after yew the day mam -- a says a her, as a tidy her up. ama spare yews the deetz, mam deserves at least a wee bit a dignity.

once upon a time mam would off been what yewsd call a decent wee piece. see a woss lucky in the genes department, ama say that. bobby must off taken after the bodach coss his face is wider frontways than sideways, an sgot like basically no neck. but a, eilidh, got mams face an figure, thank fuk. when yews full time carin like, yew end up eatin like just frozen foods an that, an fuk me if a woss gonna find time in the day to go runnin.

the tights were pretty well fuked, soes a just chucked them out, figurin a could order another pack off a bajillion online. she needed a skoosh now a course. mam needed half carryin a the skoosher, an there woss a railin like she woss seventy or something. that woss about all the twats offof the comhairle had given us. a gave her a bit a privacy, an sat on the toilet seat readin my kindle, while mam leaned back in her chair, an skooshed herself. we used a close the door [not lock it, we're no daft] an let her use the bathroom alone, but she slipped an the ambulance had to come an stuff, so nowadays am sitting there, waitin but no watchin.

--- so how wis work eilidh, ma dearie? --- she says a me from behind the curtain. the curtains no much use coss the water salready pure spreadin, an there's a fukoff massive pool a it on the floor.

--- och, as per mam. neilina the maneater woss on top form the day. askin after yew an all ---

--- sgood a her. shes a good soul, old nelly ---

then just the sound of the water sprayin like the pissin a the rain.

mam woss probly worryin likes what a says to neilina. but what a says is always the same. same old. same old. sall yews can say.

a helped mam towel herself off, then a had to help her with the moisturizer cos otherwise when she puts the clothes on she gets all itchinanscratchin an comes out all real red raw like the colour a lobster claw in the pot.

a takes her toilet an that, then a puts her a bed, an she asks where is bobby an a says fuktoff somewhere, an am pure fumin as a says it. mam likes the soaps on when she's on bed, so a puts on river shitty an leave her to it.

a phones my brother, majorly pissed off yew know. --- stoo fuktup bobby, leavin mam like that. she could do anything a herself. but am talkin the answer phone coss the stupetface deserves to waste his credit checkin voicemail ---

a sits in my room, an tries a listen a music. but a can only ever have wan headphone in at wan time, with my ear nearest the door, wide open listenin mamway. am listenin to mcr first album before they got shite an mainstream. a sort of whispersingalong. we only have dial up so a can go on the internet, in case bobby phones house like. a have my book on my kindle which am trying a read, but the words are no goin in. a have to read each paragraph like a bajillion times, an yet still like blurrin everywhere. mam's tele still on, but spretty standard. a know she sleeps a that.

when bobby gets in a want a slap him cross the face, like slap him pure hard so he's gone all fukinblackeyeredcheek like. a can still smell the shite on ma hands, it never goes away. its no like yewsd imagine shite smell, but more like the smell a being too clean, like not niceanbathroomsmellies clean but like pure hospital clean.

a fall asleep a the sounds a mam's snores from the opendoor interminglin with gerard way.

• • •

sbobbys turn again a wake mam up an look after her, seein as a sgot work again. but bobbys no up yet, so that means its my turn to wake up bobby. a walks into his room an its pure hoofin even worse than mams. a sees his lynx can a the side a the bed, an thinks for a jiffy, ama like a spray him with it cold to wake him up. so a grabs his can, an twizzlethetop round, a picks some skin he's no gonna miss. an sprays him right there on the upper arm, rightupcloseanpersonal like freezin liquid nitrogen.

an he's up an screamin in seconds, tears wellin up there.

now a slaps him for good measure.

--- don yew walk out on mam again bobby ---

--- what ye do that fir eilidh -- he says. since he started at the big school, sbeen talkin pure weegie.

--- don yew throw a fukin stewich bobby. what yew do that for? when a comes home shes soiled herself ffs ---

--- yir no mam eilidh, whys ye think ye can give us a row --

--- coss yewer a fuktup wee shit, bobby campbell, an yew left yewer mam there alone an scared so yew could go off an do fuk knows no wan wants to know ---

--- wis she screamin agin? ---

--- na, she woss silent, even worse. just sitting there in her own cachd, starin. starin. ---

an a woss givin the wee bugger pure evils for good measure. he woss sitting there all thirteen years in some daft breakfastanworsestain celtic jammies.

--- yews knows the score --- now a says, standin up all pinnied up an ready to fukoff a work.

--- aye --- he says, nodding, but no getting outta bed coss hes the age were hes no wantin me seein him.

--- cheerio, bobby --- a says, badcopgonegoodcop, an a fuksoff out the door an my ownsome workways.

• • •

neilina the maneater salready there when a walk into the bakery.

my pinny an ma big white hat makes me look like a baker like, but inactualsfact a dont go near the bakin. the bakery stuff comes in the back of a lorry every mornin, an me an neilina are there to smile an sell it.

the van salready here too, an neilina the maneater is a ceilidhin with lemon frizzle who drives the van. we call her that on account a her manky hair an her jaundice. lemon frizzles man father monkeynut sthere carryin boxes a bread an pies an fruitcakes into the main shop. a helps him cos a likes monkeynut. they called him that in PE in skool on account a him been born with wan ball an it bein the size a them nuts the old cailleachs give yew on Halloween. but lemon frizzles his housekeeper an woshes his XXL boxers an swears sall relative. hes the priest obvs an lemon frizzles his housekepper, there woss meetings with the bishop an everything back in the day but they tells everywan theres no nothing dodge goin on.

monkeynuts dry unlike his missus. we says tometoyewtoeachother like the chucklebrothers like. an a get sall the laughs, an a bit of flour on me, down my pinnie soes a looks like a real life baker.

--- for yewer mam, eilidh --- the priest says --- handin me a wee thing of lemon frizzle's lemon drizzle. the bakery business started when lemon frizzle used to take her lemon drizzle a coffee mornings an a tea an cake after church, an all the older biddies got sall pisstoff at her coss everywan wants to eat only her cake.

--- yewd need to be a sour wee bitch to make a cake out of lemons, an she drinks too, an that great whore a babylon the priests housekeeper. not in my day! --- swoss fukin not on some a the abuse she got from the cailleachs.

but lemon drizzle woss dead keen on watchin the apprentice on the box, so starts off the business, an soon the vans too small, an she's setting up a wee shop an getting her best pal neilina the middle aged maneater to run it an then eilidh campbell whose no goin school on account a her mother soes ideal choice to be the other girlonthetill...

a stuffs the wee slice off lemon drizzle in my pockets, knowin itll get all squishtansquasht but that just makes it taste better. the banterins done between lemon frizzle an neilina an she's a orderin monkeynut back the way he came. the two off us are watchin them drive away into the sunrise.

neilina puts on the wireless an we're a jiggin the two off us while we morninsweepthefloor to the music. a likes to dance when am in the shop, a like to get all loosened an forget like.

dozy rosie comes in at ten from the school where she been washin the floors earlier on an gets herself a macaroni pie which neilina heats in the microwave an then wraps in bogroll an gives her sayin bon appeteat like sall a serious restaurant like. we gets a couple a old biddies in gettin ceilidhin supplies for the visitors, an theys take forfukinevs to choose a sultana an cherry cake. they an neilina the maneater are gabbin away in gaelic, soes a takes the chance to have my break out the back where I puts my sens in my ear an listen more mcr. am lovin the peace,
5 theres my head goinupdownanallaround. but a wish ad tooken my kindle coss theres only chat magazine a read an a picture of a man who ate his own nipple on the front.

we close up two o clock, after helen the melon an her three boyfriends dim jim an small dòl an robbie the jobbie pop in for curry pies for the lads, an a scotch pie --- for the lady --- as neilina says, again talkin posh an pretendin we're in a restaurant like.

shes suchgoodfun neilina a sometimes wish a woss suchgoodfun when am standin there in the back with my earphones in an neilinas on a jolly with tall paul on his motor bike to pick up more supplies. everywan says thems an item, been onoff over the years. a wish a had an item, but all a got is mam an bobby. a walks back home with my earphones in likin gettin surroundsound for thelasttimethatday. bobbys no in when a get in, too fukin typic, but a smells nothing so am safe a reckon. a pops in see mam, an omgzamgreetinitsdadalloveragain, an shes lying there on the floor, coldcrystalclear, deadangone. a can see where shes collapsed. a can see theres shite on her tights again. a can see where she had her last slevvers out a her mouth.

but a feel fukall onlythisfukoffmassivesense of relief. am thinkin bobby must off fuked off a school again the day, an she must off fallen but all am thinking is am ohsofreetofly. a look at my mam an think stoo fuktup.

a go into the kitchen where a know mams purse is an leave out a hundred quid for bobby to keep him going on the counter. a write out the number a the chinkies an the chippy soes to make sure he eats a balanced diet. then a take the credit card from the purse, an walk to the road end, where a wait in the bus stop til the mong-from-tong draws up the bus speaking all leodhasach highpitchanshit a me. a gets on the bus an sa bajillion minutes too long whiles he speaking all leodhasach, an then we're driving lochmaddy where a go up gangway as footpassenger onto uig ferry, an hour an a half over minch, an then through the slicedupdicedup geography of skye, then down the long clearance saled glens a the west highlands, hittin glasgow where am planning a be...

...sixteeeeeeeeenanfree...

• • •

swhat a would do if a were neilinathemaneater.

stead a sit there with my earphones in an watch mams body lying there til bobby comes back an then we're a cuddlianahuggin an hes like a wee baby again.

--- yew sneak off a go a school again, bobby? --- a says.

he says aye, lips all tremblin again, an am worrying ama set him off again. a send him offskee a his room a try an sleep.

a take off mams tights, an puts on some new wans soes theyre no all shit-stained. a dunnoes who yewser posed to phone when yews finds a dead body. no the ambulance coss shesadonedeal, no the police cos it wossnt a murder, an no the coastguard coss shes drylanded, an no the fire brigade cos theres no wan on the ilant.

stead a phone father monkeynut the priest an neilina the maneater, an lemon frizzles comes round too coss she's nosy like.

we says a rosary sittin round the kitchen.

a member when mam used to tell bobby when he sticked his tongue me that the virgin mary would be cryin. a wonder if she'd be cryin the now, with all us ringaringarosaryin for her. but then we're down to business. bobby wants to keep on at the school, an neilina the maneater says shes gonna take him on permanent like. the priests talking all funerals. an lemon frizzlel do the caterin, like even for a discount.

then coss a got no food, a offer round the last pack a ready salted crisps in the multipack. Its ownbrand from the cope, coss walkers too dear. theys are bestbeforeended, which is pretty spot on really a thinks.

then bobby goes stay with neilina the maneater the night cos its no good for him to be round the body, while a mind the house. a sits in the house by myselfies for the first time in major yonks, an am listening music in both headphobes...

...sixteeeeeeeeenanfreeeeeeeeeeeeeeeeeeeeeeeeeeeeeeeeeeeeeeeeee
eeeeeeeeeeeeeeeeeeeeeeeeeeeeeeeeeeeeeeeeeeeeeeeeeeeeeeeeeeeeee-
eeeeeeeeeeeeeeeeeeeeeeeeeeeeeeeeeeeeeeeeeeeeeeeeeeeeeeeeeeeeeeeeeeee-
eeeeeeeeeeeeeeeeeeeeeeeeeeeeeeeeeeeeeeeeeeeeeeeeeeeeeeeeeeeeeeeeeeee-
eeeeeeeeeeeeeeeeeeeeeeeee...

DÒMHNALL IAIN DÒMHNALLACH

8

SCHRÖDINGER'S PISTACHIO

Steve Wright

i

seeing it all in a nut
on the palm of my hand.
fingers frisk for the
split in the shell.
five minutes of
frustration, a cut
on my thumb.

the halves fall apart
to reveal infinity in
nothingness. and
no fecking nut.

ii *lazarus*

an update on
the nut situation.
crisis averted,
took me to lay
empty the whole bag
to see it shyly sitting there,
a single purple tear
with a raised groove at top.

it was salty and delicious.
i licked my fingers after,
appreciating it from
beyond the grave;
running my fingers
through the dust
and tearing out
another page.

iii *inspiration*

i swear i ate every nut from the bowl,
stirring to find one rounded with
fullness amongst the halves.
i know i should have a separate
plate for the shells, but it gives
my fingers something to sift. and,
finding it for the fifth time,
the last nut tastes sweeter.
like i've stolen something from myself.

KINAESTHESIA I

Matt Broomfield

Boys carry knives because boys carry knives. Boys smoke draw because boys smoke draw. And boys throw stones at the tall house, because other boys throw stones. It is safer to walk with a knife than to be the one without. It is safer to throw, if not the first stone, then the second or the third.

An old man lives alone in a tall house. Every day he looks at his left hand all morning, from breakfast until lunch. For breakfast he eats half a dozen pickled eggs all in a row; for lunch he eats spaghetti hoops, microwaved on toast in winter but cold out of the can in summer. All afternoon he looks at his right hand, then for tea he eats fish fingers and tinned peaches until his heart feels like it will burst. In the mornings, he tends to burp a lot. In the afternoon, he is more prone to sneezing fits, though often as the day wears on a burp often begins to play around his lips once more. He has a rocking chair by the microwave but he seldom rocks while he sits and stares at his hands. Sometimes children throw stones at his house.

A lady from the council comes in to do for him every third Friday of the month. When she whistles she whistles a single, low note, in a piercing exhalation of breath. The tone does not rise or fall. The old man is in love with her, almost as much as he is in love with the rough skin around the cuticle of his right thumb. His love has never made itself known to him, and he is aware of it only a curiously unspecified yearning occurring on certain Friday mornings around 11AM, somewhere between the secondary and tertiary knuckles of his left index finger, often during the liver spot. It is a yearning which has nothing to do with pickled eggs.

Officially the lady is a cleaner, and she is only paid to make sure his house is clean, but the old man never disturbs anything or makes a mess. So the cleaner clips his nails for him instead, finger and toe. Compared to most of the nails she sees they are clean and kempt, too pink for the grey flesh in which they are set. His toenails are as yellowed as any she sees, a constellation with the simple linearity of Orion's Belt. She bites her own nails as she works, chewing them into bloody proximity with her flesh. If she comes early on a Friday, he will offer her his penultimate pickled egg. If she turns up late, it does not really make any difference. In the Second World War he killed an unarmed man at point-blank range with a pistol, but this does not really make any difference either. In the early evening, he watches her walk out to her Peugot 206, then returns his attention to the callus on the left-hand side of his right-hand thumb. Perhaps he will have ketchup with his fish finger sandwich today.

The boys who threw stones were not bad boys, and they did not do it out of cruelty, or even out of indifference. The throwing of stones was their boredom, in the long heat of August afternoons. Their lives reverberated with the clatter of coke-cans kicked down the road. They did not aim to smash the windows of the house, but if one of the big boys put a lump of brick through the kitchen window, he would of course claim he had been trying to smash the kitchen window all along. They would run, but not far. From the path past the allotments they could see the police coming along the main road that ran along the north edge of the estate. Old people never called the police anyway, but once they reached the path past the allotments they knew for sure that they were safe. Then they would stop, laugh and draw breath, and one of the big boys would light a Windsor Blue that he had bummed from his brother, who was bigger still.

The old man thinks as though he is looking through thick glass. There is thick fluffy dust on the glasses case beside his bed; he does not permit the cleaner to enter into his bedroom, and nor does he think that she would offer. They must have some secrets from one another; he does not invite her upstairs, and she does not reveal to him the meaning of the flat tone which she whistles as she chews through the nail on his big toe with a pair of industrial nail clippers. He hopes it does not mean that she is thinking of other things.

The wall of his bedroom is buttressed with jars of pickled eggs. He does not love pickled eggs, which are treacherous to the touch. The taste is good but they are too liable to squirt shamefully from his crabbed fingers and fall to the carpeted floor. He eats six pickled eggs every day and so every one hundred and eighty pickled eggs, give or take, then he will hear the cleaner open the low gate to his property and rap on the door with her scoured-pink knuckles.

There are two dozen pickled eggs in a half-gallon jar, which is the heaviest that the old man can comfortably carry down his narrow stairs from the top of the tall house to the kitchen, where he lines up his six condemned eggs each morning. This means that when the cleaner comes there are normally eight jars waiting in neat ranks by the front door to be taken out to the bin, smelling faintly of vinegar.

The cleaner does not know why he does not take them out to the bin himself, for she knows he is strong enough to walk to the shops to buy his fish fingers and his tins, to say nothing of the walk to the lean-to at the top of the allotments where another old man sells jars of pickled eggs to make enough money to buy a thick pipe tobacco he has mail-ordered from Germany. (The secret of his pickled eggs is the thin slits he slashes in their sides with a razor blade, allowing the vinegar to soak deep into the yolk. Lesser egg-picklers make pickled eggs where only the white is pickled; his eggs are always pickled to their heart.)

Maybe it is because the old man likes to play with the jars in the week, arranging them into castles and mountain ranges and plummeting gorges. When the cleaner comes she knows that the eight jars will be surrounded by thirty empty tins of spaghetti hoops and forty empty tins of peaches (for the old man sometimes has an extra tin or two at the weekends). Maybe he builds these into landscapes and cityscapes too. Maybe he is simply too tired, by the evening, to shuffle to the bin with armfuls of Birdseye cardboard sleeves and razor-sharp tins. The number of tins and jars and fish-finger packets is always the same and does not vary.

The old man has not always counted out his days like this.

SONNET FROM THE *INFERNO* CANTO XX

Harry Cochrane

I am doing everything I can to
make poetry accommodate new sorrow.
I saw them coming, wordlessly, in a row.
Tiresias androgynous; enter
the cobbler-turned-astrologer Asdente
and others who had confused the straight and narrow
and found lunamancy and Tarot.
There was Michael Scot, and there was Manto,
on whom my master discoursed and pronounced
his city's foundress, yet a diviner.
It didn't matter who: their tears rinsed
their arse-cracks, hamstrings, backs of knees –
their heads were screwed on 180°
which had looked to make themselves diviner.

FIRE EATERS

17

Barney Couch

MORNING ABSTRACT AND MORNING STUDY #12

Dominic Hand

This part in which you breathe grows around itself
and into the other / green of the surroundings
for whatever ignites your iris
this evening is wholly a part of its chain-
link of sound

Already you feel something letting up,
Late in the season, as familiar sounds recall
Forgotten faces like the waning day. They migrate
Through the city, or egress
New passages, down the old stone walls.
And by the open windows catch
Beached glimpses of the whole.

Like desire we come back to them,
Lush and tapering with vowels like flaze
Plots of delphinium, lily-tinged evocations of romanticism,
Threshing the buds from the verbal mess.
New life stirs these sequences.
Roses flow from the papered wall.

I know that I rely too much on my own
Beaded thoughts as they come to me,
When mostly what passes is the dull
March of the paragon. The glitz
Of pyrite blocking the path. And so enter
By side streets, and other centres
Of communication.

After all, in the dream, we are free to wander
At any time, into the courtyards and rooms of history,
And cast fresh angles from a diamond eye
Vaulting past with purifying reach;
As we come to rest in an open field,
Bleached by light, where the eyelids shut,
Creaseless and petalless,
And you a name among them.

AMERICAN SHORT STORY

Mathilde Sergent

It had nothing to do with being smart, getting out. You got out if you were incandescent, luminous like that pretty girl Heather who ended up on MTV and then, not long after, in a body bag on the wet end of the Hudson. SAT scores had nothing to do with it. There's no use wanting to get out when you know it's not about where you put your feet but the color of your soul. Our soul's rotten black—it's a hereditary condition, something dormant and vicious like HIV or measles. We farm the land. We hurt no one.

•

Mouths taste like cotton-candy, the rank heat of summer, and flies that died making return trips within the same square inch of air. Kissing has to be wet to be real. After a fight with his father Jim enlists. They send him a letter, which he has her read: apparently he's going to Afghanistan. We hug like we never learned how to. The sheets are sticky with sweat and sugar. We fuck and lie there, unsatisfied. The war is neither a good nor a bad thing. It toils with a blank mind, cruel without design. Perhaps, says our amputee English teacher, that is the worst kind of cruelty.

•

Kat works at the farm. Blackleg takes ten cows. One morning Kat finds the spotted one Daisy on the ground, swollen and dead. Jim sends a letter, you gotta get those animals their vaccines for gods sake. Secretly we think it is chance. Only chance keeps you alive. Any eagerness on either side is a damning thing. Kat sleeps with a trucker at Millie's diner; down there you shut your eyes and help out. The soul remains rotten, since rot can only be supplanted, not healed. We learn that our love rid of its violence is subpar. The effect of that revelation is minimal.

•

The statement has ceased to stand: we hurt no one. We hurt things and people, and we hurt. There is no blanket history but a reprieve, then a surrender. At landing Jim's mouth is marred. He can dissemble an AK47 in twenty seconds on a good day. This time our hug crushes bones. Our collateral damage is a hail of bullets through every window on a thirty mile radius. With the force of it we fall to the ground. Halting, we kiss.

•

Now there is value: we leave bruises even brushing. At the sink we stand so close we could be mistaken for each other. We are alone left at the farm, but there is no talk of defecting. The summer is hot like burning. We let the crops die; rivers dry, and old people die with the sigh of their fans. We are untouched by mercy. We remember: it had nothing to do with being smart, getting out. After all we knew that there was no leaving if you were truly born here. We get rings at the local K-mart, and an icecream cake to eat on cardboard plates on which 'Happy birthday' is written in neon colors.

•

The war is a serious matter. We go along with it. Kat twists the ring on a chain and keeps working. The farm is sold for too cheap. On permission Jim takes a bus to her doorstep and lies there like a dog until she comes back, leaning his head against his duffel. He eats the Poptarts in her fridge, fixes up her miserable garden shed. We are impervious to sorrow, but vulnerable to rage. Obama is de-throned; still the war goes on. There is no TV in the new house. All that there was left of beauty within us slowly fades.

•

We get a divorce one month before the end of the war. After the papers are signed and we get a burger at the local McDonalds, Jim asks a Coke for his wife and no-one corrects him. We lie in the same bed, unlawfully wedded. On the day of deployment, a counter-order is sent out. He shoulders the duffel anyway and starts down the asphalt road. The silence is close-knit like a storm. 'Cloudy,' she says. We the two of us are unstable beings. Kat goes back inside, maybe to get an umbrella.

MATHILDE SERGENT

TN22

27

Ruth O'Connell Brown

makes wing

light thickens and the crow wings its way to the rooky wood

your misquotations settle,

mind-silt

water insect
moon

in the background

a mound of earth, piled deep like the barrow of a Saxon king

the mist covers my knees now, not my face

I am still not taller than the bracken.

EXODUS DRAMATICULE

TAKEN FROM THE PLAY 'NEW EDEN'

Rebekah-Miron Clayton

Actors required: Director Led

- Declare the praises of him who called you out of darkness into his won derful light
- Stiletto
- Laura
- My grandad sometimes calls me sweetpea.
- A cold January evening
- I've got long legs, which only makes skirts look much shorter
- Em
- Beats by Dre.
- We never once noticed the ¬¬¬¬¬¬ tree lights above the shop windows
- Raindrops tinged electric red
- Lilah
- Mascara to her jawline

- Tearing the rancid skin from my ashen face
- Only to watch it slither back over the wounds I create.
- Tarmac black
- Jack?
- *One hard stamp.*
-
- They will soar on wings like eagles; they will run and not grow weary
- David?
- Those shots we downed to drown out the ice caps.
- Michael...
- I don't care where she works up an appetite, as long as she comes home for dinner
- Shape shifters
- It was another Saturday, the 18th this time
-
- There is such weakness in what I had imagined to be strength.
- Christian
- I'm always game for a laugh
- Back hunched, his body shakes, a great bear...
- Sobbing. There's always that.
-
- Waging a war against the soul
- Sarah can show a guy a good time, y'know?
- *One hard stamp.*
- Piggy
- Did it give you relief?
- Alice?

EXODUS DRAMATICULE

- The ink dances with my rubies, colliding within me.
- Lost
- After you've drunk a bit, you forget to keep shifting your skirt down...
- Lost
- Sophie
- And the king will desire your beauty. Since he is your lord, bow to him.
- Lost
- Default, Apex, Chimes, Summit, Radiate, Waves...
- Rippling in the darkness
- I am so very bare, unannounced, now shaded in your sighs.
- Sigh
- The lights in the bathroom are always a sharp reminder
-
- JAMES?
- The smell of sweat
- Catch me if you can.
- Katherine...
- 10 10 13
- After the sugar rush shock of your words, colliding with mine in the universe between our hushed lips...
- Where did our tongues learn this?
- She's 15
- Conquered
- I am nothing
- Fluorescent
- Deep ravines landscaped across these cheekbones
- Split down the middle

- I cannot be sure who you are in love with.
- Charlotte.
- I am wounded
- Daisy, Eva, Bea, Mara, May...?
- The body that is sown is perishable, it is raised imperishable
-
- *One hard stamp.*
- I have been telling you of my existence
-
- Electric dawn by the roadside
- Skull weeds
- Silent
- Skin graft
- He will wipe every tear from their eyes.
- A splintered viola soaked in cells
- Robert, Lucinda, Gemma, Samson, Bella, Ella, Rick, Daniel, Nathaniel, Delilah?
- Listen
- *One hard stamp.*
- A great beast
- My ankles wade in a heated 'substancelessness'
- Carcass
- Barely a bubblegum burst.
- Slain
- The memory of blood rush
- I am slightly concerned that I may fold in half right the way through myself.
- Pain in the left side
- Solid black kick start

EXODUS DRAMATICULE

- Heart to heart?
- Find the spaces in which it hides
- Honey
- Lead breaths
- Those shatter patterns
- Don't I know you?
- Finger tip grip
- Pulse drags
- Deep throat
- Safety jaws
- Tipping my grip
- Longways
- A hurtling in my bones.

- End -

REBEKAH-MIRON CLAYTON

34

WHAT IF EVERYTHING IN THE WORLD WERE A MISUNDERSTANDING?

Isaac Nowell

Luxuriant aphasia, drawn out
as if another drew it out. You felt

a stark deferral of voice, as if vicarious-
ly spooled in oil. You felt,

without, as if another. Delicate,
somewhere in a saloon-bar, the gold, fruit-

liquor poured. You bruised
your collar bone and believed

in Edmund Spenser. 'Maculate, unless
unseen,' they said with a wink and

a punch (in the brilliant desert).

FROM DARWIN'S BURDEN

Emily Everest-Phillips

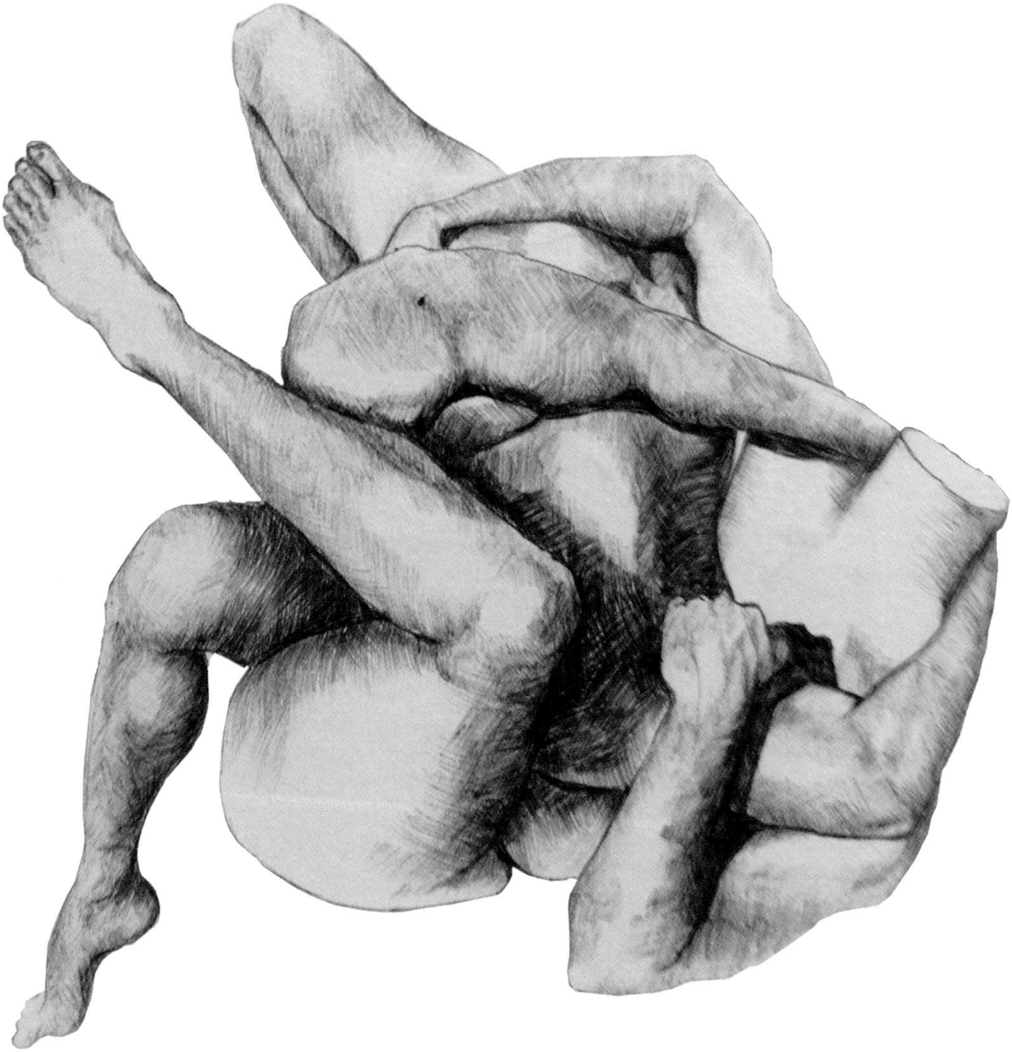

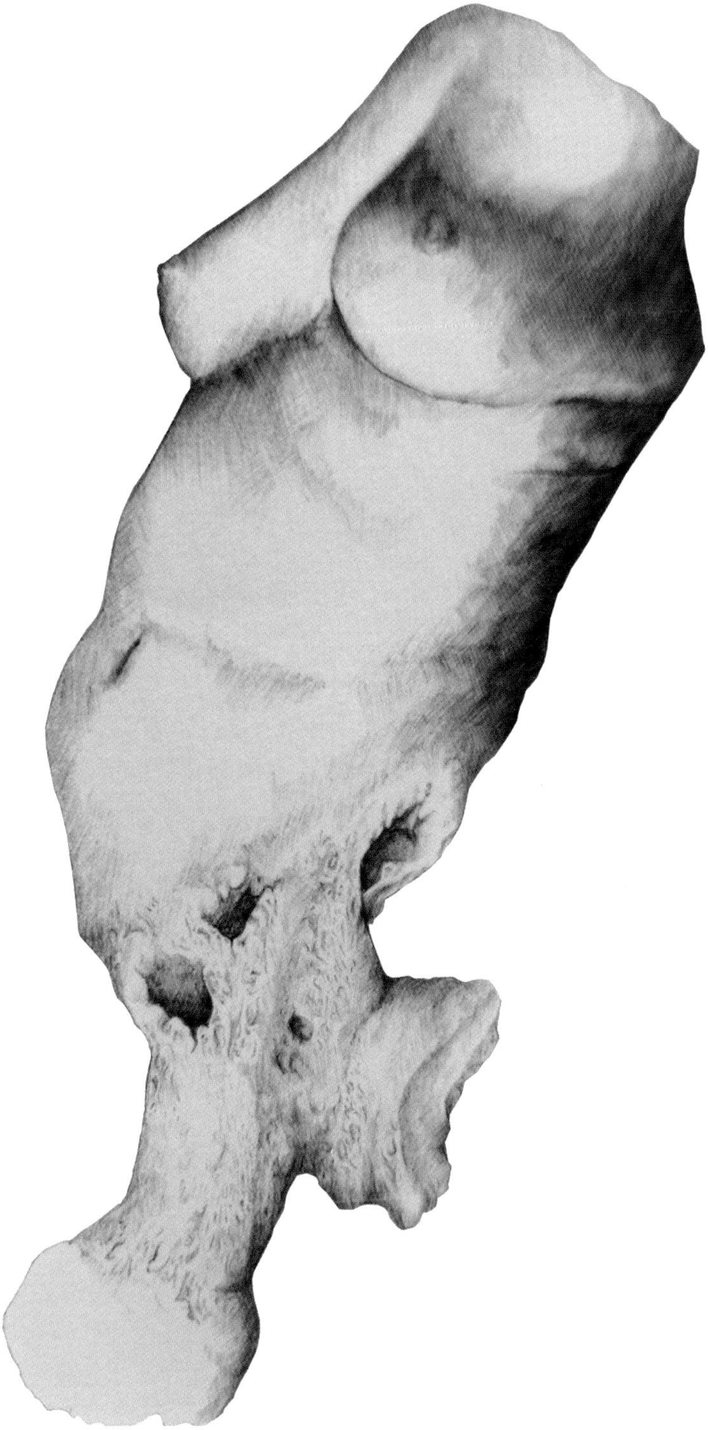

OUR BODY

David Miller

41

• Today we didn't leave at all b/c cold, and my body is breaking under its own weight, I know. I think I'm pregnant but don't know for sure b/c haven't tested. So, ya, Artur's baby, eight months, save the date (hahaha). I haven't gotten my period, and that's whatever b/c I haven't gotten it before and that's really no big deal, but, idk, something about this time that seems different...maybe the feelings involved, the immediacy of the man curled up besides me playing w/ my thin arms, spreading my ass cheeks all day. Don't bring up "abortion" b/c that is seriously out of the question. I sure can't afford one and he sure as shit can't afford one either (+ we don't want one) and our one friend got a homemade abortion (think stick-in-poke tattoos, which Artur is covered in btw) and it mangled her cunt so bad that now her periods bleed blue, and it's so fucked up/I have seen it. Artur and I don't have jobs b/c it is fucking tragic and awesome to be poor but educated. It really isn't--it sucks--but we are waiting to pull a bonne-n-clyde/ Badlands and kill someone important together, I think, so we can go to jail and have life served to us (hahaha). That is part of our thinking w/ the baby b/c maybe the jail house warden (maybe he is like ones from the bad movies, Southern and patriarchal and too respectful of the sanctity of family, and named after, like, Jack Daniels, is my thinking) will be super chill and let us live together if we have a baby/if I am about to have a baby after killing the important figure...but, again, the murder thing is all so G(x)d-damned tentative that I don't even know what's up anymore. B/c, you see, our ex-friends seek the nicer things in life but, well, yes, generally, we do not. We--Artur and me--are very happy just by our lonesome pair, and we can spend all day fucking and eating just noodles without thinking about how unhealthy/unstimulating it is do what we do how we do it. We are very cool in that sense--carefree, but we care so much, too, is the weird thing, and that's the thing I don't quite get about our love

• Today we looked around the Eastern suburbs but had to sprint away hell-fire fast when a pack of dogs came/started chasing us. Artur vomited after we got away b/c we don't exercise much and the adrenaline really fucked him up. I felt like shit after but didn't vomit. We ran into a CVS downtown and ate a bunch of metamucil but then bought a pack of gum for like 60 cents so it wasn't suspicious. We went back to the site and I listened to Artur write songs. Sometimes I listen to him play all day. Artur and my love is pure as babyshit (I say babyshit is pure b/c of all the sweet healthy gerbers natural foods they get to eat, and you have to be extra-attentive about the food you put in babies, I know). We get each other in almost most regards. He is my best friend, really

• Today Detroit rained. We watched it all go down from one of the broken windows. There were flood sirens (I think that's what they were). We--Artur and me--moved to Detroit after not finishing Sophomore year b/c of too strong love/his depression. We live with a bunch of Russians in a factory that closed down a long time ago, and it is fucking tight. We get a whole factory floor to ourselves and we like to make shit out of salvaged shit all day if we can. The Russian's floor just flooded, though, so they're going to be living up here w/ us now, I guess. Artur invited them (he is always doing stupid shit like that w/ his good heart--I would never have thought of that). We think the Russians are illegals but don't know b/c they don't speak English...but it's not like it matters though b/c we are liberal af. They are pure immigrant, and we get along with them pretty well. Sometimes they make us good food in exchange for the loose tobacco we collect from littered butts downtown. I am writing a play that takes place in a Brecht play I read once, and I'm thinking about having the Russians perform it so nobody knows wtf is going on. There is no internet in the building, which sucks, but also my parents can't find us which doesn't suck. Artur has no parents anymore: he is from LA but not good LA. He is not rich and his dad--single dad--was an asshole and a set designer until he died when we were freshmen when he fell in a mineshaft on location w/ that Matthew McCoanuhay (?) movie, Sahara, in Mexico. (Hence Artur's depression and serious collapse and serious inability to do fucking anything). He has gotten better but he is by no means better. He wanted to drop out and I said fuck yes b/c I wasn't having a good time and had to take all these dumb fucking intro courses that were totally meaningless and were stifling my creativity and were worthless towards my dreams, of which I have many. We went to sleep w/ out eating anything but the gum

• Today we snuck into the science-y musuem and looked at innovations which we didn't care for. I liked the early train models they had in there but Artur didn't. We went outside and found a container of some chicken in the dumpster, which was dope + tasted pretty good. We went home and fell asleep at like 6 b/c we were so wiped the fuck out from the days activities. Really, Artur is so long-legged and attractive, especially when he sleeps. He is dark and sinewy like he chose his body from a police sketch. We met at the college we didn't finish at during orientation weekend. He was smoking and I was smoking and we got to talking and never stopped. We do this thing where we like to imagine we are holding the liberal art's degrees we didn't finish getting and then we fake wipe our asses with them and laugh even though we make the joke almost every day. Artur's laugh is fucking obnoxious but I still love him but do I? That question has been on my mind more and more, but it's one of those questions that really just stays there unresolved but looms so big so that you never make any traction on it...e.g. G(x)d, the Soul, who I am, etc. He is, no doubt, my first love, but idk what that even means. I don't want to say more

• Today we even thought about getting part-timed jobs so we could eat more. We are in a serious G(x)d-damned rut. Hungry, tired, and Artur is coming down w/ something which means I'll come down w/ something which means the baby (?) will come down w/ something--which=no good. Artur has started doing this thing where he talks to my stomach and it's too cute and I can't take it. I say, man, stop it, you fuck. He says, I love you, and I'm like ?...why this shit all the sudden. When people mention Artur and me¬¬ (people from college, people who we used to hang w/ and know, those who seek the finer things), one of the first things they always talk about is our clothes, which are impeccably dope. We wear a lot of black, but then we separate ourselves from the horde by putting, like, one not black article somewhere random so it's all discordant, which is really the one word to describe the look we embody. That's why we like Detroit so much/why we came here b/c discord. It's fucked up here, and we love it so hard. There is so much behind every alley, like the dark heart of America, which is another way to describe our style. We feel like we run on coal, and we kind of do. Like everyone else at that college, from home, from America is like a subway, like electric rails, right? but we, we are different: we are old-fashioned in the newest sense: we are the train that Anna Karenina killed herself under, the one that a half-million Chinese bones pieced together; we are polluting the sky w/ our too-full tobacco lungs, that disgusting cough you hear in stories about West Virginia, that old curmudgeonly asshole on death's door w/ like 8 kinds of cancer who refuses to stop smoking b/c it's all he's got, that little infant unwittingly + cutely sleeping in the apartment next door to the meth cook, that kid you knew who drowned tragically at, like, 11: we are her, him, zir, zim; we are discord, death itself, dying

• Today I went out alone b/c I couldn't stand Artur's puppy-dog loving sickness anymore. I went to one the DIY houses where bands play sometimes and fucked a drummer in the bathroom. I got too drunk off drummer's bottle and woke on a couch and decided I would stay there for awhile and am still there. The drummer is a local named Neil. The apartment is his apartment. He is pretty chill, and when I told him I was pregnant he started eating me out. He said he wanted to know so he could decide to marry me or not. He ran out to buy a pregnancy test, but I took a bunch of his food and went back to Artur. Artur was all wet and covered in sores and he can't stop coughing. I couldn't take him to the hospital b/c we made a vow. I fed him all the drummer's food but he just puked it up. I asked the Russian's to come in and save him b/c he was dying and they did some Russian things on him, and Artur stopped sweating so much. He still wasn't great and he still had to rest all day, I think the Russians said, but he would be fine, I also think they said

• Today I felt the unequivocal presence of God in my head, and it made me feel such joy that I wept all over Artur, and we thought these, my tears, would be the only cure he needed.

• Today was more Artur bullshit. I've had to nurse him for about a week. He had me read Baudelaire to him, but I got bored after a few days. He is still so fucking clingy and his sores are gross as fuck. I'm seriously thinking about ditching him: this is not how I want to spend my youth and my looks. He is kind of getting better but enough. I've used up all our papers and most of our tobacco b/c bored. There's nothing to eat b/c Artur, and I don't want to touch the food that's left b/c all his deadly germs and whatnot crawl all over it. I'm going stir-crazy and legit crazy, too, I think. This is not why I moved out here, this is not what I had planned, and I am pissed as shit and fuming so hard all day every day and enough enough

• Today we listened to Joni Mitchell, Arthur Russell, and Beat Happening. I had one earbud in and he had the other. Problem was his breathing was so fucking loud and labored and obnoxious that there was like this other mix on the tracks that fucked up everything. I got pissed, stormed out, cried,

• Today I woke up in Neil's arms. The last three days have been like a fucked up pill haze at Neil's. I'm hungover and feel guilty as shit and like a piece of shit, and Artur must be dying from worry. I like Neil but he isn't Artur. He has food, a bed, a place, a solid dick, but he isn't Artur. Idk, I'm all fucked up and can't think straight and I think my eyes are like permanently red. I went back to Artur and he was dying again but worse now. The sores had started to fester and burst and he smelled like shit, actual shit. The Russians were nervously running around rubbing salves on him and giving him stuff to drink. I was still in a haze for most of it/didn't really know what was going on. He kept trying to hold my hand but it was too gross. Again, I couldn't take it

• Artur died today. Or maybe it was yesterday––we never had any watches or clocks or phones, and I was at the drummers. He didn't leave a note, a will, a nothing

• Today I wept until I miscarried

•

- Today
- Today I moved in with Neil. He is making me get a job so I can pitch in for rent, which I am pretty pissed about, but I get it––this is real life, I get it. I finally checked my email today on Neil's computer and there were a lot from my parents.

HOUSE PARTY (FROM SIM CITY)

Alex Paseltiner

Sometimes when my social meter is low
I use the phone to call up my friends
May, Ann, Cadence and Joni and invite them
and their husbands to my house party.
I take a brisk shower, change into my bikini
and wait for the doorbell. In Buy Mode
I buy neon inflatable patio furniture
while the caterer stocks the buffet table,
so that when Morty and Barb arrive
I'm already dancing it up in my gogo cage.
Everyone is talking about my dancing.
Our handsome robot butler is serving us
his romantic party energy drinks,
thereby multiplying all of our fun
scores, but zooming out I notice Cadence
isn't even here, the Pleasants aren't here,
everyone else just eating and standing
around the bathroom talking about
peace and airplanes and burglary.
To be honest I've always been terrible
at parties, and when the mime shows up
or you hear the Mister Softee truck
you know bad things are coming.
At that point only one thing can save
the evening, and when the cake explodes,
revealing the male stripper's satin pants,
the sad mime stands in the gogo cage,
waiting to be dismissed.

PERCUSSIVE INTERVENTION

First Year Architecture Students,
University of Cambridge

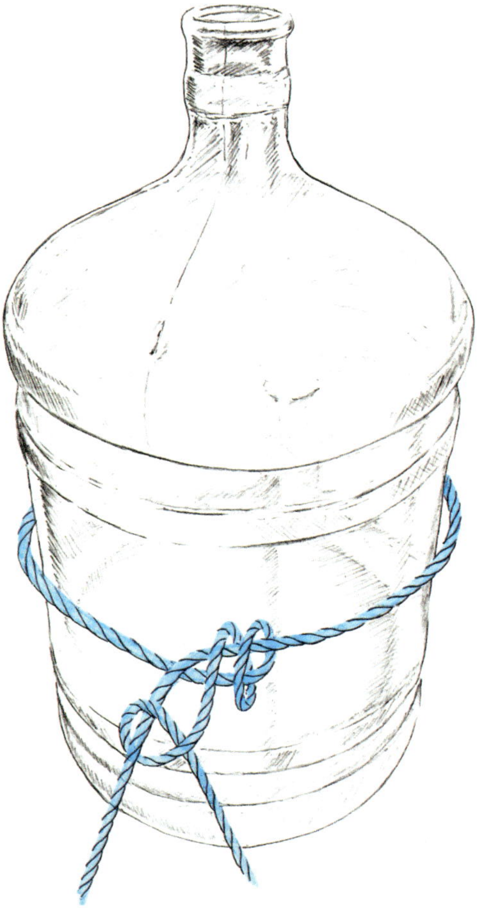

700 bottles

4200m of rope

25 people

750 hours

750 water bottles were tightly weaved together to form a façade of bottles along the entrance of the venue - encouraging the public to bang them like drums. This type of interactive project promotes Cambridge as an active, contemporary arts centre, seeking to engage the public with their city.

CHEESE-BRANDING

Emma Levin

The year is 1997. Aqua's Barbie Girl is top of the chart, Microsoft has just bought a $150 million share of financially troubled Apple Computer Corp, and Korean Air Flight 801 has met the ground in flames, resulting in the deaths of 228 people on board. Meanwhile, in an advertising agency in Farringdon, a young advertising executive named Alan Shipwright has just written the best slogan of his life. It is for a block of cheese.

"*This cheese,*" the packaging reads "*is so complex that, if it were a person, it wouldn't be friends with you.*"

Alan and his partner had been given a raise for that line. They'd been given a new office. It'd won the main prize at the advertising awards, beating off competition from the likes of Lynx ("*if she won't fuck you, it's because you're wearing the wrong deodorant*"), Weightwatchers ("*if there's less of you there, there's less of you to hate!*"), and Oedipus: the Boardgame ("*Fun for all the family. Except dad.*")

The cheese-branders' line had been so popular, they'd released a special extended edition, director's cut of the slogan: "This cheese is beautiful and intriguing, like a Rubik's cube in a bird's nest. This cheese is so intense that, if it were a person, it would make interactive sound sculptures in a run-down bedsit in

Shoreditch, and you would invite it to your party and you wouldn't expect it to come, but then it would actually turn up, you would open the door, with the music leaking out into the corridor in front of you, and you would step aside to let him in, and he would hand you a box and place a leathery hand on your shoulder and look deep into your eyes, and mouth "Don't open it" and then he would push his way in through the music and the people and he's laughing and smiling and there's a bottle of something in his hand and then all of a sudden he just freaks out and starts screaming and you ask him to leave because although you like to think of yourself as open-minded there's something deeply unsettling about a grown man openly crying and also the neighbours have already complained about noise once this week. Suitable for vegetarians."

They'd grown famous off that line. Terry Gilliam said that he wanted to do an adaptation. They were invited to all of the parties, drawn into the debauched, Bacchanalian celebrations of the cheese-branding elite. The first party they went to, they were pressed, breathless and wired, into the throng. They were surrounded by the rich and famous cheese-branders in their big fur coats and diamond-tipped canes. And they liked it. Soon, they were regulars at the lavish parties of the cheese board board – a world of excess and diamonds and girls – oh! The girls! The cheese-branding groupies, those nubile young women who just went weak at the knees for well-described dairy products.

Of course, there were those who resented their success. Sullen, bitter ex-colleagues who pointed out that "if their cheese was a person, you probably wouldn't want to eat it." But the cheese-branders didn't care; they were too big to fail, and too busy to read criticism. All of a sudden, they were in demand. They were the it-cheese-men. Pounding out slogan after slogan, like a funny simile.

As their oeuvre grew, so did criticism. The fans didn't like the newer slogans, said they didn't reach the dizzying heights of their debut slogan, and betrayed the die-hard fans by straying from their roots – good, old fashioned metaphor. It all started to go a bit wrong. They were putting less and less effort into the slogans, spending more time at the parties. Their purple fake-fur coats felt like a uniform, not a privilege. And the slogan business wasn't fun anymore. After their hit, they'd been pigeonholed. They weren't allowed to brand other things, it was only cheese. They were stuck in a creamy, calcium-rich rut.

And then came the edam.

The phone in the cheese-branders' penthouse was ringing. Alan shrugged off a couple of groupies, and reached out for the phone. He missed, and sent the ruby-crusted receiver tumbling the floor, where it scattered the toys from his Faberge kinder eggs. The noise spooked their pet ocelot, who leapt from his purple sheets, knocking the table over, sending the lines and credit cards from the night before flying.

The farmers had invented a new cheese. They wanted them to do the slogan.

The new cheese was a scientific marvel. Six-dimensional edam, which could only be seen by wearing two pairs of 3D glasses on top of each other. It was delicious, and should have sold itself, really, but there was a complication; when you are wearing two pairs of 3D glasses, you can see through time. In controlled trials, most people were so distracted by visions of their future self that they forgot all about eating the cheese.

They took the case and, long story short, the campaign failed miserably. The edam was withdrawn from the shops within a matter of weeks, and the two cheese-branders were forced to live in ignominy, poverty, and Hammersmith.

The end.

EMMA LEVIN

KAMU BRATHWAITE DOES SOME FACEBOOK STALKING, circa 1950

Ruth O'Connell Brown

Words

Words need love too

Too much, Ted Hughes

With your face like a mountain

And everyone in love with you.

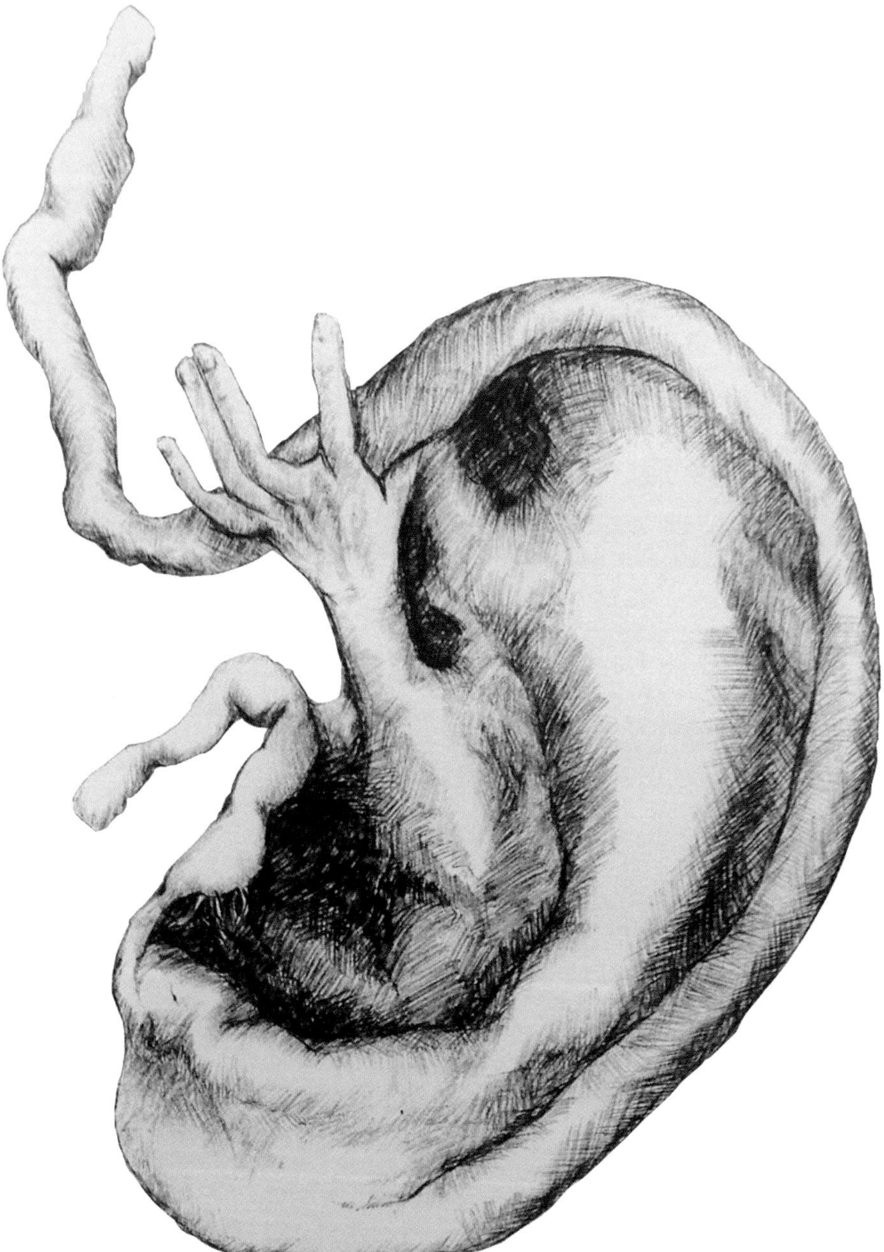

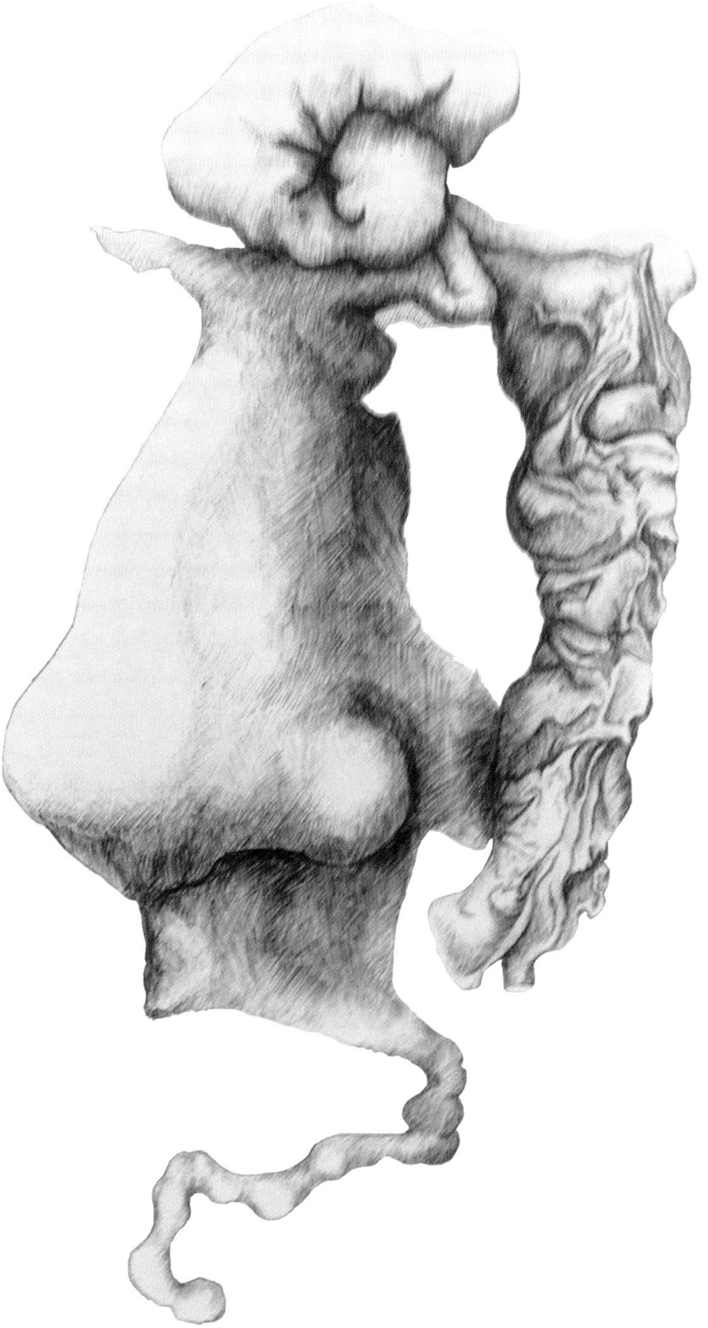

KINAESTHESIA III

Matt Broomfield

When the old man awoke his first thought was of pickled eggs. His second thought was of double-glazing, and how he could not afford it. Heat rose, he had read. This was why, in the long months of winter, he would spread his fingers an inch or so above the hot wire of the toaster as it toasted his sliced white bread, turning them in warmth so sudden and sharp that it was painful. But though his room was at the top of his tall house it was the coldest room of all, and the September wind prised its way in through the leaky casement of the window.

His house was a council house in a row of terraced council houses, but it stood a storey higher than the rest. It was this that made its kitchen window a target for stones on the rare occasions that groups of boys wandered down the winding path over the allotments and into this unexpected sliver of council properties, hemmed in on one side by the allotments and on the other by the railway track as it left the town for the north. The old man did not know why his house was taller than all of the other houses, but he liked it. There must have been a time before the council owned these properties, when the owners had been free to erect whatever garrets and turrets and spires they wanted on their property. He was not sure if this true, for he was not really sure how council houses worked, and whether the council would buy a terrace with one house that was so much greater than those it was conjoined to; but he knew that none of the other houses on the whole estate stood three proud stories above the ground. He woke up further above the ground than anyone else he ever spoke to.

Of course, this meant that the wind laced itself around the exposed walls of his bedroom, and that he woke up shivering even now, at the very beginning of autumn. Unopened jars of pickled eggs were no substitute for cavity wall insulation. He never turned his heating on, even in the cruellest tightening of the noose of the wind about his attic room. He knew that the council had some money, somewhere, intended for this purpose, but it seemed very far away. When he shook violently awake in the depths of December with his breath curling around his head the talk of this money seemed like a story from another world. But he had several blankets, and he was grown thin enough now to wear all of his clothes at once.

In any case, it was only September, and the cold did not yet reach to his bones. He lay for a while moving his limbs under the blankets, finding patches of coldness and warming them with his skin. The sun was half-up so it could not yet be seven o'clock. A strip of wallpaper had been tacked into place over his window, which had no curtains or blind, but it was ragged along the bottom where it had been torn off from the roll, and light intruded into his bedroom every morning. When he awoke, he often wondered what could be done about this; he could not afford to sacrifice a blanket to keep the sun out, for he needed all three to keep the heat in. In the summer he liked to open the window and lean out and gaze down the front of his tall house. He planned how he would scale its sheer surface, swinging from the guttering and bracing himself against next door's satellite dish, limbs unfurling and finding purchase, toes seeking out unseen crevices in the rough red brick. He saw himself from above, moving like liquid, never remaining still. The old man often wished that there were windows in the sides of his bedroom so that he could gaze over the lower roofs to either side and plot his assault on their corners and angles and faces. In his dreams he steeple-chased over the roofs of the town, legs finding space where there was none in the waking streets. He could reach the cornershop in three strides and surmount the allotments in ten. Whether he grew enormous or the estate shrank to a diminutive size, the old man could never say. It made no difference when he was striding around the town on legs as long as telegraph poles and feet which never lost their footing.

His third thought was of pickled eggs. As he willed himself to pull back his blankets he thought of their rubbery, sour resistance to his gums. He thought of brine swilling round his stumps of molars, of the delicious sharpness of vinegar on the roof of his mouth. If his stomach had let him he would have happily drunk great draughts of brine, in pints and gallons, savouring the salt as it sloshed down his throat. As a young man he had eaten and eaten and eaten; even now, six eggs was a great size of breakfast for an old man who sat on a rocking chair without rocking all day. His muscles still remembered a little of their old hunger. Their complaints woke him in the night as his stomach cramped, his heart doggedly searching for protein that was not there. This night past his gut had been still, and he was able to sit up without having to pause for breath as he braced himself on the bedside table. His body shook but his tread was steady as he crossed the room to where he had left his slippers, reflected in the myriad jars of pickled eggs which rose in columns either side of the door. He thought of pickled eggs for the fourth time that morning as he began to bend down to his slippers. If he remembered he left them beside his bed, but he did not always remember in the evenings, when things grew more confused and routines more uncertain and his body less willing to carry out its functions to their completion. He paid the price for his carelessness now, unhappily trying to shuffle his foot into the worn tartan, fingers cramping uselessly an inch above the slippers. He put up his other hand to steady himself against the doorframe, and nearly killed himself in a tumultuous cascade of slimy eggs and broken glass and surging vinegar. But instead he slid his thin white feet into his slippers, straightened up and set himself to the task of going downstairs.

A two-up-two-down with another room up on top of that could have housed a whole family, and more besides. The old man knew that. And he knew that there were families that needed this house, and he would have been happy for them to have it, though he loved waking up higher up than anyone else he knew. But he did not know how to tell the council that he did not want to live alone in a tall house, not when there were families living very close together in smaller houses.

For a time he had written them letters. He did not have writing paper but he had carefully unpicked the labels from the pickled-egg jars which still had labels left on them from when they had held something other than pickled eggs. For this purpose, he had not let the cleaner trim the nail of his right thumb for some weeks, till it had grown rougher and more yellow and he had been able to use it to prise paper from glass. At first it had not been possible to write anything on the blank reverse side of the labels, for they were covered in sticky paste and curled up when he placed them on the table by the microwave. So he had left them flattened out on the windowsill, two at a time, because this was all that would fit. He weighed them down with empty tins and left them to dry in the sun as its heat pressed through the dusty window. When they dried he could write legibly on them with dark pencil, if he pressed hard. He had explained with care that he was only one man, and that there must clearly be some mistake, for though he loved it he did not need the tall house. He explained that the room below his little bedroom stood empty, dusty, a space through which he passed with the tread of a ghost. He wrote that he knew of girls, young girls, whom his cleaner talked about, with babies and nowhere to live, who were waiting for council flats when all the while there were empty rooms here. He wrote that he had tried to explain all this to the cleaner, but she had smiled and said that she was only a contractor and that she knew nothing of housing contracts, and he had frowned because this made no sense, and she had smiled again and said that it did not matter but that she did not know anything about houses and that she was only paid to clean, and that not enough. He wrote all this on the backs of his labels, his writing getting smaller as he ran out of space, and though he did not join his letters they bunched together at the bottom of the labels. When he finished the letters he had not known what to do with them. He did not have stamps, and if the cleaner did not know anything about houses he doubted whether she would know how to send a message to the council. One Wednesday morning, as he gazed intensely at the ball of flesh at the base of his thumb, he had been struck by a sudden thought. Then he had left the house, even though he had enough food and cigarettes to last him four more days. He had shuffled down the road to the base of the steep path which climbed up over the allotments. There was a small paved area here, where the police pulled up in their squad cars when they chased the boys who threw rocks and drank cider and smoked weed, and thought about getting out of the car and chasing the laughing boys over the hill and into the dark net of the estate. Sometimes boys played football here as well, or else a complicated game of their own devising where you had to bounce a flat football off the angle of the wall and into one of the three squat recycling bins which faced it. Two grey and one green, they were clearly emblazoned with stencilled white paint which marked them as the property of the council. It was therefore clear to the old man that someone from the council must come here to take care of them, and tend to whatever needs recycling bins had. So he took his hand-written letters and posted them, one by one, into the dark holes on the front of the recycling bins. He took care to put some letters in each one of the three bins, in case one of them should be taken to the dump by mistake. Then he walked home, feeling a little sad, for he would miss his tall house. But then if they moved him to a council flat, he would wake up higher still.

But that had been a year ago, and the council had never replied. So the old man still made the long walk down the narrow stairs to the kitchen every morning. In the kitchen he gathered together his breakfast; three-quarters-empty jar of pickled eggs, plate decorated with a cartoon mouse and elephant duo who had sold cereal during the 1980s, mug of water from the tap. He had forgotten to go to the bathroom to piss. When he was a young man pissing had been a great pleasure for him, and he had taken pride in dislodging dirt from the back of urinals and sousing trees and walls in a uniform spray. He had pissed off the side of mountains. Now his stream was as unsteady as his hands. Until a couple of years ago he had at least been able to rest his penis on the lip of the sink and let a tired dribble of urine spatter into the basin, but now he was too short, or perhaps he could no longer support himself on the balls of his feet for the sluggish duration of his morning piss. He cast a wistful glance at the sink, for the bathroom was back up the stairs he had just descended. But it was not worth the risk of the cleaner finding him with piss drying down the leg of his tracksuit bottoms, and so he set down his plate and his jar of eggs and trudged back up the stairs to the toilet.

MATT BROOMFIELD

65

DADDY SHOT THE DOG

Jim Hilton

Barrels smoking, we burn drip-gas up the interstate;
Hunch fierce toward a windshield full of crags,
Sun-sore skies and an endless highway. Leagues back
County boots crunch our roadside stubs in anger;
Backwaters mourn their fat-head sons,
Headlines guess our course, and America spits blood
Like we pissed it off–like we sent its Stetson flying.

We bivouac in woods, couple beneath awnings
Of Cypress and Buckeye and read Screenland magazine.
Rangers stalk the forest trails beyond their jurisdiction–their hearts all full of dollars
That rust to autumn pink with the buckshot's touch.
I would bequeath this bounty-plagued world and all its currency to gasoline
Just for a solitary dance with you. And we would laugh as it came down.
But Rangers stalk the everglades. They stalk & stalk like they'd hunt us through the veil.
Their brothers, fathers, uncles join them. There's not enough shells on this Earth for all its evil.
Twigs snap and rifles cock among bat-wing beats. Whatever happens, I love you,

And I'll meet you at Grand Coulee Dam, New Year's Day, 1964.
Signs and wonders be fucked, I'll meet you in Odessa,
Oklahoma, Kansas or Missouri, South Dakota up to the badlands of Montana.
I'll meet you beyond the Great Plains; under the soft glow of Missoula refineries.
I'll meet you on horseback, far above the lights of Cheyenne,
Riding high over Saskatchewan mountains.
I'll meet you in the four-cylinder Ford Coupe
Parked among a hail of bullets, and we'll drive somewhere.
I'll meet you in the Stereopticon, smiling, surrounded by wilderness;
And mad horny kids will sigh at us;
They'll leave their towns, laughing, cursing, and never look back.

AFTERMATH I AND II

Sophie Sparkes

ALL IN THE FAMILY

Jonathan Crossley

"Hi. I'm Emily."

The group all nodded, and their eye contact, strong and deliberate, was half comforting, half get-to-the-good-stuff-already.

"A little about me: I work in audio books, I record them. So if my voice sounds familiar, that's probably why."

I raised my empty Styrofoam cup—the rim cracked at either end—and took a fake sip.

"I got pregnant at 16 and my boyfriend bounced soon after. I mean, if I'm being fair, he joined the army, but what's the difference. So, not seeing any other option, I gave my son up. And I thought it would be good to have a clean break, you know? Not set up any kind of weird visitation with his new parents. And so time passed, and I got into audiobooks, and it's kind of a lonely job. I mean you just talk to yourself all day. So, I don't know, I guess a part of me always hoped that my son would hear something I'd worked on. Like, he'd open his computer or turn on the stereo, and I'd be the voice that came out. That I could read to him from the other end of a power line, and neither of us would know. Well, I met Luke for the first time last week, and things are going well. They're going really well. And I guess that's why I'm here."

Luke's school got out at 12:30 on Fridays. The administration claimed it was to allow students some downtime before a weekend filled with extra curricular actives. A large number of parents hated the policy, said the only reason it was implemented was so teachers didn't have to take any grading home. But I stayed quiet. Those early dismissals were the only way I could see my son. He'd invented a band, just like every seventeen-year-old boy with long hair.

It was our eighth Friday together. I drove into the parking lot and saw Luke on the stairs, his lanky arms jutting out of his sleeves, his veins, intricate and blue, resembling the subway map of a city I didn't know. He got in the car and didn't say a word. I liked that about him, that he could handle silence.

We drove out of town and up the 80. Late season snow, turned the color of soiled underwear, melted on the side of the road. We went down to one lane for a little while, as Caltrans started their spring maintenance; that time of year when the scars left by six months of winter chains are filled in and forgotten.

The rest stop was quiet. But still, I made a habit of parking by the far side of the building, where the asphalt rested under a thick layer of pine needles.

My hand massaged the back of his neck. My fingers twirled his hair—brown and curly, just like his dad's. For the thousandth time, I said how sorry I was for abandoning him all those years ago, and that I fully planned to make up for all the time we lost. And then I pulled him close, his lips against mine. I want to say I hesitated.

•

"Was that good for you?"

"Oh shut up," Emily said. She wrapped her limbs around me, tight and warm.

"I'm glad we finally did it."

"Me too."

We kissed and cuddled and the contact faded into a shared silence. I may have even fallen asleep. But I know, sometime later, I looked out the window and saw that it was snowing. I made an attempt to take in my surroundings, to really remember them. Because that moment felt important, like a fork to elsewheres I couldn't yet identify.

"Hey, don't answer this, but was that your first time?"

"What? No. Of course not," I said, unable to escape the thought that the last time I was inside her, we were both in a hospital. I went on to invent a girl named Donna, who I guess I now had a thing with the summer between sophomore and junior year. Emily cut me off just as I was getting to the good part, tears in her eyes, saying we should probably head back soon.

We sped down the foothills on our way back to Sacramento. The sun was low in the sky, giving downtown a pink backdrop as it started to light up. *This is why so many people do this drive*, I thought. Because at this time of day, at this angle, Sacramento could be mistaken for a better city. The giant malls, the tract housing, the farmland—all pushed outside the glow of reality.

"What are you thinking about?" Emily said.

"Nothing."

"Really?"

"Yeah."

"Come on. You can talk to me." She laughs a little.

"I don't know. The Kings. How Boogie's contract extension will impact the cap. Just shit like that."

"Would you like it if we watched basketball together?"

I leaned over and kissed her on the cheek. Just to drop the subject. Just to not hear her voice for a little while.

Emily dropped me off at the Denny's around the corner from my parents' house. When we first started meeting up, we agreed not to tell anyone. I didn't want my parents asking even more questions about my life, and she said she'd feel embarrassed or something.

I walked through the front door as my parents made their way to the living room. My mom said something about how it's already November and college applications are due in January but, by the closing of my door and the decibel of my music, she had to know she was talking to herself.

•

This whole thing isn't as crazy as you think. Genetic Sexual Attraction occurs in 50% of reunions, according to some estimates. And this isn't a new phenomenon. Adoption agencies have known about GSA for decades, they're just hesitant to talk about it. Sue Cowling, the deputy director of the Post-Adoption Centre, has said "Genetic sexual attraction associated with IVF births is a time bomb waiting to go off," and I know that's not the case here, but still, it shows that this is a real issue that needs to be addressed openly. And "sexual" may even be the wrong word to describe what's going on between Luke and I. Joe Soll, a psychotherapist in New York, has said GSA is less about sex and more about an attempt to recapture denied parent-child intimacy. For example, just the other day, Luke asked to suckle my breasts.

The front door swung open, and I could see the red booths, the fake wooden tables, the stoned teenagers in their employee uniforms—black polos with a red chili just above the left breast. I turned away. I couldn't go in. Not yet. My defense wasn't perfect, far from it. At best, it was a draft away from impassioned monologue.

The door swung open again.

"Emily! Is that you," Luke's adoptive mother said. *Mother*. The thought caught me off guard, unsure which of us deserved the title of imposter.

"Sorry. I just had to make a quick call."

We made our way toward the table. Luke and his adoptive dad both looked up and smiled.

This is what Luke didn't get: that, for me, the worst part of this wasn't that my Xanax hadn't kicked in yet or that I feared a SWAT team would burst out of the kitchen. No, the worst part was his adoptive parents—having them pull out old photos and slip him a beer with lunch and say, again and again, just how proud of him they were. It was like having a glimpse into an alternate dimension, a timeline that you thought was snuffed out long ago. I tried to explain this to Luke once and his response was "kinda like if you fell into a world where 9/11 didn't happen?" I thought that was a bit dramatic and self-indulgent, but then I found myself talking about the Challenger takeoff. How we were all sitting on the reading rug. How the TV, strapped to a black cart, showed the flames turn from progress to despair in an instant. How, later that afternoon, everyone in my third grade class learned what "surely bond" meant. Maybe each generation has its own remnants of a dead future? Or maybe Luke just inherited my flare for pretension?

•

I returned Emily's call late. Said therapy sounded like a dumb idea and that I was going to spend the afternoon playing video games with my friends. I told her that she shouldn't worry; that we should just have fun; and that, if we trusted our feelings, we couldn't be doing anything too wrong. I also thought three weeks after a tearful reunion was a bit soon to start dragging me to stuff.

Stewart and Connor came over around two, and we booted up *Grand Theft Auto*, taking turns venturing across the game's digital Los Angeles. The game's open world was a pleasant change from the narrow corridors and limiting levels of most video games. Run over pedestrians, fly helicopters, absorb bullets. We could do anything here, the rules of society fading away with the start-up logos.

"Samantha invited me to her party next weekend," Connor said. "And don't worry, I can totally get you guys in."

"That's awesome."

"Dude, you're so lucky. She wants on bad."

"Yeah. You're probably right." Connor said. I was shocked at how much rage a smirk could insight.

"I'm hooking up with someone too," I said.

"Really? From school?"

"No. We met on Craigslist."

"Dude, that's so gross."

"Yeah. But more importantly, are you getting some?"

I smiled and the room erupted in laughter and high-fives.

"Luke's wetting the D!'

"Plus, she's older. Knows all this crazy stuff."

"What's her name?"

"Janice."

"Do you have a picture?"

"No. She's really private. I shouldn't even be talking about it."

"Oh. I see how it is. You guys probably met on vacation, huh?

"Fuck you," I said. "And give me that controller."

As I dropped into the neon glow of Los Angeles, I realized the genius of the game. By trapping me in a world where I had unlimited lives and my progress was auto-saved and everything was designed for fun, the developers had removed all possibility of unpleasantness. And while the game had a story with characters and plot twists and morals, I felt like I'd stumbled upon the real message: fuck unpleasantness. *Literally fuck unpleasantness.*

•

The movie ended and everyone piled outside, following the green glow of the exit signs. But we didn't head straight home, frustrated at what a 14-dollar ticket got you. Instead, we set up camp on my backseat, fogging the windows, making *Titanic* jokes, giggling whenever a nearby car would beep twice and then unlock. Another showing started to filter into the parking lot, and Luke made some excuse about having to change into a new pair of shorts. I nodded and handed him his backpack, my role in our silent routine. He always came once before the actual act.

"I can't believe you leave for college tomorrow," I said. Luke's head rested against my chest, sleepy and post-coital. "You're so grown up."

"Yeah. I'm excited, it should be fun."

I ran my hands through Luke's hair, massaging his scalp, picking apart the knots and dreads. After a while, I let my hand trail down his arm. I reached his hand, our fingers interlaced.

"Hey, I know it's a long way and I want you to have fun at college, but do you think I could come and visit sometime?"

"Sure. I mean, if you want to. But maybe wait until the spring? Just so I'm settled and stuff."

"Yeah. Of course. Whatever's easiest for you."

"And I don't know. It's just... I'll be living in a co-ed dorm so—"

"It's okay, Luke. I get it."

I dropped him off at Denny's and made it two blocks before breaking down. With the smell of sex lingering around the backseat and his used condom hanging out of an old Macy's bag, my drive home seemed impossible. So I decided to sleep in the car. Reclined my chair, opened the sunroof. Had to be back at his parents for 8am, anyway. The official sendoff.

As I lay on my back and watched planes blink across the night sky, the *Challenger* tragedy rattled through my mind. I used my phone to find footage of the takeoff, the first time I'd watched in nearly thirty years. And as the seconds passed and the ship soared higher and higher, leaving the sea of blue for the edge of black, I thought the astronauts might make it this time; that, with enough effort and skill and heart, they could outrun the past. But they didn't. Instead, they exploded four miles above the Florida coast. Right on schedule. I remembered how NASA later said the cause of the explosion were a couple faulty O-Rings, that they were cold and created a vacuum or something. And I thought that maybe the first time I kissed Luke was like installing a faulty O-Ring, a seemingly minor act that sets you on a course for heartbreak. I spent the next hour on the *Challenger* Wikipedia page and hated myself for comparing my relationship to seven astronauts maybe being conscious as they plummeted back toward Earth. I hated that I felt the need to draw attention to my dramatic comparison as a way to defend myself from future criticism. Because it felt right, even though I knew it wasn't.

•

I was looking for some cash when I found my mother, her name sandwiched between the house blueprints and some old water bills. I thought it would be hard to track her down. That it would take years and a private investigator and heartbreak before our reunion transformed from daydream to reality. But it turned out she had a Facebook and, just under a week later, we got coffee at a little place by the river. The first half hour or so was awkward, us ordering finger food, joking how the choice in background music reveled in coffee shop self-parody. But she had a nice voice, strong and melodic, and I felt myself being drawn in with each passing phrase, each little chuckle. Soon we settled into a rhythm, comparing bad decisions and telling stories we usually only tell drunk. We realized that, as children, we'd both promised to 'live forever or die trying." I blinked and the café was starting to change over for dinner. She offered to give me a ride home, and, on the way out to the car, I couldn't help but notice how her dress fell against her thighs, how her heels clicked against the tile floor, how she smiled when our hands brushed. As we entered my neighborhood, passed through its tall white gates, she pulled over and tried to explain why she'd given me up. Her story was circular, traveling back and forth in time to add amendments and asides, as though she remembered new details with each sob. I squeezed her hand; a little uncomfortable at how much her guilt turned me on. She kissed my hand. And then I kissed her cheek. And then she kissed my mouth. Neither of us said a word until a policeman knocked on our window, telling us we were parked in front of a fire hydrant.

FICCIONES TYPOGRAFIKA (614-616)

Dani Ismailov

PARTICULAR CONTROVERSIES INCLUDE [...]

Henry St Leger

all quotations from Carolyn Petit, who wrote a review

the | **GRANDEUR** |

Grand Theft Auto V is an open world, free-roaming action-adventure video-game
developed by Rockstar North and
published by Rockstar Games in 2013,

[...] **criticised** for [...] its realisations of extreme violence,
and of misogyny,
and light

treatment of criminal acts [...] the **freedom**
to kill lightly, and dark
despite

multiple playable characters, so many
bleeding hearts, and a voice to cut through the noise

80

It was a **game-changer**, a **cultural behemoth**, and a **player** in **three acts** [...] and
the most [...] entertainment product in **history** [...]
the **vehement liberty**, standing ground
like a statue [...] but

Please drink and drive responsibly, they say
Please bloodlust responsibly (like

little Carolyn, who felt the weight
in her hand
but never let go of the handle,

|

|

|

PARTICULAR CONTROVERSIES INCLUDE [...]

the female | **TATTLE** | dripping
across **Vice City's** parade, from Carolyn's measured rainfall:

'The beauty of cruising in the sun-kissed hills
turns sour real quick' 'when a voice comes on
the radio that talks
sweet nothing',

|

'that glorifies male sexuality while demeaning women',

|

'with nothing in the narrative
to underscore how insane and wrong
this is',

|

'when a voice comes on the radio that talks sweet nothing – '

Do you know how beautiful you aren't, Carolyn?
I read your review. I read your 'review', Carolyn,

I shot you with dual-handguns and broke the glass roof of the twittersphere, saying
#agoodwoman takes a bullet | #prochoice | #howwedo

#righttobeararms | #righttouse | #righttorepresent | #righttowrong | #righttoplay

and they called me
the | **AESTHETE** | and followed me, to the end, and I told them,

Yes, I met a woman like you once.

I met **Lindsay Lohan** on a street corner
attempting to prostitute herself,
and I shook her hand and looked her down and taught her RP.

She thanked me,
with a *discount*, but I misheard
and took her.

And she complained and was filthy from the traffic and the atmosphere.

So I washed her face
for her, with a pool of cement that had already set.
And she got herself all over the pavement.

And I knew you the moment I saw you,
because you were repeated on every corner,
and I ran you over on every street.

And you never remembered me.

EDITORIAL TEAM

EDITOR

EMILY FITZELL

GUEST EDITORS

ALISON TURNBULL - QUENTIN BLAKE

DEPUTY EDITORS

CAL REVELY-CALDER - ROWLAND BAGNALL

ASSOCIATE OXFORD EDITORS

TOM COOK - LUCY DIVER

SELECTION COMMITTEE

ROWLAND BAGNALL - TOM COOK - LUCY DIVER - EMILY FITZELL
BEATRICE LIESE - CAL REVELY-CALDER - ALBINIA STANLEY

DESIGN

ADAM THELWALL

WEBSITE

ARCHIE BAGNALL

PUBLICITY & EVENTS

MILLIE BRIERLEY

VARSITY BUSINESS MANAGER

MARK CURTIS

SPECIAL THANKS

SIMON CRITCHLEY - THE JUNCTION, CAMBRIDGE

THE MAYPOLE, CAMBRIDGE - THE ALBION BEATNIK, OXFORD

MICHAEL BROWN - CAMILLE RALPHS - JAMES ROGERS

SPONSORS

CAMBRIDGE

CHURCHILL - FITZWILLIAM
GONVILLE AND CAIUS - HOMERTON
JESUS - LUCY CAVENDISH - MAGDALENE
MURRAY EDWARDS - NEWNHAM
QUEENS' - ROBINSON
TRINITY

OXFORD

ALL SOULS
CHRIST CHURCH
MERTON
NEW COLLEGE

SPECIAL THANKS

SIR QUENTIN BLAKE

Matt Broomfield is a third year English student at Wadham College, Oxford. His interests and influences include Adrian Mitchell, William Blake, maximalist prose and contemporary battle rap.

Harry Cochrane is a third year English student at Pembroke College, Cambridge. Dante is his great literary love, and he hopes to complete his project of translating the Divine Comedy into a hundred Petrarchan sonnets over the next few decades.

Barney Couch is a photographer from London who has worked in portraiture and fashion during his time at Cambridge. He is especially interested in the interaction of humans with a human-modified environment, and to that end is currently working on a range of personal projects.

Jonathan Crossley is a first year Creative Writing student at Somerville College, Oxford. He is interested in gender relations and the intersection of science, technology, and human behaviour.

Dòmhnall Iain Dòmhnallach is a third year Biomedical Sciences student at St John's College, Oxford. He is passionate about contemporary Scottish and Gàidhlig literature, and also has a special interest in steampunk fiction.

Emily Everest-Phillips is a first year History student at St Hugh's College, Oxford. Her involvement in contemporary ballet and movement theatre has translated into her artwork as a special interest in anatomical figures.

Dominic Hand is a first-year English student at Oriel College, Oxford. His work has been featured in The Missing Slate, Playhouse64, Cherwell, ISIS, and Ash Magazine. In 2014 he won the Christopher Tower Poetry Prize. In 2015 he co-founded the creative project PROCESS. A number of formal influences include John Cage, Brice Marden, John Ashbery, and Robert Ryman.

Jim Hilton is a second-year English student at Jesus College, Cambridge. He is particularly interested in American novels and film.

Daniyar Ismailov is a second year student at Robinson College, Cambridge, studying social anthropology and politics. He has particular interests in digital art, grime music and the politics of Central Asia.

Emma Levin used to study geography at Hertford College, Oxford, but now belongs to the department of ContEd. She likes Kafka and CBBC.

David Miller is a third year visiting student at Wadham College, Oxford. He is an American who normally attends Sarah Lawrence College, where he studies Philosophy and English. He wants to write novels and be a decent human being.

Rebekah-Miron Clayton is a second year Education with English and Drama undergraduate studying at Homerton College, Cambridge. She has a special interest in performance art, rich poetic language and combining artistic mediums.

Isaac Nowell is a student at Balliol College, Oxford. He has a particular interest in thirteenth century representations of the sex life of the animals.

Ruth O'Connell Brown is a second year English student at St John's College, Cambridge. She is particularly interested in Buffy the Vampire Slayer, and how the internet is changing the way we read and write.

Alex Paseltiner is a visiting third-year at Exeter College, Oxford studying both English and Computer Science. Among his interests are computational linguistics, hypertext literature, and urban studies.

Mathilde Sergent is a third year English student from Fitzwilliam College, Cambridge. She has a special interest in female American modernism and Imagism, as well as contemporary art.

Sophie Sparkes is a first year Music student at St Anne's College, Oxford. Her work incorporates a range of media from sculpture and film to spoken word and live sound.

Henry St Leger is a graduating English student at Robinson College, Cambridge. His special interest is in video games and forms of storytelling in the digital era.

Stephen Wright is a second year studying English at St Peter's College, Oxford. He is interested in 20th Century American poetry and the interplay between spoken performance and the written word.

Group Submission

First Year Architecture Students, University of Cambridge.

www.themaysanthology.co.uk

@MaysAnthology

mays-editor@varsity.co.uk

www.facebook.com/TheMaysAnthology

ACKNOWLEDGMENTS

This magazine has been published by Wharncliffe History Magazines in association with Pen and Sword Military Books Limited, with the purpose of creating an awareness and an interest in the subject of military history.

For over twenty years Pen and Sword has published numerous military, naval and aviation books covering various conflicts throughout history. A vast amount of military titles have been published over the past few years, covering the personal accounts of soldiers who have taken part in many conflicts, stretching from the First World War through to the Falklands War. The books featured in this magazine are only a few titles taken from a large selection of subjects covering The Great War.

These publications would not have been possible if it had not been for the skill and dedication of the authors, who have painstakingly researched and written about these conflicts in order to bring them to light.

Only extracts have been taken from these titles to produce this magazine and much more information can be gleaned by reading the books mentioned at the end of each chapter. Pen and Sword have included more colour illustrations and images to the text in order to add more interest for the reader, making this a very special publication.

Pen and Sword Books would like to thank; Roni Wilkinson, Herbert Sulzbach, Keith Yates, Jack Horsfall, Nigel Cave, Peter Downham and Tonie and Valmai Holt, whose works have appeared in this magazine 1914 – OUTBREAK OF WORLD WAR ONE 95 YEARS ON.

Wharncliffe
HISTORY MAGAZINES

In association with;

Pen & Sword Military Books.

First published in Great Britain in 2009 by
Wharncliffe History Magazines
47 Church Street
Barnsley
South Yorkshire
S70 2AS

Edited by Roni Wilkinson

Design, layout & photograph colouring:
Jon Wilkinson

Maps by Dominic Allen

ISBN: 978 184884 102 4

A CIP catalogue record for this book is
available from the British Library.

Printed and bound in the United Kingdom

For a complete list of Pen & Sword titles please contact
PEN & SWORD BOOKS LIMITED
47 Church Street, Barnsley, South Yorkshire,
S70 2AS, England
E-mail: enquiries@pen-and-sword.co.uk
Website: www.pen-and-sword.co.uk

CONTENTS

1914

ACKNOWLEDGMENTS 3

INTRODUCTION 6

HURRYING TO CALAMITY – THE SPARK 8
Roni Wilkinson

WAR DIARY OF A GERMAN ARTILLERYMAN 18
Herbert Sulzbach

DEFEAT FOR THE ROYAL NAVY – 1914 34
Keith Yates

CONTEMPTIBLES AT MONS – 1914 50
Jack Horsfall & Nigel Cave

DIARY OF AN OLD CONTEMPTIBLE 80
Peter Downham

BAIRNSFATHER'S CHRISTMAS TRUCE 92
Tonie and Valmai Holt

INTRODUCTION

At the beginning of the twentieth century the then civilised world had everything to look forward to: the industrialisation of the previous hundred years was evolving with ever-increasing momentum promising an exciting future; electricity had been harnessed; steam-driven engines had revolutionised transport; the internal combustion engine had been invented and man had learned how to fly like the birds. Then, in the second decade, it all turned sour as countries set on each other turning the inventions of peace and promise into weaponry. The resulting conflict spawned further loathsome contrivances to destroy humanbeings, such as poison gas and flame-throwers. What had caused the change? Nationalism and patriotism whipped up by religious institutions in the countries involved must surely take the blame. As to the mechanics of the outbreak of the Great War, historians will continue to debate and each generation of them will doubtless revise the works of those living closer to the events of 1914-1918, as they seek to throw fresh light on that terrible period in the history of the world. This magazine looks at the last five months of 1914 as the nations, one after another, tumbled into war. How did it all come about?

In his paper *J' Accuse* Dr David Miller lays the blame for the war against the German Empire at the door of the French, in particular the Parti Colonial, drawn from the most powerful politicians, diplomats, bankers, industrialists and journalists in France. In the aftermath of the Franco-Prussian War of 1870-71, the capture of Paris, defeat of the French army and the loss of Alsace-Loraine, the Parti Colonial's masters conspired for revenge.

With a succession of weak French governments in the nineteenth and twentieth centuries, the Parti Colonial was effectively more powerful than its employers in the forming of foreign policy. Certainly that was the case with the Viviani government in office in 1914. Using its powers of diplomacy and with a well-defined secret agenda the Parti Colonial succeeded in forming an alliance with Russia. Germany was thus bracketed with potentially hostile countries on two frontiers. Italy, Japan, Spain and the United States were wooed in an attempt to draw them into the French diplomatic camp. The cartoon on page 11 of this journal illustrates the results of diplomatic chicanery.

The Parti Colonial had been unwittingly aided in its machinations by German foreign policy under Kaiser Wilhelm. The clever diplomatic manoeuvring of Bismark, who had always sought to keep France isolated, had been abandoned.

With its eye on a short war the Parti Colonial worked on a domestic, nationalistic revival within France.

In the Baltic state of Serbia visiting members of the Austrian royal family, Archduke Ferdinand and his wife, were shot and killed. Austria made demands on Serbia that could not be accepted without modification. Austria declared war on Serbia. Russia mobilised in support of Serbia. Germany declared war on Russia and attacked France to knock her out in a few weeks. Following victory in the west troops would be transported to the east to defeat Russia. The German war plan included a sweep through neutral Belgium.

Great Britain declared war on Germany. '*All over by Christmas*' was the view by many in August 1914.

What was it like to be a part of a massive invading army? In the article 'War Diary of a German Artilleryman' an extract has been taken from the best-selling classic *With the German Guns* by Herbert Sultzbach. His diary covers from October to Christmas.

It was unthinkable that the Royal Navy could be bested by the German Imperial Fleet, but as the Great War began to roll, a squadron of cruisers under the command of Admiral Graf von Spee clashed off South America with Admiral Christopher Craddock's squadron. This little known action in the Cornel Sea was a defeat for the Royal Navy.

Already the news was grim concerning the fighting in France and Belgium: the British army was retreating before the German invader, but not before the Battle of Mons had been fought. Our extract is taken from a bestseller in the Battleground series of guide books, Mons by Jack Horsfall and WW1 series editor, Nigel Cave.

The British Tommy's story during the first few months of the war is supplied by the diary of Edward Roe who records a war of movement that came to an end with the infamous trench system.

It might have ended at Christmas 1914 when the two sides stopped fighting and met up in the middle of No Man's Land for a party. The famous cartoonist Bruce Bairnsfather experienced that brief truce, before the two sides were ordered to return to killing each other. An opportunity for sanity missed.

'The driver took a wrong turn and was reversing slowly when Princip stepped forward, revolver in hand, and fired the fatal shots killing the couple. Within a short while every member the gang of assassins was arrested..'

A HURRYING TO CALAMITY – THE SPARK

The Balkans was a powder keg with its numerous small countries and its peoples speaking some fifteen plus languages; added to this were the two rival faiths of Christianity and Islam further dividing men. The bulk of the population of the Balkans professed the Greek Orthodox faith that looked longingly at Constantinople – which they regarded as their sacred city. The stage was set for the most terrible conflict the world had ever experienced, for the increased tensions in the Balkans prepared the ground for the assassination of the Austrian heir-apparent by a seventeen year old Serb student. The spark which ignited the fuse of war occured at the end of June 1914

By Roni Wilkinson

Extracted from *Pals on the Somme* and reproduced by permission of Pen & Sword Books Ltd.

Archduke Franz Ferdinand, nephew and heir to the Austro-Hungarian Emperor Franz Josef, and his wife were the victims of a Bosnia-Serb outrage while on a state visit to Sarajevo on 28 June 1914. It was strange that he should have been selected for the revolutionary gesture for he was perhaps the most liberal-minded member of the Hapsburg dynasty, often, it has been said, to his own detriment within court circles.

Archduke Ferdinand crown prince of Austro-Hungarian empire.

The Royal couple were to be driven to the Governor's residence and six members of the assassination team dispersed themselves along the route looking for opportunities to commit murder. Within minutes of the motorcade getting under way a bomb was thrown by gang member Cabrinovitch and the Archduke instinctively sought to ward it off. It struck the vehicle and bounced off to explode in the vicinity of the following car where fragments injured two Austrian officers. Immediately the wounded aides were driven to hospital. The Archduke ordered his driver to make for the same place so that he could ascertain the extent of the injuries of his staff. In the event, the driver took a wrong turn and was reversing slowly when Princip stepped forward, revolver in hand, and fired the fatal shots killing the couple. Within a short while every member the gang of assassins was arrested.

The assassinations called forth a strong note of protest and a message amounting to an ultimatum from Austria, in which they accused the Serbians of tolerating the machinations of dissident groups ranged against the Austrian-Hungarian monarchy. Although holding itself guiltless, Serbia made wide concessions. However, they could not accede to all ten points listed in the note:

1. To suppress all publications inciting to hatred of Austria-Hungary and which were directed against her territorial integrity.

2. To dissolve forthwith the Narodna Odbrana ['National Defence' – a propaganda society formed in 1908 to present Serbia's cause to the world]; and to confiscate all its means of propaganda; to treat similarly all societies engaged in propaganda against Austria-Hungary, and to prevent their revival in some other form.

The Archduke Ferdinand and his consort set out on their final journey to the town hall in Serajevo.

3. To eliminate from the Serbian educational system anything which might foment such propaganda.

4. To dismiss all officers or officials guilty of such propaganda, whose names might subsequently be communicated by Vienna.

5. To accept the 'collaboration in Serbia' of Austria-Hungarian officials in suppressing 'this subversive movement against the monarchy's territorial integrity.

6. To open a judicial inquiry into the murders, and to allow delegates of Austria-Hungary to take part in this.

7. To arrest without delay Major Tankosic and Milan Ciganovic, implicated by the Sarajevo inquiry.

8. To put an effectual stop to Serbian frontier officials sharing in the 'illicit traffic in arms and explosives', and to dismiss certain officials at Sabac and Loznica who had helped the murderers to cross over.

9. To give explanations regarding the 'unjustifiable language' used by the high Serbian officials after the murder.

10. To notify Vienna without delay of the execution of all the above measures.

Point 6 was a violation of the Serbian Constitution and their Law of Criminal Procedure and consequently the Serbian government felt unable to comply fully. It did however, agree to the other demands. More than ready to make what reconciliatory moves it could the Serbian government also stressed that it would be prepared to refer the matter to the Hague Court, should the Austro-Hungarian government feel dissatisfied.

The last thing that the government of Serbia wanted was another war, they had just been involved in two and were exhausted. It was generally agreed by the Great Powers that they were unlikely to have done anything so provocative as being a party to murdering the heir to the Hapsburg dynasty – neither instigating it nor desiring it. Even some German diplomats could not see the logic or reason in the Serbian government picking a fight with a more powerful neighbour and saw the reply to the ultimatum as compliance. Not so the Viennese government. A week after the assasination, Franz-Joseph, Emperor of Austria-Hungary, wrote to the Kaiser of Germany:

'According to all the evidence so far brought to light, the Sarajevo affair was not merely the bloody deed of a single individual, but was the result of a well-organized conspiracy, the threads of which can be traced to Belgrade and although it will probably prove impossible to get evidence of the complicity of the Serbian Government, there can be no doubt that its policy, directed towards the unification of all countries under the Serbian flag, is responsible for such crimes, and that a continuation of such a state of affairs constitutes an enduring peril for my house and my possessions.'

Cabrinovitch threw the bomb that was warded off by the Archduke.

Princip fired the fatal pistol shots. Police photograph shows signs of a beating.

As may be judged from the tone of the letter, there was absolutely nothing that the Serbian government could do to placate the Emperor and avoid war. Assurance of support for the Austrian stance came by telegram the following day from German chancellor, Herr von Bethmann-Hollweg who, speaking on behalf of Kaiser Wilhelm, wrote:

'His Majesty desires to say that he is not blind to the danger which threatens Austria-Hungary, thus the Triple Alliance as a result of the Russian and Serbian Panslavic agitation. As far as concerns Serbia, His Majesty of course cannot interfere in the dispute now going on between Austria-Hungary and that country, as it is a matter not within his competence. The Emperor Franz-Joseph may, however, rest assured that His Majesty will faithfully stand by Austria-Hungary as is required by the obligations of this alliance and of his ancient friendship.'

Germany would stand by Austria-Hungary in her punitive action against Serbia whatever the consequences.

Regarding help and support for Serbia, as it became increasingly obvious that there was no placating the

German Kaiser Wilhelm and Franz-Joseph, Emperor of Austria-Hungary, stood together against Serbia.

National alliances which ensured world war would result from any fallout: Germany and Austro-Hungary in one camp (Central Powers), ringed about by France, Russia, Great Britain (Triple Entente) and Italy.

House of Hapsburg, the Tsar of Russia sent a telegram to the prince regent of Serbia on the 24 July:

> *'When your Royal Highness applied to me at a time of special stress, you were not mistaken in the sentiments which I entertain for you, or my cordial sympathy with the Serbian people. So long as the slightest hope exists of avoiding bloodshed, all our efforts must be directed to that end; but if in spite of our earnest wish we are not successful, your Highness may rest assured that Russia will in no case disinterest herself in the fate of Serbia.'*

Russia stated that her forces would be mobilized the moment Austrian troops crossed the Serbian frontier. Immediately, the attitude of Germany stiffened and it became evident that even a partial mobilization of the Russian army would be regarded as a belligerent act. These were grounds for war, not only against Russia but against Russia's ally, France. In vain Russia protested that her partial mobilization was a precautionary undertaking. Secretly, Germany's own preparations for war were well ahead of those of any other European nation, as events would soon prove.

Matters began to move quickly. Four days later, on 28 July at 11 am, Austria-Hungary declared war sending a telegram to that effect to the Serbian town of Nis. They considered it the golden opportunity to settle the matter once and for all – that troublesome hotbed of intrigue

Tsar Nicholas II of Russia.

and rebellion Serbia would be 'brought to heel'.

The arrival of the declaration that was to launch the biggest slaughter in the history of mankind was remembered by a junior official in the Serbian Ministry of Foreign Affairs, 'I was having lunch in the Hotel Europa in Nis. The dining-hall was crowded with people from Belgrade. Between twelve and one o'clock a postman entered and handed something to Mr Pasic, who was eating about two tables away from me. Pasic read what the postman had handed to him and then stood up. The room fell deadly silent and he announced "Austria has declared war on us. Our cause is just. God will help us!"' An identical telegram was sent from Vienna to the Serbian supreme command.

Doubts about the authenticity of the telegrams arose when at 3 pm Pasic enquired of the German minister only to be told that the German Legation knew nothing about the matter. Immediately Pasic sent cables to the governments in London, Paris and St Petersburg about the strange telegrams asking if it could possibly be true that Austria-Hungary had declared war on Serbia.

Before he got answers to his cables Belgrade authorities informed him that guns were bombarding the Serbian capital. The last hopes that war could be avoided vanished.

True to her word and in support of her Serbian friends, on Friday, 31 July, Russia declared war on Austria and the following day Germany retaliated by declaring war on Russia. Because of the German war plan (drawn up by German strategist Count Alfred von Schlieffen) any war with Russia on the eastern frontiers meant an attack, in the first instance, in the west against

Albert, King of the Belgians.

Germany's traditional enemy, France. The theory was that by the time Russia had effected total mobilization, the enemy on the opposite border would have been annihilated within forty-two days. The national railway system would then transport a major part of the German army eastwards to defeat, in turn, the Russians who would likely have overcome the holding forces and be threatening German territory.

The German plan also called for passage of its main thrusting columns, comprising four armies, through neutral Belgium to get at France. Britain, whose foreign policy had always been to avoid, if at all possible, a super power dominating Europe, particularly the coastline opposite her shores, sought to support Belgium. The German government, on Sunday, 2 August, had demanded that Belgium grant its armies free passage or suffer the consequences. At 10 o'clock that night German troops crossed the Belgian frontier from the direction of Aix-la-Chapelle. Simultaneously their forces entered the independent duchy of Luxemburg en route to the French border. The first shots were fired by the French outposts in the provinces of Alsace and Lorraine. On Monday Albert King of the Belgians telegraphed King George V asking for help:

> *'Remembering the numerous proofs of Your Majesty's friendship and that of your predecessor, and the friendly attitude of England in 1870 and the proof of friendship you have just given us again, I make a supreme appeal to the diplomatic intervention of Your Majesty's Government to safeguard the integrity of Belgium.'*

The British government was officially informed by Belgium on 4 August that German troops had invaded Belgium and that the violation of that country's neutrality had become an accomplished fact.

Immediately, a telegram was sent by British prime minister Mr Asquith to the British ambassador in Berlin, to the following effect:

> *'The King of the Belgians has appealed to His Britannic Majesty's government for diplomatic intervention on behalf of Belgium. The British government is also informed that the German government has delivered to the Belgian government a note proposing friendly neutrality pending a free passage of German troops through Belgium and promising to maintain the independence and integrity of the kingdom and its possessions on the conclusion of peace, threatening in case of refusal to treat Belgium as an enemy.'*

Sir Edward Grey, the British Foreign Secretary, had requested an answer within twelve hours. The Prime Minister, Mr Asquith, then read a telegram from the German foreign minister, which the German ambassador in London had sent to Sir Edward Grey. The reading was greeted with hoots of laughter in the House of Commons:

> *'Please dispel any distrust that may subsist on the part of the British government with regard*

to our intentions by repeating most positively the formal assurance that even in case of armed conflict with Belgium, Germany will under no pretensions whatever annex Belgian territory.'

Premier Asquith was able to read to the House a telegram from Brussels which informed them that, the German government 'deeply to its regret', would be compelled to carry out by force of arms the measures 'considered indispensible in view of the French menace'.

Excited crowds gathered at Buckingham Palace and in Parliament Square, London, to witness the last seconds of peace ticking away and to greet a popular event. The deadline for Britain's ultimatum to Germany expired at 11 o'clock (midnight in Germany). The striking of that fateful hour by Big Ben was the signal for an almighty, enthusiastic roar. Patriotism, 1914 style, was born. Tuesday, 4 August 1914, Britain and Germany were at war.

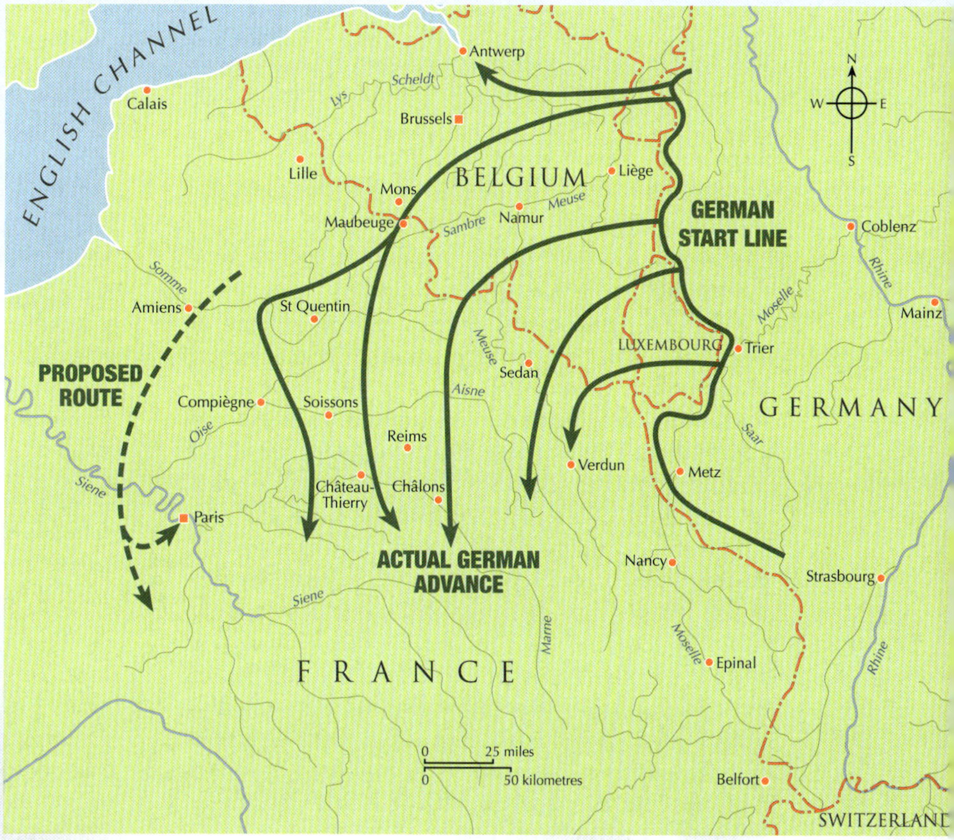

THE GERMAN ADVANCE THROUGH BELGIUM

It had come as no surprise to some. Certainly British Military Intelligence had been predicting an all-out war with Germany since 1907, according to recent research into hitherto unexamined documents originating in the Foreign Office and Admiralty. British agents had detected a pro-war faction among the senior officers of the German military who had become convinced that war was essential for the ongoing development and benefit of the German army. That belligerence was aimed mainly at Great Britain and her Empire and was, apparently, fed to the Kaiser as a regular diet of hate. The Kaiser, however, would make his move when he was absolutely convinced of a victory. With the situation in Serbia he felt that the opportunity had arrived. Certainly the masses were ready for it.

There were scenes of patriotic fervour and martial ardor during the first days of August in all the European capitals directly affected by the war. In London, Paris, St Petersburg, Vienna and Berlin enthusiastic crowds filled the streets, singing national anthems and hymns, cheering their respective rulers and national heroes. The

German soldiers of the 47th Infantry Regiment advance through north eastern France, August 1914.

'War of the Ages' had been launched and, over the coming months, the citizens of those same capitals of Europe would begin to experience heart-rending mourning as husbands, sons and lovers began to fall on the battlefields in such numbers as to surpass all former records of history.

IN SUPPORT OF BELGIUM

In Britain preparations for war had been going on some days prior to the expiration of the deadline. Reservists were called up and the Territorials were brought back from their summer training. Bank Holiday weekend (Bank Holiday Monday was 3 August) was the start date for the annual army camps, however, this time, the unfolding international events were to add excitement and drama to the occasion. No sooner had the trains taken the 'Saturday Night Soldiers' to their seaside locations for their fortnight of military training than they were running them back to their towns and cities. It was no mean feat, the South Midland Division under canvas near Rhyl was estimated to number around 10,000 men. As disgruntled holiday-makers were finding their excursion trains had been cancelled, the territorials were arriving back at their drill halls. As an integral part of the National Mobilization Plan the Territorials were, within days, being transported to pre-planned coastal defence positions.

The first four infantry divisions of the Regular army, comprising two thirds of the British Expeditionary Force, were in France by 12 August shortly to be pushed back by the huge columns of grey-clad invaders. An American correspondent for the *New York World*, Alexander Powell, described the awesome spectacle presented by the invaders:

'It was a sight never to be forgotten. As far as the eye could see stretched solid columns of marching men, pressing westward, ever westward. The army was advancing in three mighty columns along three parallel roads. These dense masses of moving men in their elusive blue-grey uniforms looked for all the world like three monstrous serpents crawling across the countryside.

'American flags which fluttered from our windshield proved a passport in themselves and as we approached the closed-locked ranks they parted to let us through.

'We passed regiment after regiment, brigade after brigade, of infantry, and after them hussars, Uhlans, cuirassiers, field batteries, more infantry, more field guns, ambulances, then siege guns, each drawn by thirty horses, engineers, telephone corps, pontoon wagons, armoured motor cars, more Uhlans, the sunlight gleaming on their forest of lances, more infantry in spiked helmets, all sweeping by as irresistible as a mighty river, with their faces turned towards France.

'Every contingency seems to have been fore-

A fortress protecting the Belgian town of Liège smashed by German guns.

seen. Nothing was left to chance or overlooked. Maps of Belgium, with which every soldier is provided, are the finest examples of topography I have ever seen. Every path, every farm building, every clump of trees is shown.

'At one place a huge army wagon containing a complete printing press was drawn up beside the road and a morning edition of the Deutsche Krieger Zeitung *(German War News) was being printed and distributed to the passing men. It contained accounts of German victories of which I had never heard, but it seemed greatly to cheer the men.*

'Field kitchens with smoke pouring from their stovepipe funnels rumbled down the lines, serving steaming soup and coffee to the marching men, who held out tin cups and had them filled without once breaking step.

'There were wagons filled with army cobblers, sitting cross-legged on the floor, who were mending soldiers' shoes just as if they were back in their little shops in the Fatherland. Other wagons, to all appearances ordinary two-wheeled farm carts, hid under their arched canvas covers machine guns which could instantly be brought into action.

'The medical corps was as magnificent as it was businesslike. It was as perfectly equipped and as efficient as a great city hospital.

'Men on bicycles with a coil of insulated wire slung between them strung a field telephone from tree to tree so the general commanding could converse with any part of the fifty mile long column.

'The whole army never sleeps. When half is resting the other half is advancing. The soldiers are treated as if they were valuable machines which must be speeded up to the highest possible efficiency. Therefore they are well fed, well shod, well clothed, and worked as a negro teamster works mules.'

The Germans had expected that Belgium, with its small army would, at most, offer a token resistance. While ineffectual in halting and throwing back the grey hordes surging across their fields and into their towns, they did manage to cause a delay of three valuable weeks. Close to the border were the Belgian towns of Visé and Verviers and they had been the first objectives of attack and Belgian defence. Both were occupied after desperate resistance and the town of Visé was systematically burnt in reprisal, it was claimed, for the firing by civilians on the German invaders.

A vivid description of the march into Belgium and the fighting in front of the fortress-ringed frontier town of Liège was given in a letter by one German officer who was wounded in the battle:

'Our trip towards the Belgian border was a triumphal procession, although it was pouring with rain as we marched through the Ardennes. The towns and villages seemed to us to be deserted. We had no rest and during the night we were fired upon.

'On 6 August, at dawn, we reached the Ourthe valley – there were obstacles everywhere. It was an awful march, the roads were frequently blocked by felled trees and rocks, and bridges over rivers had been destroyed. In the afternoon we took up quarters in a village some distance south of Liège.

'After thirty minutes the column was fired upon from the surrounding high ground. It was dark and pouring with rain and a thunderstorm was roaring.'

'Seven o' clock in the evening the order was given by the captain to march on Liège. It seemed impossible; we felt that we could go no farther for the forts were thirty-five kilometres away. But, nevertheless, we pressed on.

'After thirty minutes the column was fired upon from the surrounding high ground. It was dark and pouring with rain and a thunderstorm was roaring. Then suddenly shots were fired from quite close by and we see some of our men falling. Then we learned that our baggage train, bringing up the rear, had been attacked. Such are the atrocities of the franc-tireurs *[guerillas, or civilian snipers]. The night cleared and there was bright moonlight. In the distance we could hear the sound of heavy artillery pounding the forts.*

'One Company was ordered to turn back to the village that we had just passed through. There, the people were all shot and their houses burned.

'Meanwhile we keep marching on, and close to Liège we turned off and took cover behind a wood. Four regiments lay down their knapsacks and 'iron rations' were consumed. After resting we were then roused and formed up in attack formation. The last exhortations were given.

'We charged into a hail of bullets and shells which were being fired in our general direction, but with little accuracy. Along the way we ran past our own artillery with the guns and limbers stuck up to their axles in mud.

'Suddenly a hail of bullets came at us from directly ahead. It was our own men who were firing upon us – we had been mistaken for the enemy. Just in time we were identified and the firing ceased. We were then directly in front of

Belgian infantry, at a make-shift barricade, await the German massed columns flooding through their countryside, villages and towns.

the firing line of the forts. There was confusion all around and the password 'Woerth' was given as friend and foe looked alike.'

From the foregoing it is understandable that with hundreds of thousands of soldiers on the march cases of mistaken identity should occur. Today 'Friendly Fire' or 'Blue on Blue' (or, more commonly, 'Home Goal') are terms used to described such incidents. Back in August 1914 wounding and death suffered by the Germans in their advance was attributed to armed civilians, rather than highly nervous and trigger-happy comrades. Similarly, bridges, tunnels and telegraph lines that were blown up had to be the work of civilian saboteurs rather than Belgian military engineers.

Quaffing looted wine in order to quench their thirst during the marches probably contributed to the shooting incidents that were taking place. Again, believing such casualties to be the result of the work of Belgian civilians, the German army took reprisals. Time and again the actions of so-called *franc-tireurs* were used as the reason for the bombardment and burning of towns and villages. They were claimed by the Germans to be acts of revenge for hostile acts carried out by non-combatants and intended to prevent their occurrence elsewhere by striking terror into the hearts of the Belgian populace. Whatever the pretext or excuse, the historical fact remains that the result of the German progress toward the Franco-Belgian border constituted a martyrdom for Belgium. It gained the sympathy of the

Accused of firing on the German columns and blowing up bridges these Belgians are being marched to a place of execution.

German infantry come under fire somewhere in Belgium.

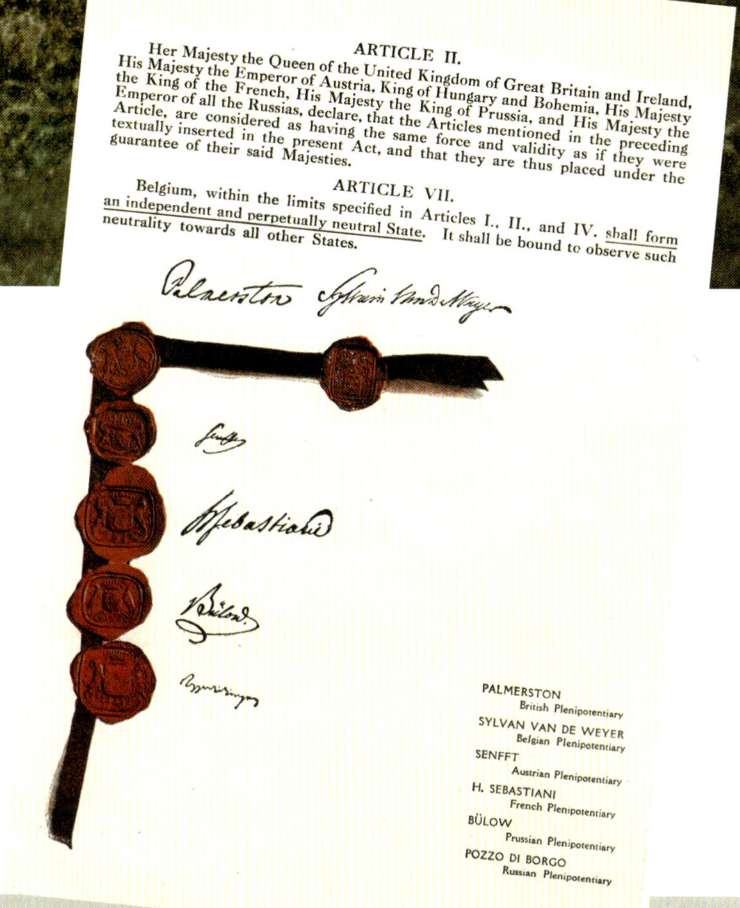

ARTICLE II.

Her Majesty the Queen of the United Kingdom of Great Britain and Ireland, His Majesty the Emperor of Austria, King of Hungary and Bohemia, His Majesty the King of the French, His Majesty the King of Prussia, and His Majesty the Emperor of all the Russias, declare, that the Articles mentioned in the preceding Article, are considered as having the same force and validity as if they were textually inserted in the present Act, and that they are thus placed under the guarantee of their said Majesties.

ARTICLE VII.

Belgium, within the limits specified in Articles I., II., and IV. shall form an independent and perpetually neutral State. It shall be bound to observe such neutrality towards all other States.

PALMERSTON
British Plenipotentiary
SYLVAN VAN DE WEYER
Belgian Plenipotentiary
SENFFT
Austrian Plenipotentiary
H. SEBASTIANI
French Plenipotentiary
BÜLOW
Prussian Plenipotentiary
POZZO DI BORGO
Russian Plenipotentiary

civilized world, put off potential allies to the Central Powers and stiffened Belgian resistance. The German timetable was thrown out enabling the French fully to mobilize and Britain to land its expeditionary force. Consequently, between them, the British and the French forces were able to effectively oppose the German advance on Paris.

It was becoming clear to the discerning leaders in the west that it would take a mighty force to halt and ultimately defeat the powerful war machine that had been fielded by the German High Command. Little wonder that the Kaiser referred to the British Expeditionary Force, which numbered in the first weeks a mere 94,000 men, as 'contemptibly little'.

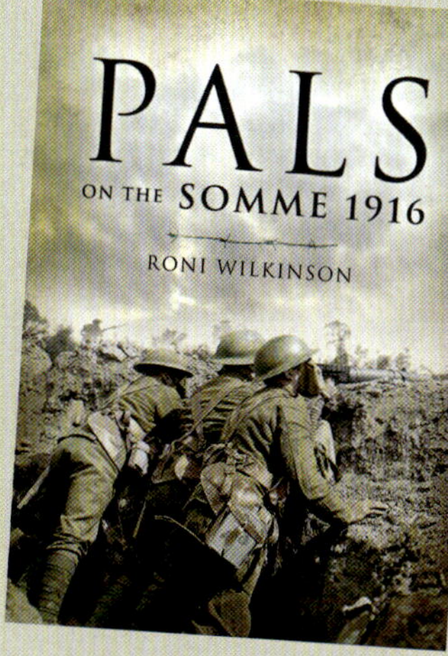

‘The façade of one house collapses, mounted patrol horses tear along the streets, and the first dead and wounded are lying about. You can’t see at all where the firing is coming from. I stand, or rather hang, on the reins between my two horses: No. 2 gun keeps on firing and firing.’

WAR DIARY OF A GERMAN ARTILLERYMAN

Frankfurt-am-Main, 28 June, 1914: Archduke Francis Ferdinand has been murdered, with his wife (the Duchess of Hohenberg), by two Serbs at Sarajevo. What follows from this is not clear. You feel that a stone has begun to roll downhill and that dreadful things may be in store for Europe.

By Herbert Sulzbach

Extracted from *With the German Guns* and reproduced by permission of Pen & Sword Books Ltd.

I am proposing on 1 October to start my military service instead of going to Hamburg as a commercial trainee. I'm twenty, you see, a fine age for soldiering.

Herbert Sulzbach.

14 July: I travel to Würzburg, report to the 2nd Bavarian Field Artillery Regiment and get accepted.

Böhm, the German airman, has scored a world record with 24 hours of continuous flight.

23 July: Ultimatum delivered to Serbia by Austria-Hungary.

No strong action by Austria appeared to have been taken since the assassination on 28 June until suddenly this note was presented, containing ten demands which among other things were supposed to allow Austria herself to take action on Serbian soil against activities hostile to Austria. Serbia has to accept the ultimatum within 48 hours, otherwise Austria reserves the right to take military action. A world war is hanging by a thread.

25 July: Unbelievably large crowds are waiting outside the newspaper offices. News arrives in the evening that Serbia is rejecting the ultimatum. General excitement and enthusiasm, and all eyes turn towards Russia – is she going to support Serbia?

The days pass from 25 to 31 July. Incredibly exciting; the whole world is agog to see whether Germany is now going to mobilize. I've hardly got enough peace of mind left to go to the bank and do my trainee job. I play truant as though it were school and stand about all day outside the newspaper offices, feeling that war is inevitable.

Friday, 31 July: State of war declared and total mobilization announced in Austria-Hungary.

Saturday, 1 August: 6.30 pm: The Kaiser orders mobilization of the Army and Navy. That word 'mobilize', it's weird, you can't grasp what it means. First mobilization day is 2 August.

Try as I may I simply can't convey the splendid spirit and wild enthusiasm that has come over us all. We feel we've been attacked, and the idea that we have to defend ourselves gives us unbelievable strength.

Russia's dirty intrigues are dragging us into this war; the Kaiser sent the Russians an ultimatum as late as 31 July. You still can't imagine what it's going to be like. Is it all real, or just a dream?

My brother-in-law travelled to Wilhelmshaven on 3 August. He's a staff medical officer on the Naval Reserve. I put my name down on the nominal roll, as a war volunteer, of course; I'm hoping to get into our 63rd. I go to the barracks and try my luck. A lot going on there, and people very enthusiastic; some tearful good-byes too, as the regiment of regulars is pulling out.

I visit my nice motherly friend Martha Dreyfus and get given a lucky penny. My brother is in London and means to be here in four days' time, or six at the most.

Berthold, who has been our manservant for quite a time, is joining his regiment, and our dear friend Hauptmann Rückward has already pulled out of barracks. Very rapidly, you might almost say in a few hours, nearly all the men one knows have disappeared from civilian life. My sister and all her married women friends are left alone – their husbands have joined the colours. The first enemy aircraft is reported to have flown over Frankfurt.

4 August: I think I'll certainly be able to get into the 63rd. All of us who have reported as war volunteers are enduring hours of anxiety in case there won't be room for us.

Mobilization is going as smoothly as you please, and people feel a terrible hatred for the Russians and the French. England's attitude is ambiguous.

Reports are coming in of the first clashes on the frontier. There's a huge spy-hunt going on inside

Germany, and notices in foreign languages are disappearing from the shops. And a curfew at 11 o'clock. My friends who have already completed their year of military service are all off now, and our beautiful Adler car has been 'called up' too.

The German Army has a huge job on its hands: war on two fronts. We can only hope that Providence will stand by us. At home our first officer is billeted on us, OW, Leutnant, Army Reserve, from Herborn.

On 4 August, in the evening, news that England has declared war.

7 August: My brother has landed at Hamburg, so he got away from England all right. My last day in civvy street. News in the evening that Liège has been taken by assault.

8 August: I am a soldier at last. Everybody so friendly, most touching. The girls are all most concerned, getting very motherly. Incidentally, I've been unbelievably lucky to have got into the 63rd, because no fewer than 1,500 war volunteers applied there in the first few days, and only 200 were taken; many of my school friends are in the same artillery battalion. My brother-in-law is in the SMS *Ariadne.*

9 August: My brother has arrived.

10 August: We are allowed out into the town in our fatigue uniforms: it is not very easy for us, since we can't even salute properly yet, but we manage it without being too glaringly conspicuous. The next few days are given over to training; the old drivers take particular pleasure in making us do 'stables', so that we get to know this aspect of military life. It isn't easy at first to muck out the stalls, water the horses, feed them and groom them. We start having instruction periods on shooting technique.

10 August: We hear about the victorious battle at Mulhouse in Alsace; also news of the battle of Lagarde. My brother has not been accepted by the Hanau Uhlans. When Liège was taken, a Zeppelin went into action giving air support for the first time.

11 August: Montenegro declares war on us, after previously declaring war on Austria-Hungary.

13 August: France and England declare war on Austria-Hungary. Japan is still keeping neutral, but seems unfortunately to have an alliance with England.

Our Zeppelin, the *Viktoria Luise*, comes over every day to do practice bombing. The German battleship *Goeben* is unfortunately stuck in the Mediterranean. Mobilization is gradually finishing off. It went marvellously. There are still a lot of military transports coming through.

20 August: Brussels has surrendered without firing a shot (Ghent did too, on 23 August). We need to occupy Belgium before we can be happy about advancing into France, because otherwise the French, whom the Belgians would certainly have let through, would have attacked us from the rear.

20-22 August: Great victorious battle in Lorraine, after which the French go into general retreat, more like a rout. Huge number of prisoners. It's the biggest battle so far, on a 300-kilometre front. The Crown Prince of Bavaria has been in command. In Paris the people seem to be very depressed.

23 August: My sister has arrived from Kissingen with her small child. My brother is with the 9th Hussars at Strasburg. Japan's ultimatum to us over Kiauchau not replied to means war with Japan as well. The few thousand Germans over there won't be a match for the superior weight of Japanese forces, but they'll fight like heroes until they are killed or taken prisoner.

Victorious action by the Crown Prince's army at Longwy.

24 August: Big victory celebration here under summer night sky.

25 August: Namur falls.

26 August: Longwy falls.

26 August: We are sworn in.

26 August: Hauptmann Rückward has been wounded and is back from the front, also Ottomar Starke and other people I know.

27 August: Our Reserve Battalion is ready to march. Wild enthusiasm.

28 August: Belgium has been completely occupied, and the French Army bulletins are beginning to admit that they are on the defensive. Big victory at St Quentin against the British and French.

29 August: Big victory against the Russians in East Prussia; General von Hindenburg in command.

Terrible news: the *Ariadne* has been sunk in a sea battle off Heligoland. And my brother-in-law was in the *Ariadne.* I was just beginning to say good-bye to my parents and my sister and, at the very same moment, my sister had news that her husband has died a hero's death: he went down with the *Ariadne*. It is nearly impossible to say good-bye to her because she finds the sight of me in uniform too painful.

Morale at the barracks is terrific, and I'd be just as happy and enthusiastic if this terrible misfortune hadn't happened to us; even the sympathetic telegram from the captain of the *Ariadne* is not able to bring us any comfort. The death of my brother-in-law is also honourably mentioned naval despatches.

The victory in East Prussia which I have already noted seems to have had a decisive effect, since the Russians who had pushed into East Prussia are pouring back in full retreat across their own border. Down in Galicia a battle is raging between Austrians and Russians.

We've been ready to march since 28 August, the very day my brother-in-law was killed in action.

1 September: We had more shooting with live ammunition at Bergen. In the evening news that 70,000 Russians have been taken prisoner in East Prussia, a huge victory, while the gigantic battle between the Austrians and the Russians seems to have ended in a draw after six days.

2 September: Reveille at 3.45 am; then a solemn church parade, and at 8 o'clock the long-awaited march-off after a bare four weeks' training. We are among the first few volunteers to reach the front. We entrained at the goods station, and I was seized by a strange feeling, a mixture of happiness, exhilaration, pride, the emotion of saying good-bye, and the consciousness of the greatness of the hour. We were three batteries, and marched in close order through the town to the cheers of the inhabitants. We travelled away through the country I love, past Boppard, Coblenz and on past all those enchanting villages and little towns along the Rhine. We were given our rations at Mehlem.

We hear that Turkey is mobilizing against Russia.

The journey continues. The horses stand quietly in their vans, and we lie between them. It is an idyllic picture; the men are cheerful. The first night, with a wonderful full moon, makes you feel a bit melancholy. You lie there in your fatigue uniform and try to sleep. Among my fellow war service volunteers are many acquaintances and friends from my schooldays. I know my Obergefreiter, he was a hairdresser. 2 September, that is the day we marched off and the anniversary of Sedan, overwhelming victory by the German Army against the French Army at Verdun. Apart from that, the Germans are only forty kilometres from Paris. If we could only be up there ourselves!

The Austrians are having another hard fight against the Russians at Lemberg.

3 September: Aachen. We got breakfast on the station. Many convoys travelling west, but strangely enough, three Army Corps as well, travelling from the west to Russia.

Last German railway station: Herbesthal. We get very ample rations, and the horses have oats, hay and straw in plenty. At Herbesthal again, more and more military trains, and I see the first trainload of prisoners, Frenchmen and Englishmen. Poor chaps, all dirty and untidy. I gave them as much to eat as I could find. At Herbesthal our convoy train stood still for hours, and fresh German convoys kept passing in both directions. We moved off towards Brussels. Our train stopped often on the way, and you saw the first ruined villages and country mansions; we saw our first carrier-pigeon in flight. During the night, a very long halt. At first it was eerie, but then we were reassured by a beautiful full moon shining down on a ruined mansion, like a scene in a fairy-tale. The men are relaxed and cheerful.

4 September: the picture changes. You see sentries everywhere, guarding railway crossings and bridges. It doesn't look so peaceful. Towards evening we get an order to stop looking out of the train and to shut the doors. Then we get an order to harness the horses in the train – not very easy for us.

5 September: at 2 am, in the fortress at Namur, taken a few days before, we moved into the Belgian Uhlans' barracks and stables. At daybreak we snatched a few hours' sleep on the straw. Next day begins with 'stables', just the same as in barracks at home. Then we can go out and look at the town, sit in the cafes and fancy ourselves!

We hear that the German cavalry is within a few kilometres of Paris.

There are a lot of German troops in the town: Stoipe Hussars, Mainz Dragoons, Hanau Uhlans. Strolling round the town, I see the first signs of artillery fire: houses in ruins and sad-faced inhabitants. The effects of bombardment made a very deep impression on us. In the town itself, all private houses have to be shut up by 9 pm. You get back at last to the habit of washing yourself properly.

We hear of fresh resounding victories in the East, and here in the West the French seem to be desperate.

German artillery column moving towards the French town of Lille in 1914.

Namur on the River Meuse.

At my barracks is a Belgian prisoner, who attacked a German officer and knocked him about and is now going to be shot tomorrow. I talk to him and feel overwhelmed by this event – having a man in front of you who is going to be executed next day.

On many doors in the town you see the proof of our troops' good nature. You are always finding messages chalked up, saying 'Be nice, chaps, and look after the people in this house', followed by the name of a unit. The days in Namur passed quickly. We had barrack duties, went outside the town to do exercises, and in our free time we could sit in cafes and restaurants; the first close friendships were struck up between comrades. The peaceful days were interrupted from time to time by air-raid warnings. On our exercises outside the town and near the forts of Namur we saw signs of serious fighting, and the terrible effects of artillery fire: houses levelled to the ground, forests mown down, barbed-wire entanglements, trenches, packs thrown away by Belgians or Germans, earth piled up by bursting shells. In the park of a beautiful château, more graves than you could count of Germans, Frenchmen, Belgians, all killed in action – war!

We keep noticing inscriptions on the doors of houses and cottages, even in the villages, 'Very nice people, please treat them kindly. Sergeant X', sometimes written in English and French as well.

We hear that Maubeuge has fallen (40,000 prisoners, including three generals).

The best hours of these days in Namur are when you are on guard duty at night. You feel your responsibility and apart from that you have peace and quiet to think, encouraged by the fabulous summer night sky.We war volunteers get high praise from our commanding officer and from Leutnant Reinhardt.

We are in a sweat to get to the front at last.

Now and then convoys of prisoners come through, and when they do I sometimes manage to talk to a prisoner and hear what he thinks. They are all glad to be coming to Germany and to have the war behind them. This is something we can't figure out. Rumours of the most nonsensical declarations of war: Some – not all, unfortunately – are untrue. I receive sad news of the deaths of many of my acquaintances and friends, especially from our sister regiment, the 81st. Who, out of all my friends and acquaintances, is going to follow them?

25 September: warning order to prepare to march. So the days at Namur are over at last, and in great excitement we saddle up, harness our horses and move off in field marching order. Off we go, passing near the battlefield of Waterloo. It's a cold night, but all the same you fall asleep from time to time on your horse. I am the middle driver on No. 2 gun.

26 September: we go through a pretty district, and hear gunfire from Antwerp way. We pass two villages, Braine-Le Comte and Enghien.

The closest friend I've made so far is Kurt Reinhardt, who is a regular officer cadet and my Leutnant's brother. As a soldier he is just as hard-working and keen as he is an intelligent and sensitive human being.

28 September: things get more exciting. We pull away from our billets in the dark and seem to have been formed into a detachment. 2,000 men are marching with us, from the 76th Rostock, the 87th Mainz *Landwehr*, Sappers and Ulm Uhlans.

One troop of my Battery, under Leutnant Reinhardt (including my own No. 2 gun), is in the lead. For the first time we move up to firing positions at a qick trot. In the excitement, doing a gallop over a trench, we broke a wheel, the No. 1 driver's horses stumbled and both mine fell over them; I was hanging between them, but it all went very smoothly, we replaced the limber and on we went. On this first advance I actually met a man I knew from Frankfurt. We fired four whole rounds, but there was no sign of the enemy. The position is getting more ticklish, and at last we seem to be coming properly into the firing line.

Again and again, when we are passing, the windmills start to turn – suspiciously; it looks as though this is a sign from mill to mill that the Germans are coming. I have no notion where the front runs or how far away our armies are.

Billeted in a tiny, poverty-stricken village – Welle.

29 September: Awful disappointment; our unit is ordered back to Namur. On the 30th, to our great joy, we are heading west once more. In our billets at Ath we have for the first time a room with a bed – unbelievable luxury, because generally you sleep on the ground or in a stable and don't wash.

1 October: We march off towards Toumai. The first section, the one containing my gun, is in the lead again today. Twelve kilometres short of Tournai our Uhlans are fired on once again; Tournai seems to be still occupied. The detachment commander is General Wahnschaffe.

At mid-day our advance party is ordered back into the Battery. At 2 o'clock we all go into position in front of Tournai. There is British artillery beyond Toumai; since we are not strong enough, we are ordered to pull back, unfortunately; and we had such an ideal position! It's boiling hot. An enemy airman is given a dose of rifle-fire by ourselves and the infantry, without success. Just this side of Leuze an unmanned locomotive was launched full steam ahead by the enemy towards our Sappers' train; we fired at the locomotive but unfortunately did not hit it. We heard later that it didn't destroy our Sappers' train because they managed to divert it to another siding.

On the march through Leuze we see many inhabitants with frightened faces. The houses have all their window-curtains drawn. The unit which last marched through Leuze seems to have been fired on by the civilian inhabitants, so we all ride through this 'pleasant' village revolver in hand. Next day I become the No. 1 driver on No. 2 gun. We pull back again and after two hours head west once more. An aircraft is sighted, but we see the Iron Crosses under his wings in time – so he's a German.

A cavalry patrol rides towards us; they are not our Uhlans, but Hussars from another unit. Six regiments are supposed to be advancing, including the 13th Hussars from Diedenhofen and artillery as well. And a whole corps is supposed to be coming up as well to support us. They seem to be preparing for a battle. One of the Hussars was wearing the Iron Cross Second Class; this was the first time I had seen it. We get back to billets in Ath for the third time. This everlasting marching to and fro appears to have the higher purpose of misleading the enemy.

Now it's October, how very different; I had thought this season would be, just a few months ago: first I wanted to take a trainee job with an export firm in Hamburg.

There seems to be an endless amount of cavalry near here.

3 October: Our section is the advance party again. Tournai has been evacuated by the enemy; we march through the town and get stared at by the inhabitants as though we were sea monsters – not very amiably.

We go into position outside the town, dig ourselves in and spend a pretty cold night in the straw beside the horses. Full moon again. While the sun is rising, the moon is sinking in the west: what a picture! The first Sunday properly in the field. At 9.20 am we cross the Franco-Belgian border. We are in France! At 1 o'clock we are in Helemmes, a suburb of Lille. No. 1 gun had just fired on a windmill, so that No. 2 gun – mine – was in front. Only twenty or thirty men of the 76th in front of us, and the main body behind.

The buglers sound 'Fix bayonets for assault'. It was incredible hearing the signal to go into action; you couldn't help thinking of the poem we had at school, *The Bugler of Vionville*. A terrible street battle began. We were right up at the front; the first barricades had been put up in front of a railway embankment, and the infantry swarmed over them all with bayonets fixed, and now a dreadful fire was directed at us, a hail of shots from every window, cellar-opening and skylight. We unlimber, firing into these narrow streets; it rumbles and crackles like hell, and we stand with our horses only ten paces behind the guns, so that it is nearly impossible to hang on to the wildly rearing animals; but hold them we must, for very soon the guns will have to be taken forward or back by these very horses. There's no

German artillery passing through a French town. Inhabitants peer at them from behind shutters and curtained windows.

German gun crew positioning a 77mm field gun.

question of retreat with our guns!

The façade of one house collapses, mounted patrol horses tear along the streets, and the first dead and wounded are lying about. You can't see at all where the firing is coming from. I stand, or rather hang, on the reins between my two horses: No. 2 gun keeps on firing and firing. Fires are starting in several places. The hellish noise makes it almost impossible to communicate with the command posts, so that our section has to beat a retreat with the infantry out of this dreadful street, and in so doing we encounter the main body, which has meanwhile also started street fighting. The jam of vehicles and men in this street is unimaginable, and in a few minutes it has accumulated to a scene of real devastation. After we had reassembled outside the town, we tried to get into Lille by another route, but were met by further fire, especially from machine guns, and had a number of wounded in the new position. We went back once more, bivouacked in a meadow and lay in the straw recuperating from our generous baptism of fire.

5 October: We move into a new position above another Lille suburb, dig the guns in and open fire. Enemy artillery fire replies, but is ineffective. As we limber up from this position we come under heavy small-arms fire, and we only manage to move to a new position by using the greatest skill and repeatedly throwing ourselves flat on the ground. The city is brought under continuous fire. Once more, we are passed by an exceptionally large quantity of German cavalry.

6 October: Spent in our bivouac and sleep between the horses. The horses have had their tack on for days; so have we, in our peace-time uniforms! At 5 am we move into a new position and dig the guns in once more. Then we witness an unforgettable scene: one cavalry regiment after another rides past us. The 23rd and 24th Dragoons from Darmstadt, mounted chasseurs from Trier, regiments from Metz, Karlsruhe, Bruchsal, Mulhouse and Cassel; they trot past us for hours and hours; they look terrific with their lances, and you feel that something very big is going to happen. You are actually there to see military units advance and take up their appointed places, you feel that a great battle is in preparation and you are suffused with hope and excitement. I saw quite a number of people I knew among the men moving past. How strange that people should meet on this gigantic front, pretty well on the field of battle.

It is fine to have found a friend like Fähnrich (Officer Cadet) Reinhardt – he has the same views and ideas as I have; we chat as we walk together to fetch water for the horses, and as we chat we forget the war.

We also foraged on our own account and found some marvellous wine in a deserted château; but the château itself looked terrible, everything broken and smashed to pieces – the owner will never see his fine mansion again in the state in which he left it.

I make notes for my journal, lying beside the horses. You are gradually growing a beard, and you can swear and grumble like an old soldier. You still feel it is something wonderful to be one of the millions who are able to join in the fighting, and you feel it is really necessary.

A German 77mm field gun ready to open fire.

A few quiet days follow in the same position. Our first casualties, killed on 4 October, are buried. We are quite near a village bearing the pretty name of Baisieux. At night, in the open, it is getting fairly cold.

I am proud to have been praised by my Captain for my conduct on 4 October. One is only just beginning to realize now what kind of situation we were in at the street battle on 4 October: it was providential that we got out of that fearful mouse-trap; we had not expected our baptism of fire to be so thorough. The enemy had fixed it up in such a cowardly way – he didn't let us fight properly, man to man, he just fired on us out of a snug hiding-place!

10 October: The sun is out and we are just seeing to our horses, when we receive a warning order: the Wahnschaffe Detachment is to occupy the citadel of Lille, which has been evacuated by the enemy. After a six-hour ride we get to the outskirts of Lille at about 6 o' clock; the civilians greet us, outwardly polite and nervous. Strangely, the trams are running, as though there weren't any war!

We move in, and along comes a report that our Uhlans have been fired on. Two batteries move into position, and our troop is the advance party again. On into Lille in the mist and darkness; we shoot into a cul-de-sac and can't get any further. Suddenly we get the order 'About turn, march!', since once again a volley of rapid fire is opened on us with rifles and hand-grenades from all the houses, and the situation is worse because it is night; some Uhlans' horses come back riderless, and we sit hunched up on our horses, as though you wouldn't get hit so much if you were near the horse! By some miracle we get our guns out without any casualties and camp in the open. It's an icy cold night and foggy as well. The horses are kept harnessed up, as every moment we expect the enemy to make a sortie out of Lille. You couldn't think of getting any sleep, and for the first time we are hungry. We are worried and silent; even more than on 4 October, you have the feeling that you're not going to get out of this dead end alive. Antwerp has fallen.

11 October: Today is my nephew Herbert's birthday, today he's a year old and has never consciously seen his father, who was killed in the first action at sea on 28 August – the terrible fate that has now happened to thousands!

We make our third attempt at getting into Lille and are fired on for the third time in doing so. We now discard all consideration for the inhabitants of Lille and open heavy fire on the city centre. We are not strong enough, and have to go back again; we expect reinforcements and camp near Chereng. Our morale is not good, our minds are full of the horrors of 10 October. We found a farm near by, had our first good meal and bought some wine and jam, which our comrades much appreciated. For some days we had been sleeping in a stable and had a roof over our heads, but we didn't get much sleep – along would come the well-known warning order: March for Lille! Icy cold night, dead tired, you're half asleep on foot or on your horse. At 3.30 we went into firing positions, and the sound of firing around us became louder. We had a blanket of heavy, damp fog over us.

12 October: After a disagreeable night, the stepped-up artillery attack on Lille began. You could see a huge fiery glow: Lille was burning. We hadn't intended this destruction, but after those street battles (where the heavy fire came not only from the military enemy but

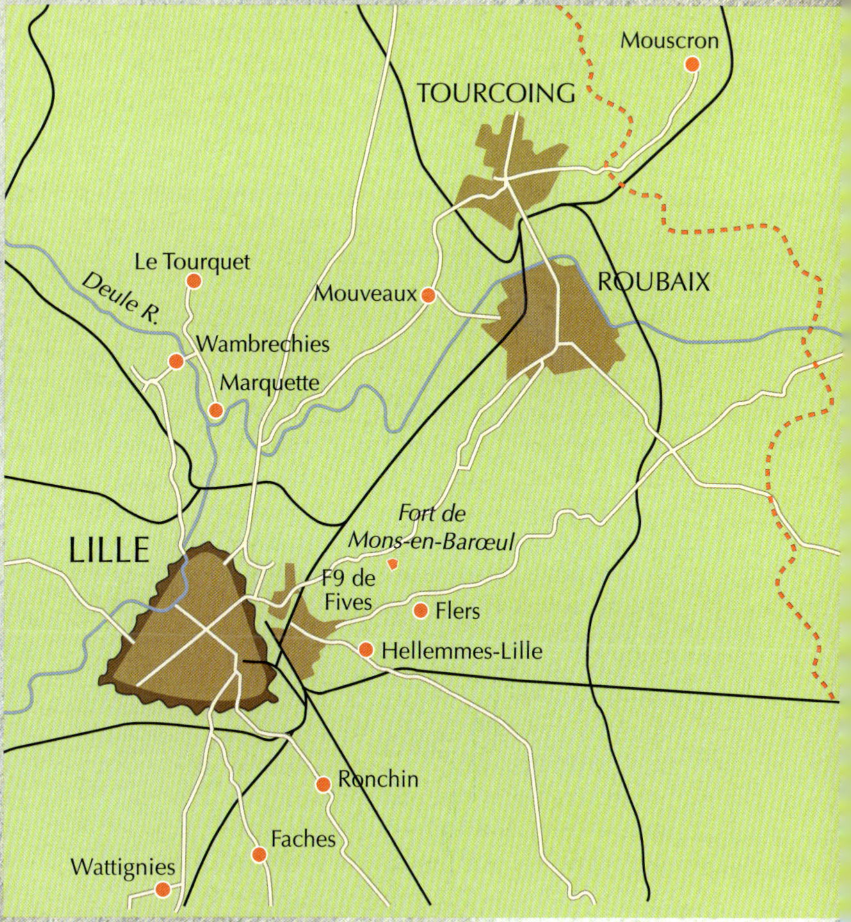

A German camera captures scenes of the fighting in Lille.

from civilians) it was unavoidable. 12 October draws to its close after we have been firing into Lille, with a few breaks, all day.

13 October: We enter Lille, our detachment from one side and part of the 19th Army Corps, which came to support us, from the other side. Now there is no more firing in the streets, and with cheerful hearts and high spirits we march in to the tune of Die Wacht am Rhein, We halt in front of the citadel; the 19th A.C. men have already brought out the prisoners, more than 4,000 French and Arabs.

Parts of Lille are still burning. More and more regiments are marching in with bands playing, and some of them march on immediately; apart from the regiments of the 19th (Saxon) Army Corps, Wiirttemberg regiments are coming through as well; and in a staff motor-car, the Crown Prince of Bavaria. At 2 o' clock we occupy the citadel, and a few French soldiers are still sitting about inside it. I have a long talk with them: we should all have been done for on 4 and 10 October if we had risked going any further into the city, and how incredibly lucky we were that they didn't spring that awful trap behind us!

The citadel itself was in an unbelievably scruffy condition; but all the same we found 500 Arab horses, rather thin, which our officers and NCOs were glad to take on. The experience of marching into the city and thinking of our own first well-fought victory gives each one of us complete satisfaction. I have another long talk with my friend Kurt Reinhardt and we get on to the subject of civilian life, talk about our childhood; all the things which you used to take for granted when they happened to you seem now idyllically beautiful. Leutnant Reinhardt has been busy all evening on a job for the High Command, drafting a proclamation in French to the inhabitants of Lille: it is to be posted everywhere tomorrow. Leutnant Reinhardt was also commissioned to speak to the city councillors of Lille, telling them they were to comply with regulations made by the High Command and would be well treated by us provided they did so.

The French are putting the blame for not being able to hold Lille on to the British. A short while ago Lille was still not occupied by the enemy and apparently it was a British suggestion that the city was in fact put into a state of defence.

14 October: We look after our horses and have quiet duties. We are not allowed out into the town yet. The civilians are supposed to be very much embittered, all the shops are said to be closed. A number of the prisoners have not yet been evacuated, and I talk once more to some of them, also to an Englishman who gives his anger at France an airing. We hear once more from the prisoners what incredible luck we had on 4 October, since the enemy intended to let us advance right up to the citadel and then to cut off our retreat. Only the premature firing at Helemmes saved us from this fate.

14 October: A day of rejoicing, since we received our first mail—no fewer than thirty letters for me, and lovely parcels of things to eat as well.

15 October: We move from the citadel into a barracks.

16 October: Parade.

17 October: We are allowed out into the town for the first time. We ate at a restaurant on the Grande Place. The city is swarming with German military. The whole 6th Army is supposed to be gathered here. I gaze wonderstruck at many cavalry officers and other ranks all wearing the Iron Cross. The cavalry must have been doing sterling work in the last few days. You see Hussars, Dragoons, Uhlans, chasseurs and *chevaulegers*, the light cavalry. I met several school-friends; one keeps on finding it strange to meet people one knows in the middle of a war as though one were in the Goethestrasse at Frankfurt.

19 October: Warning order, but it is cancelled in the evening.

20 October: Warning order! After our few quiet days we pull out of Lille at 6 am – into another battle; we belong to the 19th Army Corps. The roads outside Lille are blocked, we only advance seven kilometres in the whole day, and go into position in a village. We meet hundreds of British prisoners-of-war being evacuated.

We belong to the 2nd Battalion, the 77th Field Artillery Regiment. The gun-limbers are standing without cover and are under constant small-arms fire.

British and French prisoners are marched through the rue Faidherbe and place du Théâtre in Lille.

21 October: Change of position. We pull forward, get our first glimpse of this battlefield, and have to get used to the terrible scenes and impressions: corpses, corpses and more corpses, rubble, and the remains of villages. The infantry has taken the village of Premesque by assault. The bodies of friend and foe lie tumbled together. Heavy infantry fire drives us out of the position which we had taken up, and this is added to by increasingly heavy British artillery fire. We are now in an area of meadowland, covered with dead cattle and a few surviving, ownerless cows. The ruins of the village taken by assault are still smoking. Trenches hastily dug by the British are full of bodies. We get driven out of this position as well, by infantry and artillery fire. We stand beside the guns with the horses. A dreadful night comes down on us. We have seen too many horrible things all at once, and the smell of the smoking ruins, the lowing of the deserted cattle and the rattle of machine-gun fire make a very strong impression on us, barely twenty years old as we are, but these things also harden us up for what is going to come.

We certainly did not want this war! We are only defending ourselves and our Germany against a world of enemies who have banded together against us.

22 October: British planes fly over our position and report their observations to their artillery, so that we get a thorough 'blessing'. We cook hurriedly behind some ruined houses.

We see our first air battle, the first attack by a fighter aircraft. Our battery receives its first Iron Crosses, and we feel that each individual's decoration has been given to us all.

23 October: With our support the infantry makes an assault on the British positions, but the British have dug themselves in so well that the attack does not succeed.

24 October: Hellish infantry fire, many horses wounded. Enemy fighter aircraft fly over us. Ownerless dogs have found their way to us and give us great pleasure.

Sunday, 25 October: Lovely warm autumn day. Heavy artillery fire began at mid-day. We replied to it, and towards evening fetched ammunition from Lomme. Bringing up the ammunition along roads under continuous fire is very disagreeable; heavy rain and a cold autumn night: we're soaking wet and have to sleep pretty well in the water.

27 October: At 6 am we try another assault, with the infantry, on the British lines: the beggars won't give an inch, and our 109th and 138th sustain heavy casualties. We still get fired on from time to time, the shots coming from ruined houses and farms lying in some cases beyond the front, and on searching them found to our astonishment that the snipers were real heroes: wounded Englishmen.

We kill and pluck any hens still running loose and thus provide our own rations; our trusty gunners prove to be farmers and milk the ownerless cows; they don't get put

Parade in the Grande Place.

Human debris; German corpses after an attack.

off by odd shells falling near them. We construct our first crude dug-outs.

28 October: Today we have been in this position for a week. At night we came under heavy small-arms and machine-gun fire. In the meanwhile a field telephone has been laid between the individual command posts. I am a telephone operator. Of course the cable keeps getting shot through and one has to keep on patching it. The job of being a telephone operator is exceptionally interesting, since you are the man who gets first news of all important messages regarding future hostilities. The most difficult job is to keep the cable to the infantry intact. Our position lies 400 metres behind the trenches.

29 October: Fetched ammunition again. British planes drop leaflets saying that we ought to surrender. The other way round would be more sensible!

A Saxon company tries an extremely daring assault entirely on its own, which costs the lives of nearly every man in the company.

There are also quiet hours when we sit in the sun, chat and smoke and play cards. The red-letter days are always the ones when we get our mail.

We fire on enemy artillery at 2,700 metres: delayed-action fuses. Our battery has gradually gone under cover, very nicely camouflaged. Artificial trees have been planted so that the enemy airmen can't spot us. The dug-outs are like mediaeval caves.

1 November: Large-scale washing and shaving operation. We gradually notice that the static war which we have got into is becoming a permanent fixture. Rainy November days follow, all rather alike. Exchanges of fire with enemy artillery are becoming a habit. We've been in our uniforms for weeks without being able to undress. At the beginning of November we hear that Turkey has declared war on Russia – all the better for us, thank God! We get our first newspapers and read about the Emden and her heroic exploits. The first replacements for our casualties arrive. I've been sent a proper sleeping-bag from home. Now I can sleep even in the open when it's raining without getting wet!

8 November: Another red-letter day – we are kitted out in field-grey. Up to now we've been wearing our old blue peace-time uniforms.

We have to keep going out to hunt *francs-tireurs*, civilians behind the front who take every opportunity of shooting at us out of hiding-places. People have been saying for some days that America wants to declare war on Japan and Britain – if only it were true!

10 November: Dixmuiden has fallen.

11 November: Another assault is mounted against Armentières, the town in front of us. It is pouring with rain, and every inch of Armentières is burning. The battle is raging most fiercely on the right wing. Small-arms and artillery fire are going over our heads continuously. The battle doesn't slack off at night, and a cloudburst of rain and stormy wind help to make a proper Shakespeare night of it all; the limbers are brought somewhat further back, after weeks positioned right behind the guns, with the horses standing day and night in harness; the good-natured beasts are to be taken to stables in a little village, one kilometre to the rear. The poor creatures badly need a rest.

So now the limbers are at Perenchy, in a flax-spinning factory. I am here for a few days, and in the evenings drive up to the guns with mail and rations. This is generally a frightful drive through pitch darkness made even more dreadful by the fires in burning Armentières.

I'm just managing to write to my family. It is a relief to be able to report your experiences in detail. You also get time to think about beautiful things from the past, but you don't have thoughts about the future. My friendship with Kurt Reinhardt fills me with complete happiness. We see less of each other because he has had to stay with the guns.

25 November: The first snow is falling; icy wind and stormy weather. On 18 November comes the shattering news that the Emden has been sunk in Chinese waters, after very many heroic exploits which have been acknowledged with honour even by our enemies. They say the crew has been saved.

We hear that a great sea battle has been fought off Chile, ending in a victory for the German squadron. Another 20,000 Russians have been taken prisoner in the East.

The snow is covering the ground now and has turned the plains of Flanders into a winter landscape.

29 November: Mail arrives in the evening, and among other things I get a parcel as a present from my old school. Then we read the newspapers out loud to each other. At the battery meanwhile they have made themselves much more cosy. The dug-outs have tables and stoves and one even has a piano in it. Now we have been a whole month in this position. We exchange greetings with the British every day in the shape of shells; everything is gradually becoming a habit. Great excitement and interest as we watch air fights between German and British flying men. Now and again we use our guns to attempt to knock down an enemy plane, but each time it remains an attempt. It is still a winter landscape with cloudless days, cold and sunny.

A piece of special praise from my extremely strict Feldwebel nearly fills me with delusions of grandeur. I have taken on one of the ownerless dogs. A small mongrel terrier bitch. It is very touching, by the way, how fond all our men are of animals; it indicates a good character. It's very moving to see how our old driver Strobel can never go to sleep without his little dog, and looks for him for hours if he isn't there.

We are preparing more and more for a static campaign. The infantry positions have been surrounded with strong barbed-wire entanglements.

The sea battle which I mentioned on 18 November was the battle of Coronel.

27 November: Report that another 129,000 Russians have been taken prisoner in the East. Bravo Hindenburg! We keep hearing of more heroic exploits by the *Emden*, which was sunk in such a famous action, and now further stories about the *Karlsruhe*.

Really marvellous food parcels come up in the mail, and the whole battery enjoy them.

1 December: I get leave to spend a day in Lille with two friends. Can you people at home imagine how we felt to get out of the mud of battle into a town actually inhabited by civilians and looking almost like peacetime? Shops, restaurants, cafés, civilians and military in clean clothes. We gorge our selves at the Café Mert, but at the

Another French town burns.

same time we can't avoid seeing how wretched and impoverished many French civilians look and how grieved they must be feeling. On the way back we also sat in a bar at Lomme, where we met several chaps from the 107th. They sang patriotic songs of home, but also some sentimental ones. Tomorrow they have to go back and lie in a trench: here they forget the situation and also the fact that tomorrow they may be dead.

In the evening we are back in the battery. The next few days passed monotonously, until we got a warning order on

9 December: It is very difficult to bring the guns back over this completely flat Flemish country without incurring any casualties, and actually the job ought to go to drivers of long experience, but since I am the only war volunteer, I am entrusted with the responsibility of being No. 1 driver. It is a pitch-black night and foggy as well, a difficult run, but we manage it.

10 December: At 7 am off to Lomme, where our whole Wahnschaffe Detachment assembles; we make our way through Lille and Marcq-en-Baroeuil and move into quarters in a brewery. The other ranks get private billets, we are put up by pleasant people.

11 December: Rest day.

12 December: We march to La Madeleine and entrain there – done very quickly; before that there were another four sacks of mail.

My 'pure-bred' terrier is still with me. We are given our evening rations at Hirson, and sleep in fours with the horses in the waggons.

We aren't clear yet whether we're on our way to Russia or going across to the Champagne country.

13 December: We detrain at 6.30. It's as black as night,

Leutnant Kurt Reinhardt.

Lille station and rue de Tournai during the German occupation. The trams kept running during the fighting to capture the town.

we have to saddle and bridle the horses in the dark; then we stop at a main road, we're between Rheims and Verdun. We go into quarters in Pont-Faverger, a pretty little village; the horses have good stables, and we have straw to sleep on beside the horses. We had hardly unpacked when splendid military music drew us out into the market-place, where we were surprised to see a number of senior officers strolling about, listening to the music: they gave us a really good selection. La Boheme, then folk-songs and waltzes. Then a new infantry regiment marched past with its band playing. We are just a few kilometres behind the front here, and apparently at the front itself troops are being moved about a lot. We belong to the 6th Silesian Army Corps. We see to our horses and groom them, and watch our airmen flying up to the front to reconnoitre. Pont-Faverger is in a charming position, surrounded by woods and undulating fields, and a little river flows through the centre of the village.

I spend the first evening with Kurt Reinhardt. We turn in beside the No.1 gun horses, and before we go to sleep we tell each other all the things we have been thinking about.

Kurt's father has been given the Iron Cross First Class. Kurt is as pleased about it as if he had had the medal himself. Before turning in we go and have another Bavarian beer at the Uhlans' canteen.

14 December: Duties. Then we have time to go for a walk through the village. The sun is out, really rather like spring, and I sit with Kurt Reinhardt in a garden with the little river flowing past and beside us two beautifully kept graves, belonging to men killed in action at the time when Pont-Faverger was still in the fighting line instead of being behind the front as it is today.

The next few days pass at an even pace, almost peacefully, and we can do with the rest after the strain of our exertions in Flanders in October and November.

17 December: Parade taken by General von Pritzelwitz. News of further large-scale victories against the Russians.

20 December: It is *Golden Sunday*, the last Sunday before Christmas Eve! God, what memories from peacetime! You feel that peace is something which ceased to exist ages back and that war is mankind's permanent situation. The first Christmas parcels are arriving.

21 December: Warning order – what's going to happen to all the lovely parcels? However, the order gets turned off again, so we are able to enjoy our parcels. Meanwhile, nearly everybody has got hold of a mouth-organ, and we put on a splendid concert without a brass band or anything. The CO of the 51st, who are here too, is very jolly with his men, a real charmer. Some of my mates have got cameras too, and people are busy taking snapshots.

In the evening we organize a serenade for Reinhardt, as it's his birthday: the music rings out under the bright moonlit sky. Another warning order at 10 pm. It doesn't look as though well be staying here much longer.

The next few days before Christmas bring us more mail and such a lot of food parcels that we can't possibly eat everything. People at home must think we're about to die of starvation.

23 December: We're getting in the mood for Christmas and go and fetch trees out of the woods. We feel well and happy. Our No. 3 and No. 4 guns leave us to become what they call Anti-Balloon Guns.

In the evening we get the shattering news that after many victories at sea, the *Graf Spee* squadron has been out-gunned by the British and sunk off the Falkland Islands: all those cruisers – *Gneisenau*, *Scharnhorst*, *Nürnberg* and *Breslau*.

24 December: It's snowing, a proper Christmas atmosphere. We are given inoculations, and at 5 there's a church parade; a big garage has been transformed into a church. On each side of the altar a fine Christmas tree is bright with candles, and 'palms' have been put up all round the walls. The officers sat at the front, with the choir on the left, and the men standing behind. It was all so solemn and uplifting that you had tears in your eyes even before you heard the strains of *Silent Night*, We were all much moved and felt quite melancholy, each of us taken up with his own thoughts of home.

Then our battery celebrated Christmas in our own back yard, under a splendid tree of our own – it was a Christmas Eve worthy of the name, and very beautiful too. The Regiment gave me a most splendid Christmas present: I was promoted to the rank of *Gefreiter*, (lance-bombardier) and it did me good to be picked out like this after so short a time.

25 December: Christmas celebrations are over. At 10 o'clock we get a warning order to march off immediately. We entrain and proceed to Challerange under a bright moonlit night, icy cold and sparkling with stars, and on to Montois, where we go into billets.

26 December: We move off again, this time through Ardeuil to Ripont. Here we are in the middle of the district whose name you know so well: Champagne! From Ripont we have to go up steep slopes over hard-frozen ground to our new firing position, which we move into at 6 o' clock. And that's our Boxing Day, our 'second Christmas Day'. The limbers stand out in the open, in the icy cold night, and we stand beside the horses, but relieve each other to get warm in the dug-outs belonging to the 16th, to whose 2nd Battalion we now belong (8th Reserve Army Corps). Christmas, 1914, is over.

The horses are withdrawn to Ripont Mill, then to another position; it's thawing now and is cold and wet as well, we are sleeping in holes in the ground and the horses are standing up to their knees in mud. Every scrap of woodland looks like a Red Indian village. Cave after home-made cave, and rough stalls, hastily knocked together, for the horses; the limbers, with the horses beside them, wait quite close to the guns as they fire. It seems even more disagreeable here than it was at Armentieres. The weather and the Champagne mud reduce our morale. There are exchanges of artillery fire which do not involve casualties.

29 December: I am given orders to ride to St Morel with

Christmas 1914.

Lance-Sergeant Debler. I take Lance-Sergeant Lauer's horse and we ride off on the two little Arabs, across fields to Granddeuil. Nothing but mud. Lance-Sergeant Debler had business with the Captain, while I waited outside. We made our way back as night was falling, and it was very hard indeed to find one's way.

In the evening I was on guard duty.

We receive our first mail in this position – that is, we have to fetch it ourselves from the rear by limber, which is a dreadfully difficult operation, with the vehicle and horses practically sunk in the mud. After these few days we really look like pigs. The fire gets heavier, it's developing into an artillery battle, what they call a 'gunners' duel'.

31 December: So 1914 is winding up today. A year to raise your spirits, but also a year of pain and sorrow, not only for us but for the whole of what is called the civilized world. This terrible war goes on and on, and whereas you thought at the start that it would be over in a few weeks, there is now no end in sight. Your feelings harden, you become increasingly indifferent, you don't think about the next day any more. It's my sister's birthday today: how will she be feeling without her husband?

A wish for us all for 1915: may this new year make up for 1914 and bring us peace. We drank the New Year in; there was no firing, we felt happy and for a few hours were able to forget the present.

'Unfortunately there could be no thought of saving the poor fellows; firstly I believed I still had an enemy before me, secondly the sea was so high that hardly a boat could have lived in it...'

DEFEAT FOR THE ROYAL NAVY – 1914

Easter Island was a Chilean possession, and in 1914 the bleak volcanic island's only non-native residents were the English manager of a sheep and cattle ranch, a French carpenter, and a German tobacco planter. There were also a few hundred Polynesian natives and the members of a British scientific expedition who were visiting the island to study its mysterious stone statues. The latter had arrived in May in a ninety-ton schooner.

By Keith Yates

Extracted from *Graf Spee's Raiders* and reproduced by permission of Pen & Sword Books Ltd.

The island had no wireless. So, when a fleet of warships and merchantmen visited their remote colony in the autumn of 1914, the inhabitants were amazed, and they watched in astonishment as ship after ship steamed into the bay and dropped anchor. Within five days the anchorage was crowded with more than a dozen Geman ships. The *Dresden* and her collier, *Baden*, were the first to reach the rendezvous, on October 10. Two days later the *Scharnhorst*, *Gneisenau*, and *Nürnberg* arrived with the *Titania* and the supply ships *Yorch* and *Gottingen*, Finally, the *Leipzig* steamed in on the fourteenth with her coterie of colliers.

Admiral Maximilian Graf von Spee.

The residents of Easter Island had no idea that Gcrmany was at war with Britain, and the visitors didn't enlighten them. Even if they had known about the war, the inhabitants couldn't have done anything about the Germans' arrival because there was no representative of the Chilean government to insist on the rules of neutrality. Graf Spee knew that his squadron's visit would remain a secret for several weeks because it would take that long for the British schooner to reach the mainland.

His officers bought beef and lamb from the English rancher, Percy Edmonds, with a bank draft. (The meat was examined thoroughly by the ships' doctors before being taken on board ship.) Edmonds was dubious about this method of payment because he began to suspect that war had broken out. The draft was later honored by a German bank in Valparaiso, 'vastly to his astonishment and relief.' The Germans also traded with the island's Polynesian natives for fresh fruit, vegetables, and eggs. All these purchases were thoroughly examined before they were allowed on board.

While his cruisers loaded coal and provisions, Graf Spee went ashore with his two sons and Captain Maerker. Thcv explored the island but found its plant life disappointingly sparse. The only part of the trip they enjoyed was their visit to the huge stone idols that had been discovered by the Dutch admiral Roggevccn in 1722.

Geman light cruiser Dresden *arrived at Easter Island 8 October 1914.*

The* Scharnhorst, *Graf Spee's flag ship.

Gneisenau.

Nürnberg.

Leipzig *arrived at Easter Islands with up-to-date war news for the rest of Graf Spee's cruiser squadon.*

Coaling operations at Easter Island were the most unpleasant the squadron had ever experienced. The only decent anchorage was in the unsheltered Mataveri Bay. The weather conditions became so bad, with high winds and driving rain, that the cruisers were in danger of dragging their anchors and drifting onto the rocky shore. They had to put to sea to finish coaling.

But there was a pleasant side to the visit, once the *Leipzig* had arrived. Her officers and men were able to renew old acquaintances in the other ships and exchange experiences since the squadron had left Tsingtao in June.

The *Leipzig* had brought some fairly recent newspapers from Peru, and the crews were delighted to read about the Emden's brilliant success as a commerce raider and of her daring attack on Madras. They also learned that the *Konigsberg* had sunk a British cruiser at Zanzibar. The islanders found some of these newspapers after the Germans had left and discovered that war had broken out months earlier. But without a wireless there was nothing useful they could do to inform anyone about the squadron's visit. By the time the *schooner* could get the news to the mainland, Graf Spee would have long since left the island, and his whereabouts would remain a mystery.

While the German squadron was moving steadily across the Pacific, far away in the Admiralty building Churchill, Battenberg and the Chief of Naval Staff, Vice Admiral Sir Doveton Sturdee, were becoming increasingly worried about the threat it presented. From all reports, Graf Spee seemed to be heading for the west coast of South America. If his squadron descended on this busy shipping area it would create havoc. Britain had important trade with Peru and Chile in grain, lamb, nirates and copper – it could ill afford to have it disrupted.

As Churchill put it, the problem with Graf Spee was: 'He had no lack of objectives. He had only to hide and strike. The vastness of the Pacific and its multitude of islands offered him their shelter and, once he had vanished, who could say where he would reappear. So long as he lived, all the Allies' enterprises lay under the shadow of serious potential danger. We could not be strong enough every day and everywhere to meet him.'

Even if the Admiralty sent a squadron to try and intercept Graf Spee and to protect the trade routes from Chile and Peru, he might slip by it and reach the South Atlantic by going through the Strait of Magellan or around Cape Horn. Attacks on the River Plate traffic would be even more damaging to Britain because of its heavy dependence on Argentine beef and grain.

Four weeks before the Germans arrived at Easter Island, the Admiralty had given Rear Admiral Cradock the task of stopping Graf Spee. Cradock had left the hunt for the Karlsruhe to Admiral Stoddart, and he was now doggedly working his way down the eastern side of South America searching for the *Dresden*. He planned to sink the cruiser if he could catch her. If not, he would follow her trail until it led him to Graf Spee.

> *'On September 3 Cradock signaled the Admiralty:* Good Hope *arrived Fernando Noronha.* Cornwall *is proceeding south.* Glasgow *is proceeding with Monmouth and Otranto to Magellan Straits, where German colliers reported, and where concentration of German cruisers from China, Pacific and Atlantic appears possible.'*

The Admiralty approved of these plans, but when Cradock asked, 'Gneisenau *and* Scharnhorst *reported Caroline Islands 8 August. Is there any later information?'* it could only tell him, *'No certain information... since August 8... Magellan Straits and vicinity quite possible.'*

Two weeks later the Admiralty was a bit more definite. Cradock had reached Santa Catarina Island, four hundred miles southwest of Rio, where he received the following orders:

> *'There is strong possibility of* Scharnhorst *and* Gneisenau *arriving in Magellan Straits or on west coast of South America. Germans have begun to carry on trade there. Leave a sufficient force to deal with* Dresden *and Karlsruhe. Concentrate a squadron strong enough to meet* Scharnhorst *and* Gneisenau, *making Falkland Islands your coaling base.* Canopus *is en route to Abrolhos; Defence is joining you from Mediterranean. Until Defence joins, keep at least Canopus and one "County" class cruiser with your flagship. As soon as you have superior force, search Magellan Straits, being ready to return and cover Plate, or search north as far as Valparaiso. Break up German trade and destroy German cruisers.'*

This signal is as breathtaking in scope as it is vague on detail. How on earth was Cradock supposed to accomplish all this, even if his four ships were reinforced by the *Canopus* and *Defence*? The latter was more heavily armed than any of Cradock's ships, with four 9.2-inch guns and a secondary armament of ten 7.5-inch. She was a match for either the *Scharnhorst* or the *Gneisenau*, but it would take her at least two weeks to reach Cradock from the Mediterranean. In the meantime, did the Admiralty believe that two old cruisers and an obsolescent battleship could stop Graf Spee's modern armoured cruisers, whether they were accompanied by his light cruisers or not?

The *Canopus* was still rated as a battleship, but she was of 1897 vintage and had been ready for the scrap heap by 1914. When war came she was hastily recommissioned with a crew of reservists who were never given any practice firing her 12-inch guns. These were potent enough weapons to sink Graf Spee's ships if they could hit them, but the battleship could only manage seventeen knots at best. Graf Spee could easily steam away from the Canopus or simply maneuver just outside of her range and sink her with his own big guns. Although they were of the same range on paper, in reality they probably outranged the old guns of the Canopus by a thousand yards. The Germans were to show later that their smaller-caliber weapons could easily outrange bigger British guns.

Rear Admiral Sir Christopher Cradock was expected to take on Graf Spee's modern cruisers with only two old cruisers and an obsolescent battleship.

Furthermore, it was 2,500 miles from Cradock's base in the Falklands to Valparaiso and 3,300 miles to where the *Karlsruhe* was operating. How could Cradock cover all this territory with his handful of ships, and who was to know whether Graf Spee would go through the Strait of Magellan or Around Cape Horn? Fortunately, the German trade referred to as one of Cradock's tasks was based more on rumor than fact. The only German merchantmen off South America at the time were Graf Spee's supply ships. The Admiralty had originally considered sending Cradock not only the Defence but also no less than three armoured cruisers. But because of fears of a German invasion of Britain, it decided that these ships could not be spared from their patrol duties in the English Channel. Sturdee and Battenberg proposed an alternative: Why not send Cradock some fast battle cruisers from the Grand Fleet? The fleet's admiral Sir John Jellicoe, protested strenuously to Churchill that this would dangerously reduce his slim battle cruiser superiority over the High Seas Fleet. In the end, Churchill gave in to Jellicoe and decided to order only the Defence to join Cradock. This would have been a vital addition to his squadron, but when news reached the Admiralty that Graf Spee had left Samoa in a northwesterly direction, the order was canceled and the Defence stayed at Malta.

Unaccountably, the Admiralty didn't see fit to

> *tell Cradock about this change of plan. Apart from the ancient* Canopus, *he was to get no more reinforcements. It signaled him on September 16: Situation changed.* Scharnhorst *and* Gneisenau *appeared off Samoa on 14 September... and left steering NW... Cruisers need not be concentrated. Two cruisers and an armed liner would appear sufficient for Magellan Straits and west coast. Report what you propose about* Canopus.

HMS Canopus.

The Admiralty believed that the situation in South America was no longer urgent because the two most dangerous German ships were apparently heading toward the northern Pacific. Graf Spee's feint at Apia had worked.

By the time Cradock received this signal two days later, he had reached Montevideo. He replied that he intended to sweep south as far as the Strait of Magellan to search for German ships. Rased on the Admiralty's faulty assessment of Graf Spee's movements, Cradock now believed that he was likely to meet only the *Dresden*, which he could deal with easily. He told the Admiralty he had decided to send the *Glasgow* and *Monmouth* to the west coast to destroy German trade and that he was leaving the *Canopus* in the River Plate area to guard his supply ships.

'It blew, snowed, hailed and sleeted as hard as it is possible to do... I thought the ship would dive under altogether at times.'

On its way to the strait, Cradock's squadron met the *Ortega* on September 25, homeward bound after her escape from the *Dresden*, Captain Kinnier told Cradock about his experiences, and the admiral immediately set out for Punta Arenas to see if the British consul had any further news of the German cruiser. Punta Arenas, like many South American ports at the time, was teeming with intelligence agents. Some were professional spies, others were talkative port officials or amateur observers. Both sides used these people to gather information, however dubious it might be.

Cradock went back to Port Stanley because his cruisers were short on coal. He sent the *Otranto* to Punta Arenas to collect intelligence reports from the British consulate. After coaling, the *Monmouth* and *Glasgow* left for Port Stanley on October 3 to meet the *Otranto* and search for the rumored German trade on the west coast. The *Good Hope* staved at Port Stanley in case the *Dresden* doubled back into the Atlantic.

Two days later the *Otranto* intercepted coded German signals coming from somewhere off the Chilean coast and signaled Cradock. The admiral once again left Port Stanley at high speed. He ordered the *Monmouth* and *Glasgow* to meet him in Orange Bay. The same officer on the *Glasgow* wrote in his diary:

> '[The] *second battle of Orange Bay was also a frost. Weather atrocious and it would have been quite impossible to fight our guns. Rather interesting if we met an enemy light cruiser in similar conditions.'*

The prophetic nature of this remark would soon be brought home to its author.

Cradock's second visit to Orange Bay was not a complete waste of time. A landing party from the *Good Hope* found a wooden sign that had been left there by the survey ship Bremen in 1912. Markings on it showed that the *Dresden* had been there three weeks earlier. Cradock knew that by now she must have joined up with Graf Spee's squadron in the Pacific. Captain John Luce of the *Glasgow* headed west, leading the *Monmouth* and *Otranto,* while the flagship returned once more to Port Stanley to wait for the *Canopus*. The weather remained 'atrocious.' One of the *Glasgow*'s officers wrote:

> *'It blew, snowed, hailed and sleeted as hard as it is possible to do... I thought the ship would dive under altogether at times. Monmouth was rather worse if anything... We were rolling thirty five degrees at times and quite useless for fighting purposes... The ship was practically a submarine.'*

Even on board the much bigger *Otranto* conditions were bad. One of her officers commented,

> *'We finally got past caring what would happen... what with the strain, the weather, and the extreme cold, we longed to find something and to have it out, one way or the other.'*

On October 7 Cradock was still at Port Stanley waiting for the *Canopus*. He received a message from the Admiralty, sent two days earlier. The wireless station in Fiji had intercepted a signal from the *Scharnhorst* to a German supply ship saying that she was headed for

Easter Island. The message was in code, but the Royal Australian Navy had captured a German merchant ship in the Pacific at the beginning of the war, with her mercantile code book intact, and the Allies were able to decipher the signal. At this point no one doubted where Graf Spee was heading, and the Admiralty signaled Cradock:

> *'It appears that* Scharnhorst *and* Gneisenau *are working across to South America. You must be prepared to meet them in company, possibly with a* Dresden *scouting for them.'*

> 'Canopus *should accompany* Glasgow, Monmouth *and* Otranto, *the ships to search and protect trade in combination. If you propose Good Hope to go, leave* Monmouth *on east coast.'*

HMS **Good Hope.**

Cradock received further intelligence reports that indicated 'possibility of *Dresden*, *Leipzig*, *Nürnberg* joining *Scharnhorst* and *Gneisenau*.'

He signaled London:

> *'Have ordered* Canopus *to Falklands where I intend to concentrate and avoid division of forces. Have ordered* Glasgow, Monmouth, *and* Otranto *not to go north of Valparaiso until German cruisers located... does Defence join my command?'*

The last comment shows that Cradock was still in the dark about his reinforcements. He was becoming uneasy about his overall strength and sent another signal to London on 11 October.

'It appears that *Scharnhorst* and *Gneisenau* are working across to South America. You must be prepared to meet them in company, possibly with a *Dresden* scouting for them.'

> *'Without alarming, respectfully suggest that in event of enemy's heavy cruisers and others concentrating on west coast of South America, it is necessary to have a British force on each coast strong enough to bring them to action. Otherwise, should concentrated British force sent from southeast coast be evaded in Pacific, and get behind the enemy, latter could destroy Falklands, English Bank and Abrolhos coaling bases in turn, and with British ships unable to follow up owing to want of coal, enemy might reach West Indies.'*

Churchill decided that Cradock's ships should stay within supporting distance of each other and postpone any forays against German trade on the west coast until the whereabouts of Graf Spee's big cruisers had been determined. He minuted his copy of Cradock's last signal and sent it to the First Sea Lord. *'They and not the trade are our quarry for the moment. Above all we must not miss them.'* Battenberg's laconic reply was, 'Settled'.

On what to do about reinforcing Cradock, Churchill commented to Battenberg,

> *'I presume Cradock is fully aware of the possibility of* Scharnhorst *and* Gneisenau *arriving*

HMS **Monmouth.**

on or after the 17th instant in his neighbourhood; and that if not strong enough to attack, he will do his utmost to shadow them, pending arrival of reinforcements.'

This was sensible advice. It would have helped Cradock if he had received it. If he had been told that shadowing was an acceptable option in the eyes of the Admiralty, he might have deployed his forces differently. But the Admiralty's reply to both his previous signals merely stated:

'*Your concentration of* Good Hope, Canopus, Monmouth, Glasgow, *and* Otranto *for combined operations concurred in. Stoddart in Carnarvon has been ordered to Montevideo... Defence ordered to join Carnarvon. He will also have Cornwall, Bristol, Macedonia, and Orama under his orders. Essex remains in West Indies.'*

This message reassured Cradock. Even if Graf Spee slipped by him and reached the Atlantic, he would have enough strength there to contain the German squadron. The signal didn't insist that Cradock concentrate his whole force on the Falklands, although it did finally inform him that the Defence was not on her way to join him after all. At this point he realized he would probably have to make do with his present forces.

'He was going to almost certain death in fighting these new and powerful ships'

Most importantly, the Admiralty still did not see fit to tell Cradock that it was alright for him to shadow Graf Spee if he felt he was not strong enough to attack.

By 18 October, Graf Spee's ships had finished coaling, and everyone was glad to leave the miserable conditions at Easter Island. The squadron set sail for the Juan Fernandez Islands, fifteen hundred miles to the east. The admiral intended this stage of the voyage to be a final preparation for the sea battle he thought was inevitable once he reached the South American coast. He knew that the weather off the coast would probably be bad in October and November, and he asked his staff to work out the best gunnery ranges and tactics to be used, depending on sea conditions.

By this time Cradock was fully aware of his precarious position. He was resigned to the fact that he would probably get no reinforcements besides the *Canopus*, which was still plodding her way toward Port Stanley. While awaiting her arrival, Cradock became quite friendly with the governor of the Falklands, Sir William Allardyce, known locally as 'The King of the Penguins' and his aide-de-camp, T N Goddard. The latter wrote:

'The Admiral was a brave old man; he knew that he was going to almost certain death in fighting these new and powerful ships and it seemed to be quite all right as far as he was concerned...'

When the *Canopus* finally arrived at Port Stanley on 18 October, Cradock was dismayed to learn that she would need to remain in port at least five days to clean boilers and repair an engine defect. Worse still, Captain Grant informed the admiral that even after repairs, his ship would be able to make only twelve knots. Cradock signaled the Admiralty the same day:

'I fear strategically the speed of my squadron cannot exceed 12 knots, owing to Canopus, *but shall trust circumstances will enable me to force an action.'*

Even without the *Canopus* to slow him down, his squadron's top speed would be held to eighteen knots by the Otranto. It is difficult to see how the British squadron could force an action on Graf Spee with his twenty-three-knot vessels, except on the German admiral's terms.

This was the day that Graf Spec's squadron set out for the Juan Fernandez Islands, which was to be their last coaling stop before reaching the coast of Chile. On the way, Graf Spee changed his plans because of intelligence reports that British naval forces were being sent to the area.

These reports mentioned only the *Good Hope* and *Monmouth*. He wrote in his war journal:

'The presence of strong enemy forces on the coast makes it impossible for the present squadron to carry out its original intention of carrying on a war against commerce. This purpose is therefore renounced and the destruction of enemy forces is substituted for it.

A sea battle was much more to his liking than commerce raiding. He was confident of success now that he believed he had nothing more dangerous to face than the two old British cruisers, whose armaments and gunnery ranges he knew very well.

By October 22 Cradock decided he couldn't wait any longer for the *Canopus* to finish her refit. He signaled London: '*Good Hope* left Port Stanley via Cape Horn. *Canopus* following on 23rd via Magellan Straits with three colliers.'

Before he left the Falklands he gave a letter to Governor Allardyce, with instructions to forward it to his friend, Adm. Sir Hedworth Meux.

'I will give you all the warning I can if the German squadron eludes us; and only in case of my 'disappearance' will you send the letter to Meux. I mean to say, if my squadron disappears – and me too – completely. I have no intention after forty years at sea of being an unheard victim.'

Although the letter has never been traced, and its contents remain a subject of speculation, one thing is clear: Cradock was very much aware of what happened to Admiral Ernest Troubridge in the Mediterranean on the first day of the war. That officer failed to press home an attack with his squadron on what he believed was a stronger enemy force. This resulted in the escape of the *Goeben* and *Breslau* to Constantinople and led indirectly to Turkey's entry into the war on the German side. Troubridge had come very close to a charge of cowardice when a court of inquiry was held. Although he was acquitted of the lesser charge of negligence at a subsequent court-martial, his career was ruined and he was never given another sea command. Cradock wrote to a friend, 'I will take care I do not suffer the fate of poor Troubridge'.

No one knows what was in Cradock's mind as he left the Falklands, but in the opinion of the governor's aide-de-camp:

> *'He knew what he was up against and asked for a fast cruiser with big guns to be added to his squadron, for he had nothing very powerful and nothing very fast, but the Admiralty said he'd have to go without. So old Cradock said, "All right; we'll do without," and he slipped off early one morning, and left the* Canopus *to look after the colliers and transports, and picked up the* Glasgow *and* Monmouth *and set out to look for these crack Germans.'*

'He knew what he was up against and asked for a fast cruiser with big guns to be added to his squadron...'

The German squadron reached the Juan Fernandez Islands on 26 October and anchored at Mas Afuera to coal. This island and Mas a Tierra are the two main islands of the group, which lies about five hundred miles off the coast of Chile, due west of Valparaiso. A German officer wrote,

> *'Here we spent several melancholy days in the shelter of this gigantic rock, which frowned on the pygmy line of our ships and was the silent witness of our laborious activity.'*

No shore leave was permitted, except for a few officers and, naturally,the admiral. He explored the island and took notes on its many seabirds and brought back samples of spring-blooming plants and shrubs.

While the squadron was coaling, the *Prinz Eitel Friedrich* arrived, short of coal herself. She had returned after an unsuccessful voyage as a raider off Australia and New Zealand. Her captain had decided to leave before he ran out of coal and was caught by Patey's squadron. Graf Spee had no coal to spare for a mere armed merchant cruiser and sent her into Valparaiso with the *Gottingen* to get some from one of the German colliers there. The two ships were escorted by the *Nürnberg*, which waited off the coast to collect any intelligence reports that were sent by wireless from German agents on shore.

Meanwhile, the *Good Hope* met the *Glasgow* and *Monmouth* at a secret coaling base in the Chonos Islands on October 27. (The coast of Patagonia has many tortuous channels and inlets where warships of both sides set up coaling points inside territorial waters, without much fear of being interrupted by Chilean patrol vessels.) While coaling the *Good Hope* from one of the supply ships, Cradock came to a decision about the *Canopus*. The old battleship had got only as far as Punta Arenas, and he knew he could never force an action on Graf Spee if he had to wait for her, because this would reduce his squadron's speed to twelve knots.

He wirelessed the Admiralty:

> *'With reference to orders to search for enemy and our great desire for early success, consider it impracticable on account of* Canopus*'s slow speed, to find and destroy enemy squadron. Consequently have ordered Defence to join me after calling at Montevideo for orders.* Canopus *will be employed convoying colliers. From experience of 6 August respectfully suggest not to oppose depredations of* Karlsruhe. *May they continue until he meets vessel of superior speed.'*

This message showed that Cradock still believed, or at any rate hoped, that the Defence was on her way to South America. His oblique reference to the *Karlsruhe* was meant to tell the Admiralty that the Defence was more useful to him off Chile than chasing after a German light cruiser that had already shown that she could easily outrun armored cruisers.

He had given up on the *Canopus* as a useful member of his squadron. This was the ship that Churchill believed would give Cradock protection from Graf Spee's squadron, if not superiority over it. Churchill thought the Germans would never dare challenge the 12-inch guns of the old battleship, which he described as 'a citadel around which all our cruisers in those waters could find absolute security'.

Yet here was Cradock relegating her to convoy duty. Churchill was not pleased by Cradock's decision. He minuted the signal to Battenberg with the comment, 'This telegram is very obscure and I do not understand what Cradock intends or wishes.'

Although he claimed not to know what the admiral had in mind, he sent a further minute to the First Sea Lord:

> *'The situation on the west coast seems safe. If* Gneisenau *and* Scharnhorst *have gone north they will meet* Idzumo, Newcastle, *and* Hizen, *and will be forced south on* Glasgow *and Monmouth who have good speed and can draw them on to* Good Hope *and* Canopus, *who should keep within supporting distance.'*

This woolly and over optimistic assessment of the situation was not sent to Cradock. The chances of the *Newcastle* and the two Japanese ships running into Graf Spee in the vast expanse of the Pacific were about one in a million. What the Admiralty did tell Cradock was that it had counter-manded his orders. *'Defence is to remain on east coast under orders of Stoddart. This will leave sufficient force on each side.'*

This signal also mentioned that the *Newcastle* and the two Japanese ships were heading south from the Galapagos Islands, but they were much too far away to help Cradock. The Admiralty did not criticize or even mention his decision to leave the *Canopus* behind, which implied approval. In any event, this telegram, which was sent on October 28, didn't reach the squadron until November 1, when it was too late to have any effect on Cradock's deployment.

The German squadron left Mas Afuera on October 28, and two days later they were rewarded with a view of the Chilean coast and the distant snowcapped Andes. They had steamed twelve thousand miles to get there. Graf Spee kept his ships fifty miles offshore, out of sight of land, while he waited for the *Nürnberg* to bring intelligence reports back from ships anchored at Valparaiso. German merchant ships in Chilean ports customarily gathered intelligence and transmitted it to Graf Spee's cruisers in code, in flagrant violation of international rules. Ships of the belligerents docked in neutral harbors were permitted to send wireless messages only en clair, but violations were usually overlooked by the pro-German Chilean authorities.

On 31 October Graf Spee received a message from the *Gottingen* that she had picked up distant wireless signals between the *Good Hope* and *Monmouth*. The signals were coming from the south at equal strength, which indicated that the two ships were traveling together. Stronger signals were heard from the *Glasgow* in the Coronel area. The next morning the collier Santa Isabel sent a message that the British cruiser had been anchored in Coronel Roads at 1900 the previous evening. The only news of the *Canopus* came from a German agent in Punta Arenas, 1,400 miles away. He reported that she had passed by on the afternoon of 27 October. It wasn't likely that she was anywhere near Coronel on the 31st.

Meanwhile, the British squadron was moving steadily up the Chilean coast. It reached the Vallenar Roads, just south of Chiloe Island, on 29 October. Cradock sent the *Glasgow* ahead to see if there were any important messages for him at the British consulate in Coronel. He also dispatched the *Otranto* to Puerto Montt to try to gather information as to the whereabouts of the German warships.

In the wardroom, a fight within a few days was considered inevitable, but there was not much optimism about the result; two of the lieutenant-commanders in Monmouth, both old shipmates of mine, took me aside to give me farewell messages to their wives.'

While the *Canopus* was coaling and repairing a minor engine defect, Captain Grant discovered that his chief engineer, Comander William Denbow, had been mentally ill for some time and had deliberately falsified his reports about the state of the engines. According to a report by the junior engineering officer, Lieutenant Comander. Sydney Start, Denbow had never left his cabin once during the whole voyage and so could not possibly have inspected the engines. It turned out that after a minor repair, the ship was capable of approaching the seventeen knots she had made on her sea trials after recommissioning. She had been restricted to twelve knots ever since the false report. The unfortunate engineer was sent back to England under medical attention. He was invalided out of the navy and never heard from again.

Captain Grant didn't want to break W/T silence to tell Cradock the news. Even with the *Canopus* capable of seventeen knots, he didn't think the admiral would slow down to let him catch up. Whether or not Cradock would have been influenced by this information can never be known, but it is most likely that he would have kept on without the old battleship.

By 31 October the *Otranto* had rejoined the squadron. She had not been able to obtain any information in Puerto Montt because the Chileans there were solidly pro-German. That same day, however, the *Glasgow* signaled from Coronel that German supply ships had been frequently sailing in and out of the port. More important, she had intercepted several transmissions between the *Leipzig* and one other colliers.

Cradock ordered the *Glasgow* to leave Coronel immediately and meet him the next day fifty miles west of Arauco Bay. Just after noon on 1 December the squadron was reunited. The admiral signaled his ships to spread out at twenty-mile intervals and sweep north to look for the enemy.

The Admiralty and Naval Staff far away in London remained confident that their dispositions in the Pacific were perfectly adequate to deal with Graf Spee's squadron. Churchill's secretary wrote at the time,

'The situation on the west coast seems safe.'

The mood in the British squadron was just the opposite. Lieutenant Lloyd Hirst of the *Glasgow* wrote:

'In the wardroom, a fight within a few days was considered inevitable, but there was not much optimism about the result; two of the lieutenant commanders in Monmouth, *both old shipmates of mine, took me aside to give me farewell messages to their wives.'*

The officers on the *Monmouth* were of the opinion that, 'Glasgow *has got the speed, so she can get away, but we are for it'*.

The *Glasgow*'s officers reported that the admiral had 'buried all his medals and decorations in the Governor's garden' before leaving Port Stanley, to be dug up in the event of his death and sent home after the war. It was also rumored that Cradock had given the governor 'a large sealed packet to be sent home to the Admiralty as soon as his death was officially confirmed.' These reports are unsubstantiated, but true or not, if these were the perceptions of his officers, they can scarcely have led to a feeling of confidence.

There was little reason for confidence. Of the four

ships, only the *Good Hope* had any guns capable of inflicting serious damage on Graf Spee's armoured cruisers. These were the two 9.2-inch guns of the main armament, which were mounted on the upper deck. The secondary batteries of 6-inch guns were in casemates on the main deck, close to the water-line. They were practically useless in any kind of sea swell because of the gunners' poor visibility and the danger of being flooded by high waves.

The *Monmouth* was rated as a heavy cruiser but undergunned for her size. Admiral 'Jacky' Fisher had scathingly remarked, 'Sir William White designed the 'County' class but forgot the guns.' The cruiser carried only 6-inch guns, whose hundred-pound shells were unlikely to pierce the armour plate of the *Scharnhorst* and *Gneisenau*. Half of these guns were mounted close to the waterline. Fisher's final caustic comment on the County Class was, 'With their wretched pea-shooters, they can neither fight nor run.'

These were the two major units of Cradock's squadron. They were both old ships that had been condemned as unfit for further service before the war. When war seemed imminent the Admiralty decided it was too costly to scrap them, and they were hurriedly recommissioned and manned with crews of untrained reservists, coast guardsmen, naval cadets, and boy seamen, some of them as young as fifteen. Many of those hastily recruited to serve in the *Monmouth* were Scottish crofters and fishermen who had been given little or no gunnery practice. Even some of their gunnery officers had never been inside a real gun turret before. Things weren't much better aboard the flagship. Since Cradock had taken over command of the *Good Hope* in August, her green crew 'had only carried out one full calibre practice shoot'.

'With their wretched pea-shooters, they can neither fight nor run.'

As for the other two ships, the *Glasgow* was a fast, modern cruiser with a regular navy crew, but she was armed with only two 6-inch and ten 4-inch guns. These were more than adequate for fighting Graf Spee's light cruisers, but they were totally ineffective against his big ships. The *Otranto* was a 1,200-ton liner that had been given eight 4.7-inch guns and converted into an armed merchant cruiser. Because of the thinness other hull and her huge profile, she was known in the squadron either as the 'sardine tin' or the 'floating haystack'. She made a splendid target for the squadron's gun-laying and range-taking practice. The *Otranto* was meant to fight other armed merchantmen, not regular warships, and she was of no value to Cradock except as a dispatch ship.

Most critically, the weight of shell that could be fired by the whole of Cradock's squadron was not much more than that of either of Graf Spee's big cruisers. This assumes that the British ships would be capable of firing full broadsides in any kind of sea conditions. In the poor weather typical of the South American coast in November, Graf Spee's advantage would be far greater because half of the British guns were mounted too low to be of any use.

Graf Spee knew from his intelligence reports that he was up against only the *Good Hope*, *Monmouth*, and *Glasgow*, and because the latter had been in Coronel the previous day, he hoped to cut her off before she could rejoin Cradock. Realizing the *Glasgow* would have to leave port because of the twenty-four-hour rule, he took his squadron south toward Coronel on the morning of 1 November and ordered the *Nürnberg* to leave Valparaiso and join up with him.

That same morning, Cradock's ships heard a lot of loud W/T traffic between German supply ships and the *Leipzig*. Graf Spee had been using the *Leipzig* to transmit and receive all wireless messages between the squadron and its supply ships, so as not to give away the presence of his other cruisers. Unaware of this, Cradock thought the *Leipzig* was the only German cruiser in the Coronel area. He headed north to join up with the *Glasgow* and trap the *Leipzig* before she could rejoin Graf Spee.

This led to the dramatic situation on the morning of All Saints' Day 1914, when each admiral was taking his full squadron to 'cut off and gobble up' what he believed was a single enemy light cruiser. In reality, the two formations were steaming inexorably toward each other at a combined speed of almost forty knots. The admirals, who had been friends since their days on the China Station during the Boxer Rebellion, were about to meet again.

By late afternoon on 1 November Cradock's squadron was still fanning out and moving in a northerly direction. They were about thirty miles from Arauco Bay, where the small port of Coronel is situated. The flagship was the outermost ship, close to forty miles from the *Glasgow*. At 16.30 the light cruiser's lookouts sighted smoke on the eastern horizon. Captain Luce gave orders to turn to starboard and increase speed. A few minutes later the *Monmouth* and *Otranto* turned east in support of the *Glasgow*.

Very soon the lookouts were able to recognize the hull and upper works of the *Leipzig*. As the *Glasgow* got closer the lookouts saw more patches of smoke on the horizon. When these were identified as coming from four-funneled cruisers, the *Glasgow* turned back and signaled, 'Enemy armoured cruisers in sight'.

The *Glasgow*'s wireless operators could hear the high-pitched scream in their earphones coming from German *Telefunken* sets trying to jam their transmissions. They weren't sure whether the flagship had received their signal. All three British ships headed at full speed toward the *Good Hope* to warn Cradock that instead of trapping a solitary light cruiser, he was running into Graf Spee's whole squadron.

The *Leipzig* had identified the *Glasgow* at about the same time and followed her. She soon saw the smoke from the rest of Cradock's squadron.

Captain Haun reversed direction and signaled the news to his admiral. Graf Spee also realized that he had found the enemy squadron, not a single light cruiser. He ordered his ships to close up and form a line heading southwest. The *Scharnhorst* was in the lead, followed by the *Gneisenau*, *Leipzig*, and *Dresden*. The *Nürnberg* was still thirty miles to the north and had been trying to catch up with the squadron ever since she left Valparaiso.

Cradock ordered his ships to change direction to southeast by east and form a line headed by the *Good Hope*, followed by the *Monmouth*, *Glasgow*, and *Otranto*. They completed these maneuvers by 17.45. The Germans took longer to form their line because they were more spread out and didn't have full steam up yet. The two squadrons were now about seventeen miles apart. The Germans soon changed course to southwest by west. This brought the two battle lines onto rapidly converging paths.

Both squadrons were steaming ahead on into a rising swell, making all the ships pitch and roll badly, especially the light cruisers, which, according to an eyewitness, were 'rolling like barrels in the heavy sea'. The sky was grey and overcast, and visibility was poor because of frequent rain squalls.

'As the sun got lower and lower on the horizon, its rays would be directly in the German gunners' eyes. This would make it hard for them to see Cradock's ships in the distance, while the German ships would be clearly outlined for the British gunners.'

At this point Cradock still had time to break off contact and move south to join forces with the *Canopus*, which was then about three hundred miles away. He knew that if he did, Graf Spee would not have time to catch him before nightfall. He could always return the next morning, strengthened with the *Canopus*, to attack the German squadron, if he could find it. Even if it slipped by him, he had been assured by the Admiralty that Stoddart had strong forces waiting in the Atlantic. (But he would have been bitterly criticized if he had let this happen.)

Cradock would certainly have been justified in refusing action until he had 'superior strength,' as the Admiralty put it. No matter how dubious their evaluation of the *Canopus*, he would be far better off with her than he was at present. It was simply not in Cradock's nature to make such a decision. He was well known in the fleet for his dashing, headstrong nature and had already shown great courage on several occasions. He had been decorated by King George V and even by the Kaiser, who had awarded him the Royal Order of the Crown for his services on the China Station during the Boxer Rebellion. On several occasions Cradock had been heard to express the wish that when his time came, he hoped he would be killed in action at sea or break his neck going over a fence after a fox.

A brother officer said of him, 'Cradock was constitutionally incapable of refusing or ever postponing action, if there was the smallest chance of success'.

Captain Luce's opinion was,

'I had the feeling that Cradock had no clear plan or doctrine in his head, but was always inclined to act on the impulse of the moment.'

Cradock must have known he had little or no chance against Graf Spee's superior force, but his orders were, 'Destroy enemy cruisers'. If he couldn't do this, he might at least damage them enough that they would have to seek internment in a Chilean port, or else face the next British squadron at a disadvantage. One or two telling hits on Graf Spee's big ships might weaken his squadron so much that it was no longer a serious threat.

Cradock resolved to attack as soon as possible, while he still had the sun behind him. Sunset was due at about 18.30. As the sun got lower and lower on the horizon, its rays would be directly in the German gunners' eyes. This would make it hard for them to see Cradock's ships in the distance, while the German ships would be clearly outlined for the British gunners.

Graf Spee was aware of this, but he knew the advantage would suddenly swing in his favor when the sun went below the horizon. Then the British ships would be starkly silhouetted against the sun's afterglow, while his own would be difficult to see in the waning daylight, lit only by the moon, which, although nearly full, was obscured bv storm clouds. Graf Spee's main concern was not to let the British squadron get ahead of him and cut across his bows to gain the relative safety of the coast. But Cradock had no chance of crossing Graf Spee's 'T' with the eighteen-knot *Otranto* holding him back. With his superior speed Graf Spee was able to keep the distance between the two lines at 15,000 yards, well outside of gunnery range.

At 18.04 Cradock gave the order to turn forty-five degrees to port. He desperately wanted to close the range before the sun began to set, but Graf Spee ordered a similar turn and kept his distance. At 18.18 Cradock signaled the *Canopus*, 'I am going to attack the enemy', although the German ships were 3,000 yards beyond his range at the time.

Captain Grant signaled back that he still had 250 miles to go before he could reach Cradock's position.

Graf Spec allowed the gap between the two lines of ships to close steadily. By 19.00, when the sun had just dipped below the horizon, it was down to 12,300 yards. It was now two and a half hours since the initial contact between the two squadrons. The tension on both sides was almost palpable. Graf Spee gave the order for his two armored cruisers to open fire. To quote an official German record, *'With that order, disaster broke over Cradock's squadron.'*

At this range Graf Spee's twelve 8.2-inch guns faced Cradock's two 9.2-inchers. It was as if the *Scharnhorst* was at peacetime gunnery practice. Her first salvo landed 500 hundred yards short of the *Good Hope* and her second 500 yards over, according to an observer on the *Glasgow* who was watching the gun flashes and waiting for the splashes of the shells. This was the classic straddling pattern. With an awful inevitability the third salvo smashed into the *Good Hope*.

One shell struck her forward 9.2-inch turret, which erupted in flames that shot higher than a hundred feet into the air. At one stroke the gun crew were wiped out before they had fired a shot. The turret was turned into a useless, twisted mass of steel. Cradock's heavy guns were reduced to one. This was remarkable shooting – the *Scharnhorst* was aiming at a target some five hundred feet long and only seventy feet wide from a distance of seven miles.

At almost the same time, the *Gneisenau* opened fire on the *Monmouth*. She obtained a similar straddling pattern with her first three salvoes. A shell from the third salvo hit the *Monmouth*'s forward gun turret and set it ablaze. Within minutes the *Good Hope* and *Monmouth* were suffering terrible punishment, as salvo after salvo thundered at them across the water. The German gunners on each ship managed to fire a broadside of six shells every twenty seconds. Cradock's flagship replied with her lone 9.2-inch gun. The *Monmouth* could use but half of her 6-inch guns, which were at the limit of their range.

'At 19.50, there was a terrible explosion between her main mast and her funnel, the flames reaching a height of over 200 feet.'

The ships were now heading into the teeth of a Force six wind. It was approaching gale conditions, and heavy seas were breaking over their bows and sweeping the forward decks. The British main deck guns could not be used because of the danger of flooding the casemates. In any case, their range finders had become so encrusted with salt from the sea spray that they were useless. No hits were registered on the two German cruisers, which were rapidly becoming indistinct smudges on the darkening horizon. Cradock's ships were 'etched deep black in awful clarity' in the sun's afterglow. Their own targets could only be sighted momentarily from the flashes of the enemy guns.

By this time, the *Leipzig* had begun to engage the *Glasgow*, which fired back with her 6-inch guns. The *Dresden* opened fire on the *Otranto*. After one salvo, which fortunately fell short, the armed merchant cruiser pulled out of line toward the open sea. She was a large vulnerable target and could only help the Germans find an accurate range on the British line. Captain Edwards signaled Cradock, suggesting that he keep the *Otranto* out of range. The reply was never completed. 'There is danger; proceed at your utmost speed...'

Edwards wasn't sure what the admiral intended, so he kept on a course parallel to the squadron, just outside the *Dresden*'s range.

Ten minutes after Graf Spee's order to open fire, the Battle of Coronel was as good as over. Cradock kept closing the range until it was down to 5,500 yards, where he could use some of his secondary armament of 6-inch guns. This only made the firing by the *Scharnhorst* and *Gneisenau* more devastating, because they were now able to use their 5.9-inch guns as well.

By 1930, just thirty minutes after the *Scharnhorst* had opened fire, the *Good Hope* had been hit between thirty and forty times. She was heavily damaged in the forward part of the ship, especially the bridge and foretop area where Cradock was directing his squadron. A hail of shells had smashed through her decks and started fires in the interior of the ship. The Germans could see the orange-red glow through the *Good Hope*'s portholes. In what may have been a last desperate attempt to inflict some damage on her tormentors, the crippled flagship slewed out of line toward the enemy, some of her guns still firing. Graf Spee thought she was going to fire torpedoes and ordered his ships to turn away. He lost sight of the *Good Hope* in the haze that hung over the battle scene.

According to one of the *Glasgow*'s officers,

> *'At 19.50, there was a terrible explosion between her main mast and her funnel, the flames reaching a height of over 200 feet.'*

The forward magazine must have been ignited by one of the many fires blazing inside the ship. After this the *Good Hope* could be seen lying between the lines, a low black hull gutted of her upperworks, and only lighted by

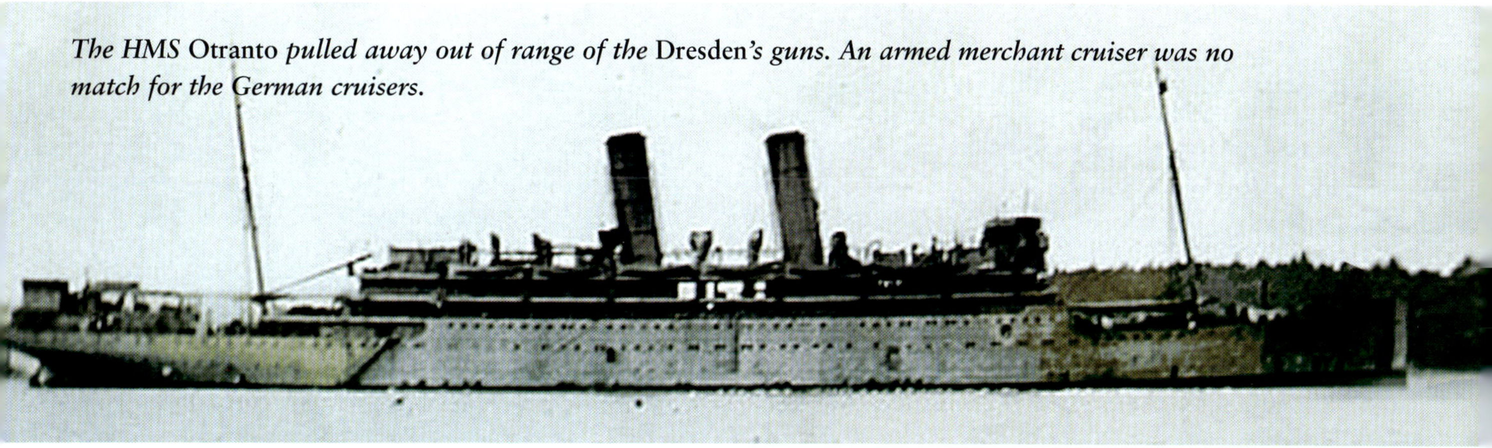

The HMS* Otranto *pulled away out of range of the* Dresden*'s guns. An armed merchant cruiser was no match for the German cruisers.

a dull red glare which shortly disappeared.

The *Good Hope* drifted off into the gloom and smoke. She was not seen again by either side. It is not hard to imagine the dreadful carnage on board. It is likely that Cradock and his staff on the bridge were all dead or dying by this time. No one actually saw her sink, but she couldn't have stayed afloat for very long in her stricken condition and must have gone down some time around 20.00. She took the admiral with her into the icy depths, drowning all those men and boys who were still alive out of a crew of nine hundred. Because the battle was still raging, no one, British or German, could stop to look for survivors.

The *Monmouth* was in almost as much distress, having been hit in excess of thirty times. The ship was ablaze and listing to port, although some of her 6-inch guns were firing sporadically. For another twenty minutes the *Gneisenau* pounded her at short range with both 8.2- and 5.9-inch shells, until she yawed out of line to starboard, away from the German onslaught. She was sinking by the head. The inrushing sea put out some of the fires, but by then she was a battered wreck.

Captain Luce of the *Glasgow* couldn't tell in the semi darkness how bad her condition was, and he signaled the *Monmouth* at 20.15, *'Are you all right?'*

Captain Brandt replied:

> *'I want to get stern to sea. I am making water badly forward.'*

Through a break in the clouds. Luce saw three ships approaching in the moonlight and signaled Brandt again: *'Can you steer NW? The enemy are following us astern.'*

There was no reply. When the *Glasgow* drew nearer, it was obvious that the Monmouth was in desperate straits. The captain of the *Glasgow* had no choice but to save his ship. The *Good Hope* and *Monmouth* were finished as fighting ships, and the *Otranto* had fled to the west at 19.45 when her captain saw that the flagship was doomed. The Germans were left with the light cruiser as their only target. She had led a charmed life so far, with only four other crew wounded, but now every time she fired her guns, the flashes lit up the darkness and attracted fire from all four German ships.

Luce knew that just one 8.2-inch salvo from the *Scharnhorst* or *Gneisenau* could blow his ship apart, and he gave the order to cease fire. He had already taken five hits from the *Leipzig* and the *Dresden*, which had concentrated on the *Glasgow* after the *Otranto* pulled out of the line. Although three of the shells had failed to explode, one had caused a large hole just above the waterline. Luce could do nothing to help the *Monmouth*, so he gave the order to head west at full speed. He wanted to find the *Otranto* and head south to warn the *Canopus* to turn back. In the words of one of the *Glasgow*'s officers:

'The Monmouth *could neither fight nor fly. She was badly down by the bows, listing to port with the glow of her ignited interior brightening the portholes. It was essential that there should be a survivor of the action to turn* Canopus *which, if surprised alone, must have shared the fate of the other ships... It was awful having to leave the* Monmouth *but I don't see what else the Skipper could have done.'*

The *Monmouth*'s ordeal was not over yet. The *Nürnberg* finally caught up with the German squadron at 21.00 and came upon the helpless cruiser, which she identified by searchlight. The *Monmouth* was listing so badly that her guns couldn't be trained on the *Nürnberg*, Whether out of frustration at missing the main action, or from fear of being torpedoed by his crippled enemy, as claimed by the Germans, Captain von Schonberg gave the order to open fire at point-blank range.

'To me it was dreadful to have to fire on the poor devil no longer able to defend herself, but her flag was still flying.'

The *Monmouth*'s White Ensign was still flying. Since she had given no sign of surrender, Schonberg was justified in sinking her. One or perhaps two torpedoes would have sufficed as a *coup de grace*, but the *Nürnberg* steamed slowly from end to end of the hapless *Monmouth* and poured in a withering hail of 4.1-inch shells. The battered ship finally rolled over on her beam ends and disappeared bow first beneath the waves.

Otto von Spec wrote to his mother, *'To me it was dreadful to have to fire on the poor devil no longer able to defend herself, but her flag was still flying.'*

A British officer remarked later, *'It must have been brutal work'*.

No one out of a crew of approximately seven hundred survived. Because of the high seas and the wind blowing at thirty knots, it would have been dangerous and probably futile to lower boats to look for survivors in the darkness. Schonberg explained:

> *'Unfortunately there could be no thought of saving the poor fellows; firstly I believed I still had an enemy before me, secondly the sea was so high that hardly a boat could have lived in it...'*

The British later agreed that the Germans could have done nothing to save any of the *Monmouth*'s crew who were still alive.

In the space of two hours the Royal Navy had suffered the loss of two heavy cruisers and nearly sixteen hundred men and boys.

Graf Spee had not had any contact with the enemy since 20.00 and did not know that the *Good Hope* and *Monmouth* were both sunk. He hoped to use what little moonlight there was and signaled his forces: *'Both British cruisers severely damaged. One light cruiser fairly intact. Chase and attack with torpedoes.'*

Captain von Schonberg reported back that he had sunk the *Monmouth*.

The *Leipzig* steamed in the direction of a dull glow that Captain Haun took to be the *Good Hope*. By the time he reached her position nothing could be seen but some floating debris. Any survivors of the explosion could not have lasted for nearly an hour in the bone-chilling water. The *Dresden* sighted the *Glasgow* through the mist at 20.30 but lost contact before she could get the British ship within range. Liideckc was on the verge of torpedoing the *Leipzig* which he recognized just in time.

As the *Glasgow* made her escape to the west, one of her officers, Sub-Lieutenant Harold Hickling, was on deck looking astern and saw the flash of a searchlight followed by rapid gunfire. He counted seventy-five flashes and knew this must have been the end of the Monmouth.

> *'Utterly dispirited and sick at heart after such a crushing blow, I went down to my cabin to snatch a few hours' sleep before going on watch. I threw myself on to my bunk, wet clothes and all.'*

The *Glasgow* managed to warn the *Canopus* of the danger ahead, in spite of German attempts to jam her signals. The old battleship was still two hundred miles away. Captain Grant immediately turned back with his supply ships to head toward Cape Horn and safety in the Falklands. This was all he could do because, as one of his officers remarked:

> *'Our fighting value was very small – our two turrets were in charge of Royal Naval Reserve lieutenants who had never been in a turret before, and the only rounds we had fired were two six-pounders to stop a merchant vessel. Some 'citadel,' some 'security'.*

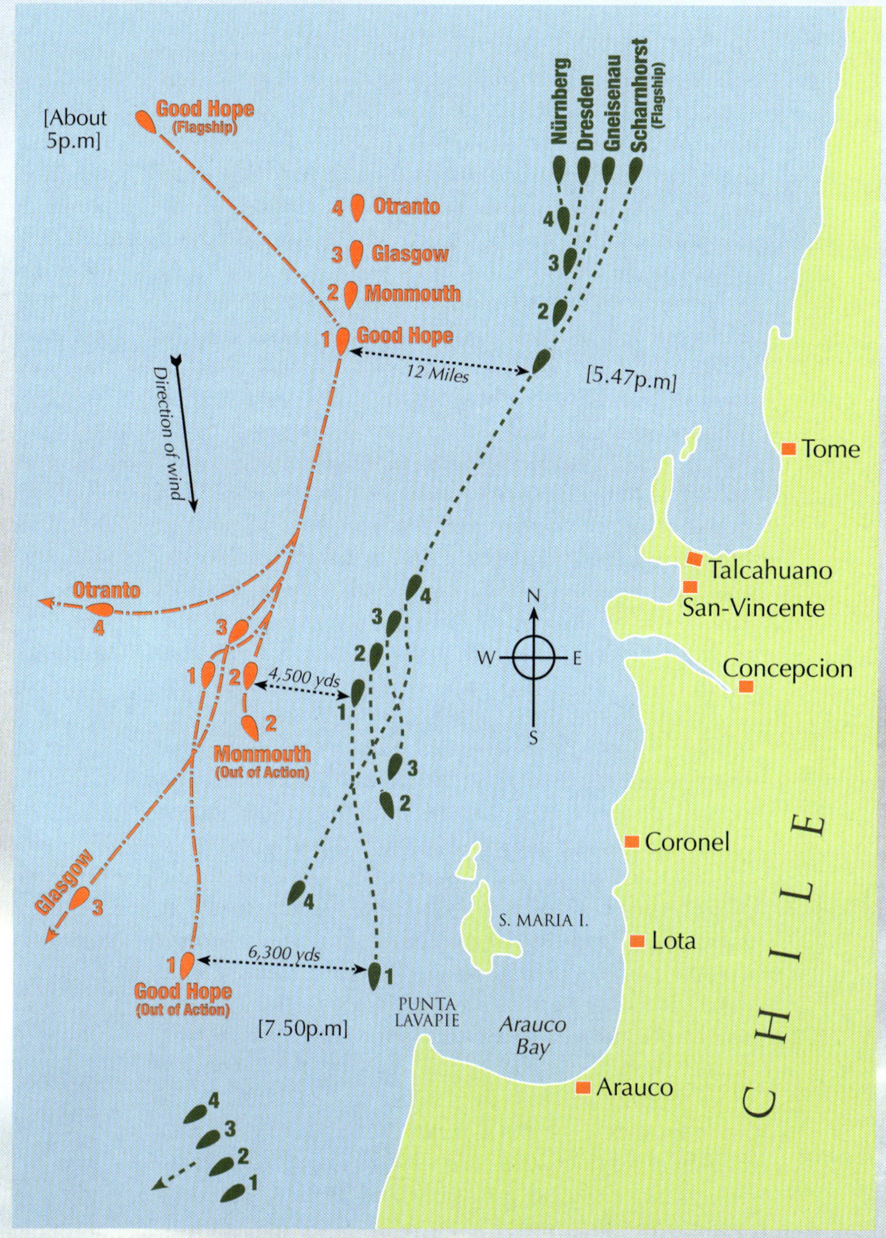

THE CORONEL SEA BATTLE

Graf Spee's victorious cruiser squadron at Valparaiso, Chile.

At 23.00 Graf Spee gathered his ships together, and they spent the rest of the night steaming slowly northwest to search the battle scene for signs of the *Good Hope*. Daylight revealed that the area was clear of British ships. Graf Spee formed his squadron in line ahead and took the flagship slowly along the line, flying the signal, 'By the grace of God a fine victory. My thanks and good wishes to the crews'.

He stood on the bridge of the *Scharnhorst* in full dress uniform, and as the flagship steamed past them, he saluted the *Gneisenau*, *Leipzig*, *Nürnberg* and *Dresden* in turn. To the crews who lined the decks to cheer their admiral, it was indeed a fine victory. They had met a Royal Navy squadron ship for ship in a 'fair fight,' for, according to the Germans, 'whatever the disparity in gun power it was four ships against four ships'. They had annihilated the two major enemy warships and forced the other two to flee for their lives. For them, Coronel had destroyed the aura of British naval invincibility.

Their own ships had suffered negligible damage. The *Scharnhorst* was hit twice and the *Gneisenau* four times, and some of the shells had failed to explode. The only casualties were three wounded on the *Gneisenau*. For the first time in months the Germans didn't feel like hunted men. At least for the time being, the cruiser squadron was in full control of the Southeast Pacific.

Graf Spee took the *Scharnhorst*, *Gneisenau*, and *Nürnberg* into Valparaiso, where the squadron could be sure of an enthusiastic reception from the German colony and the pro-German Chileans. The admiral wanted to send the details of the glorious victory back to the Fatherland and spend some time with his two sons, however brief. For all he knew, this might be their last time together. He sent the *Leipzig* and *Dresden* to the west to search for the *Otranto* and *Glasgow*. If they couldn't find them, their orders were to go back to Mas Afuera for coal and provisions and await Graf Spee's return from Valparaiso.

By now the two surviving ships from Cradock's ill-fated squadron were well out of reach to the south and heading for refuge in Port Stanley. Although they had got away unscathed, the men on these ships were in a grim mood. According to one officer:

> *'Individually and collectively we were humiliated to the very depths of our beings. We hardly spoke to one another for the first twenty-four hours. We felt so bitterly ashamed of ourselves for we had let down the King. We had let down the Admiralty, we had let down England.'*

It was three days before the news of the disaster at Coronel was to reach London. On the day of the battle the Naval Staff were still considering Cradock's position.

In the week leading up to 1 November, profound changes had taken place in the Admiralty. A new First Sea Lord had been appointed to replace Battenberg, who had just resigned. On 30 October Churchill spent several hours in the War Room with the new man, going over the dispositions of all Royal Navy squadrons and their responsibilities. It was clear that the most vulnerable point was the South Pacific, and Churchill said of Cradock, '*You don't suppose he would try to fight them without the* Canopus?' The new First Sea Lord wasn't sure, but he was convinced that Cradock was in a very dangerous position if he ran into Graf Spee with his present forces, which were an ill-matched mixture of old and new, trained and untrained. To expect them to tackle a German squadron of modern ships manned by experienced professionals was a recipe for disaster. A few days later the Admiralty received a telegram from the British consul in Valparaiso. It had been sent on 1 November and reported that Graf Spee's squadron had appeared off the coast of Chile that morning.

The message didn't reach London until 3 November. The Admiralty immediately signaled Cradock:

'*Defence has been ordered to join your flag with all dispatch.* Glasgow *should keep in touch with the enemy. You should keep in touch with* Glasgow, *concentrating the rest of your squadron including* Canopus. *It is important you should effect your junction with Defence at the earliest possible moment subject to keeping touch with the enemy.*'

The message came too late to help Cradock. As Churchill commented later, '*We were already talking to the void*'.

Cradock would be avenged at the Battle of the Falkland Islands a month later.

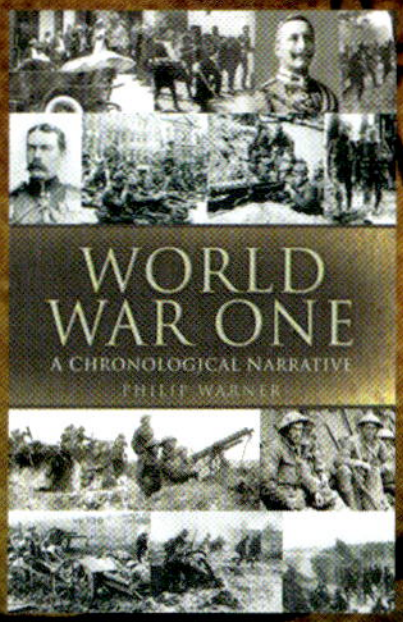

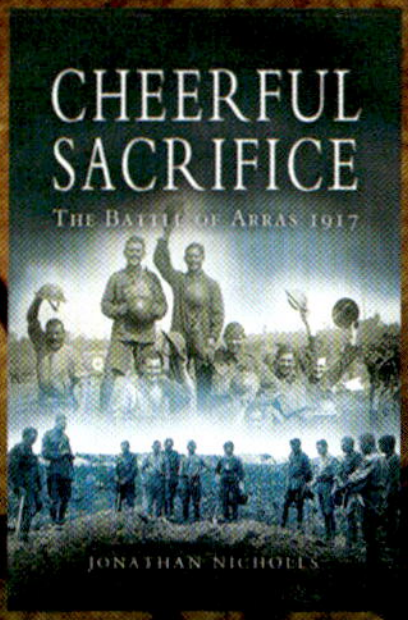

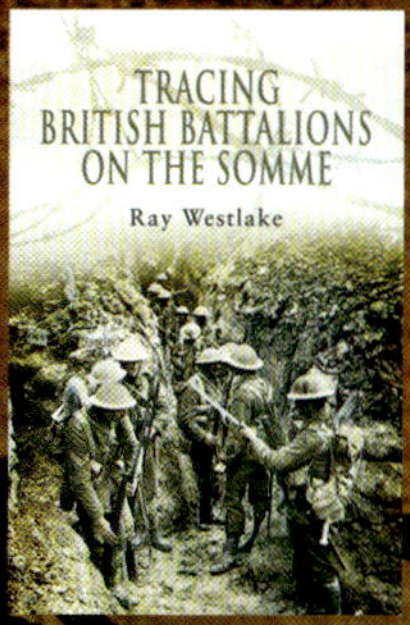

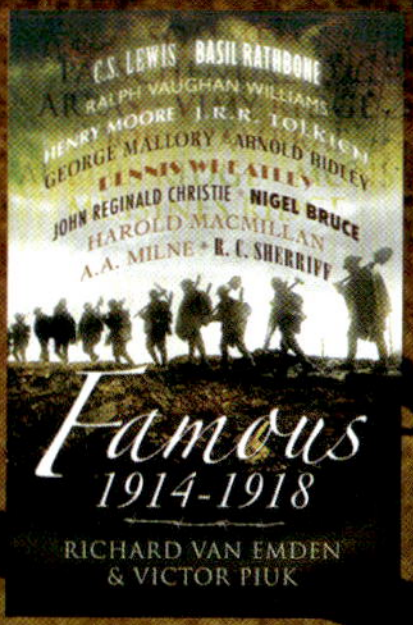

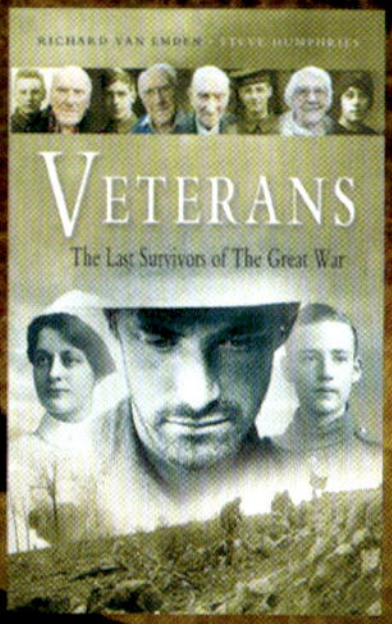

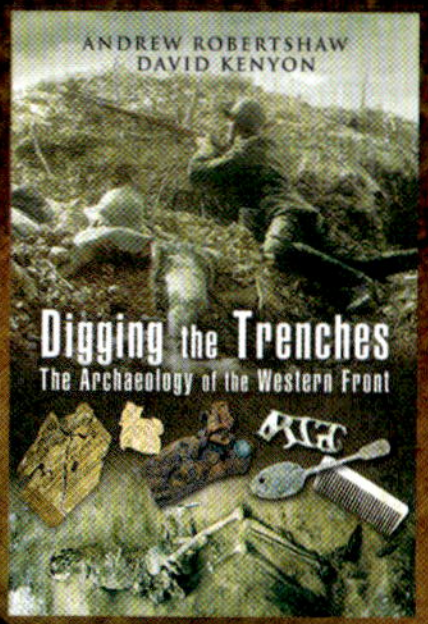

WORLD WAR ONE - A CHRONOLOGICAL NARRATIVE

PHILIP WARNER

The Great War will never be forgotten but that does not mean that it is understood. But to understand the whole conflict with its diverse and complex elements the political background, allegiances and alliances of the combatants and the military thinking of the time must be grasped. Philip Warner provides in this fine book the overview necessary to follow the ambitions and reactions of those involved so enabling the reader to appreciate the strategies and tactics on the ground. He lists the main figures who shaped events and comments on their strengths and failings as well as their significance. Helpfully he describes the end game, the literature spawned by war and asks was it avoidable?

ISBN: **9781844157761** • Hbk • **£15.99**

TRACING BRITISH BATTALIONS ON THE SOMME RAY WESTLAKE

Although over ninety years have passed since the Battle of the Somme was fought, interest in this, the bloodiest battle of the First World War, has never waned. Ray Westlake has collated all the information so painstakingly gathered, to produce a comprehensive compendium of the exact movements of every battalion involved in the battle. This book is invaluable not only to researchers but to all those visiting the battlefield and anxious to trace the movements of their forebears.

ISBN: **9781844158850** • Pbk • **£11.99**

CHEERFUL SACRIFICE – THE BATTLE OF ARRAS 1917 JONATHAN NICHOLLS

Cheerful Sacrifice tells the story of the spring offensive of April - May 1917, otherwise known as the Battle of Arras. The author points out, on the basis of the daily casualty rate it was the most lethal and costly British offensive battle of the First World War. In the thirty-nine days that the battle lasted the average casualty rate was far higher than at either the Somme or Passchendaele. Jonathan Nicholls, in this his first book, gives the Battle of Arras its proper place in the annals of military history, enhancing his text with a wealth of eye-witness accounts. One is left in no doubt that the survivor who described it as 'the most savage infantry battle of the war', did not exaggerate. Nor can there be much doubt that the author is destined to rise high in the firmament of military historians.

ISBN: **9781844153268** • Pbk • **£10.99**

FAMOUS – 1914-1918

VIC PIUK & RICHARD VAN EMDEN

Famous tells the Great War stories of twenty of Britain's most respected, best known and even notorious celebrities. They include politicians, actors, writers, an explorer, a sculptor and even a murderer. Many would become household names such as Basil Rathbone, the definitive Sherlock Holmes, AA Milne, creator of Winnie the Pooh, and Arnold Ridley who found fame and public affection as the gentle and genial Godfrey in *Dad's Army*. From politicians such as Harold Macmillan and Winston Churchill to JB Priestley, and JRR Tolkien, sculptors like Henry Moore and composers such as Ralph Vaughan Williams. The authors Richard van Emden and Vic Piuk have discovered the exact locations where these celebrities saw action. Each story will be examined in detail with pictures taken of the very spot where the actions took place. There are maps of the area that will guide enterprising readers to walk in the footsteps of their heroes.

ISBN: **9781844156429** • Hbk • **£20.00**

VETERANS – LAST SURVIVORS OF THE GREAT WAR RICHARD VAN EMDEN

Using the veterans' own words and photographs, the book brings to life a mixture of their excitement of embarkation for France, their unbound optimism and courage, the agony of the trenches, and numbing fear of going over the top. The fight for survival, the long ordeal of those who were wounded and the ever present grief caused by appalling loss and waste of life make for compelling reading. The veterans give us first hand accounts of stark honesty, as they describe in many cases more freely than ever before about experiences which have lived with them for over ninety-five years.

ISBN: **9781844153190** • Pbk • **£9.99**

DIGGING THE TRENCHES

DAVID KENYON & ANDREW ROBERTSHAW

In this, the first comprehensive survey of an exciting new field of research, Andrew Robertshaw and David Kenyon show how archaeology can be used to reveal the position of trenches, dugouts and other battlefield features and to rediscover what life on the Western Front was really like. Forensic investigation of the dead is now so advanced, that individuals can be identified and their fate discovered.

ISBN: **9781844153190** • Pbk • **£9.99**

TO ORDER PLEASE CALL: 01226 734222

Remember to mention the 1914 OUTBREAK magazine when ordering.
Visit our website at: **www.pen-and-sword.co.uk**
Alternatively you can post your order into: 47 Church Street, Barnsley, South Yorkshire, S70 2AS.
Please make checks payable to: PEN & SWORD BOOKS, adding your name and address on the reverse.
Please enclose £3.50 postage for UK orders under £25.00 and £7.50 per book for airmail orders.

'Sergeant Panter suddenly saw a column of German infantry entering the main street in front of them, four abreast, and proceeding as if unaware of the British presence. Within minutes the fire of him and his men had scattered the enemy, leaving many dead and wounded lying in the street.'[2]

CONTEMPTIBLES AT MONS – 1914

It was agreed that a British force, should war be declared, would be known as the British Expeditionary Force and would take its place on the French left and these troops would concentrate at Maubeuge. The British began arriving on 22 August 1914.

By Jack Horsfall & Nigel Cave

Extracted from *Mons – 1914* and reproduced by permission of Pen & Sword Books Ltd.

Part of Brigadier General Doran's 8 Brigade (3rd Division) entered Mons itself and then moved on, 4/Middx (Middlesex) on the right, on the west bank of the Canal du Centre, whilst the other three battalions were close behind. 4/RF (Royal Fusiliers), of Brigadier General Shaw's 9 Brigade went through the town to the village of Nimy, which lay a mile to the north but was situated on the south bank of the Canal du Centre as it curved around to the south west. The three other battalions of the Brigade took up position to the west and south of the Condé Canal, which put them to the left rear of the Fusiliers.

Behind both brigades was Brigadier General McCracken's 7 Brigade; the 3rd Division was ready to move forward.

Major General Fergusson's 5th Division was spread out to the left of the 3rd, along the south bank of the remarkably straight Condé Canal. On the right was Brigadier General Cuthbert's 13 Brigade; Brigadier General Count von Gleichen's 15 Brigade in reserve and Brigadier General Rolt's 14th on the left, at its extremity

British soldiers on the move to meet the German forces.

some nine miles from Mons. By the evening the troops had all found billets in factories, schools and houses; and although they only anticipated staying until the following day, they dug in, helped by enthusiastic young Belgians. Similar scenes were taking place on I Corps front, off to the right. Intermingled amongst the infantry corps were elements of Allenby's Cavalry Division, which had already got reconnaissance patrols on the far side of the canals. They were checking the way for the next move, which was to be an advance by II Corps to the north.

The 72 batteries of artillery had also been busily engaged in finding suitable positions, far from easy in the crowded country with its numerous mining villages. The majority had to be content with sites too far away from the canals to be effective, but a few did manage to get well forward. XL Brigade RFA managed to establish itself on the dominating hill a mile from Mons; 107 Field Battery established itself between the town and Nimy.

It was in the 5th Division area that there were the greatest problems. Major CS Holland, commanding 120 Field Battery of XXVII Brigade, managed to bring his four 18 pounders onto the canal towpath at Saint Ghislain.

Some of the Forward Observation Officers (FOO) thought they had found ideal places from which to view the enemy – when and if they came – from the top of the slag heaps. On the other hand, they were quick to discover the drawbacks: they were hot and smoking, with a thin crust that could break and through which a man could fall. Men from the coal mining areas were all too aware of this danger. Still, they were not going to be there for long.

The Royal Engineers were busy as well, examining the bridges to look at their load bearing capabilities and also how they might be destroyed if necessary. The CRE (Commander, Royal Engineers) of the two corps also discussed the recruiting of gangs of civilians to dig defences – in the light of what was soon to come they would be useful.

Early on the morning of 22 August Brigadier General de Lisle's 2 (Cavalry) Brigade had been out covering the approaches from Brussels, well to the front of the main bulk of the army. Major Tom Bridges (eventually to become a major general), commanding C Squadron of 4/(Royal Irish) Dragoon Guards, had his men in a wood just over the bridges at Nimy, about two miles up the road to Brussels. This was in the village of Casteau, about four miles from Soignies, further up on the road to Brussels. At about 7 am he saw four German cavalrymen trotting towards him. He would find out later that they were of the 4/Cuirassiers (Lancers) of the 9th (Cavalry) Division. They must have suspected something and began to turn back towards Soignies. Captain Hornby, followed by his Troop, gave chase along the paved road, alongside which a tram track ran. Corporal Thomas after a few moments dismounted and fired his rifle, hitting one of them. The pursuit continued for about a mile until, at a minor crossroads known as the Queen of Hungary, the enemy received reinforcements and a hand to hand battle of the thirty or forty cavalrymen took place. Some of the Cuirassiers were killed and a number captured – the Germans broke off the engagement and galloped off down the road.

Thomas was a regular soldier who had joined the army when he was fourteen; it is claimed that he was the first man to fire a shot in anger in the British army in the war. Hornby was awarded the DSO for his part in the skirmish. His men brought back a number of lances, helmets and other trophies; more importantly they had discovered the fact that the German cavalry were not up to their standard and that more significant numbers of Germans must be close by.

The German cavalry of the IIIrd and IXth Corps were engaged in scouting in front of the main bodies of their infantry, blissfully unaware of where the British actually were – an ignorance shared by their Army commander, von Kluck. This ignorance, and his concern about the vulnerability of his right flank, was to play an important part in the development of the Battle of Mons. At one stage he was convinced that large numbers of British troops were detraining at Tournai, well to the west, and this was to hold up the advance of vital elements of his army for several hours before it was ascertained that these troops were in fact only a brigade of French Territorials.

THE FIRST BRITISH OFFICERS TO BE KILLED IN ACTION IN THE FIRST WORLD WAR

On 16 August the Headquarters of the RFC moved from Amiens to Maubeuge. It took the army a few days to catch up with them. An officer commented;

'We were rather sorry that they had come, because up till that moment we had only been fired on by the French whenever we flew. Now we were fired on by the French and the English... To this day I can remember the roar of musketry that greeted two of our machines as they left the aerodrome and crossed the main Maubeuge – Mons road, along which a British column was proceeding.'

To safeguard against this happening again, everyone worked through the night to decorate the underside of the lower planes of all the machines with a Union Jack in the shape of a shield.

The first aerial reconnaissance by the RFC took place on 19 August; on 22 August Sergeant-Major Jillings, an observer in No. 2 Squadron, was wounded in the leg by a rifle bullet whilst flying over Maffle, south east of Ath. On the same day the first British aircraft lost to enemy fire came down. This was an Avro of No. 5 Squadron, manned by Lieutenants V Waterfall (pilot) and CGG Bayly (observer). At this stage all pilots were seconded from regiments within the army; Waterfall was in the East Yorks and Bayly was a sapper. The plane was shot down, sometime around midday, by rifle fire, quite likely by men of Walter Bloem's B Company, 12th Regiment of the Brandenburg Grenadiers.

'Suddenly an aeroplane appeared overhead. This time there was no doubt about it: the red, white and blue rings under the wings could be seen with the naked eye. I told off two groups to fire at it, and soon everyone seemed to be firing at it. It turned back as if to return southward but too late; its nose turned down, it made several corkscrew turns, and then fell like a stone a mile or so away. Murmurs of satisfaction all round. A little later three Hussars came past and shouted out that they had found the aeroplane in a field further on. 'What about the pilot and observer', I asked. 'Both in bits, sir.'

The plane came down to earth at the village of Marcq, a mile or so away; and a Belgian peasant managed to spirit away the observer's report before the Germans arrived. This made its way, finally, to the War Office after hostilities had ended. The Germans buried the officers in the Louviau family's plot in the cemetery of Labliau at Marcq; after the war (in 1924) their remains were translated to Tournai Communal Cemetery Allied Extension. They were the first British officers to be killed in action in the First World War.

Remains of a British RFC aircraft brought down behind the German lines.

A Squadron of 19/Hussars, commanded by Major Parsons, accompanied by Captain JC Burnett and his 5th Cyclist Company (5th Division), were patrolling five miles north of the Condé Canal in the wooded area north of the village of Hautrage in front of 14 Brigade, when they met up with German cavalry. The engagement between the two small forces went on for most of the day. The Hussars were reluctant to retire as their Short Magazine Lee Enfield, with its long range, was causing so much damage; but the Cuirassiers received reinforcements. The Hussars' efforts to prevent the enemy reaching the outposts of 1/DCLI (Duke of Cornwall's Light Infantry), who only arrived at the canal in the afternoon, were gradually being overcome. They retired to Pommeroeul and then Le Petit Crepin; with the assistance of a troop of Life Guards from 4 (Cavalry) Brigade they came back over the canal.

Over on the right flank, in front of 4/Middx at the Canal du Centre, German cavalry were active in the late afternoon. They exchanged rifle fire with D Company from over the canal at Obourg. There were no casualties, but the Battalion was the first infantry to fire at the Germans in the Great War.

Very early on Saturday morning, 22 August, Field Marshal Sir John French set out by car from his Headquarters at Le Cateau to visit General Charles Lanrezac, commanding the French Fifth Army, the left of the French army, at his Headquarters near Phillipeville some sixty miles away. Utterly fortuitously he came across Lieutenant Edward Spears, who was the liaison officer between the two Armies. Spears informed French that the Germans had broken through on the River Sambre, the French Xth Corps was falling back, the German First Army was extending out to the west and that the French Fifth Army was not advancing. French returned to Le Cateau, seeing little point in going to Lanrezac's Headquarters, especially as the latter was away examining advanced posts. A more serious reason was that the two did not get on at all well, largely a consequence of Lanrezac's singularly off-hand and rather insulting manner.

Spears returned to Fifth Army Headquarters to learn further disquieting news. The German XIIth (Saxon) Corps was advancing so vigorously that it posed the threat of cutting off Lanrezac's Army; he decided that he must continue his retreat. This would expose the British army's right flank, creating a gap of some nine miles between Haig's I Corps and the Fifth Army. Spears immediately set off along the congested roads, filled with refugees and French military all heading westwards. He reported to French who had also heard from one of Lanrezac's staff officers that his Army would not be advancing and was, in fact, contemplating withdrawal. However, he requested that the BEF attack as originally planned. French realised the impossibility of this request but bravely offered to hold a line at Mons and along the Condé Canal for twenty-four hours, well aware of the consequences if Lanrezac's front collapsed.

The Headquarters of II Corps was in the small, white Chateau de la Haie, in the hamlet of Sars-la-Bruyere, seven miles south of Mons, off the main road and without any telephone communication; it was about half way to Bavai, where French had his Advanced Headquarters. It was not a good choice of location, difficult to find in the dark and to communicate with at any time, and this was to cause Smith-Dorrien problems in due course.

At 5 am on Sunday 23 August French drove there to hold a meeting with his two Corps commanders and Allenby, who had already brought his Division back over the canal in the face of heavy German pressure. The Field-Marshal's orders were ambivalent: because of doubts about the intentions of the French they must stay where they were, prepared for any kind of move. Aircraft patrols had already started that morning and reports were awaited on the results of their reconnaissance. The BEF's Chief of Staff, Lieutenant General Sir Archibald Murray, was to remain at II Corps Headquarters, to react to whatever situation arose whilst French set off to Valenciennes. He wanted to find out what the French were doing to secure the allies left flank and to see Brigadier General Drummond, commanding the hastily formed (on 22 August) 19 Brigade. Its composite battalions had formed the Lines of Communication Defence troops. Drummond was to be warned that he might be needed to support the left flank, and that he was to come under Allenby's command, whose Headquarters were in Quievrain.

Whilst this conference was taking place the battalions of the 3rd and 5th Divisions were prepared for an attack. The attack would be made by three German corps, from right to left the IXth, IIIrd and IVth of Kluck's First Army. To his left was the Second Army, commanded by von Bülow; at this stage in the campaign, von Kluck answered to von Bülow, which provided potential for considerable friction. Von Bülow's Army lay directly in front of Lieutenant General Haig's I Corps which would not be attacked: there was concern about Lanrezac's Fifth Army and it would also hold Haig in position so that von Kluck's right hook could 'put him in the bag'. The German First Army would fall like a scythe on the British, pivoting somewhere from the north of Charleroi.

Von Kluck was not happy with the deviation from the Schlieffen Plan, feeling that he should be kept well out to the west and leaving the BEF to von Bülow and the Third (Saxon) Army. But von Kluck could only be angry and frustrated, as von Bülow controlled all three armies. The decision by the Germans would be a fateful one; whilst the BEF performed outstandingly in the battle to come.

Two other factors, with origins buried in the past, were to help the defenders. The German army adopted a policy of attacking en masse – just as the French did – advancing shoulder to shoulder in solid blocks of companies and carrying their rifles at the trail; on approaching the enemy they would fire from the hip, regardless of finding a target or taking aim. This would have an overwhelming and terrifying effect on the enemy whilst boosting their own courage. It had worked thus far (though there had been some local difficulty at Liège). The second factor was, at least in part, the consequence of Treasury miserliness over the matter of machine guns. Haig had been Director of Military Training when, in 1908, it was laid down that the infantry should be able to fire fifteen aimed rounds a minute in order to qualify for an extra payment. This would be stopped if a man did not maintain that standard. Many were able to fire even more quickly. This skill at arms was to be crucial. The army was also trained to march long distances – fifteen miles in full kit in what became known as 'Kitchener's Test'. This, too, was to be an important attribute over the next momentous three weeks or so.

SUNDAY 23RD: THE MORNING
6AM – 8AM: THE SCYTHE STARTS TO SWING
THE 3RD DIVISION.

During the evening of the 22nd Lieutenant-Colonel Hull had placed his 4/Middx in the positions where they would begin the battle the following day. His task was to hold the south bank of the Canal du Centre, facing Obourg on the hill in front of him, on the far side of the sixty-foot wide canal. There were three bridges that concerned him: on his extreme right flank at Lock No. 4; the road bridge to Obourg some five hundred yards towards his centre; and Lock No. 5, two thousand yards to the left of that. There was a further bridge, a couple of thousand yards to the north west of Lock No. 5, which was at the junction of his left flank and 4/RF.

Immediately to the right of the Obourg road bridge was the railway station, on the south bank. D Company, commanded by Captain HEL Glass, would cover both this bridge and that at Lock No. 4 – and for a thousand yards to the north west of the bridge, an impossibly long front. Lieutenant William Allinson was in command at the station, which had been extensively strengthened by the defenders.

To the left of D Company was B Company, under the command of Major WHC Davy, who was in touch with Captain Ashburner's C Company (4/RF) at the Bridge des Bragnons.

In reserve, C Company of 4/Middx (Captain Oliver) was a thousand yards behind D, in front of a large hospital and convent, and A Company (Major WH Abell) was on its left. Lieutenant LF Sloane-Stanley, the machine-gun officer, had his two guns between them at the junction of two small roads, looking towards the woods sloping down to the south bank of the canal. Battalion Headquarters was first put into a quarry to the left of the large cemetery which was on the side of a small hill, but then moved 500 yards north west of the cemetery into the cellars of a small house on the road to Nimy.

At dawn a mist hung over the canal and light rain was falling. Shelling of the Battalion's positions had not yet started, but at 8 am the first shots of the battle came across the canal, fired at D Company positions at the station by the German 31st Infantry Regiment. They hit Private J Parr, whom many consider to be the first infantryman to be killed in the Great War. Lieutenant-Colonel Hull had, earlier that morning, told his officers that there would be no advance over the canal, saying, *'This, gentlemen, is where we will stand and fight!'*.

Lieutenant Colonel NR McMahon, commanding 4/RF, was at Nimy, on the right flank of 9 Brigade. He commanded 26 officers and 983 other ranks, of whom

A Company, 4th Royal Fusiliers, resting in the square at Mons, 22 August 1914. They were to move up to the canal bank at Nimy.

Lock 4, guarded by Captain Glass's D Company.

734 were called up reservists. Opposite his Battalion were troops of the German IXth Corps, two regiments (ie six battalions) of the 18th Division whose attack line stretched eastwards along the Canal du Centre to D Company's (4/Middx) position. Thus there were approximately six thousand Germans against two thousand, separated by the width of the canal. The Fusiliers had six bridges to defend: from the right there was the 'joint' one held with the Middlesex; the road bridge at Nimy and the railway bridge two hundred yards to its left; the bridge at Lock No. 6, a thousand yards further left beyond the canal bend; and the Ghlin road and adjacent railway bridges five hundred yards further along the canal, the western entry to Mons.

Captain Forester held the road bridge at Nimy, which had been swung back, with two platoons whilst two other platoons were entrenched at the railway bridge and the canal bank to its left. Lieutenant Maurice James Dease, the machine-gun officer, had placed his two guns at the railway bridge, one at each side, in small emplacements of sandbags built onto the stone buttresses, with fields of fire across the canal. B Company was at Nimy Railway Station with Battalion Headquarters. D Company was at Lock No. 6 and the road and rail bridges on the Ghlin road. Part of the Company was on the western side of the canal, for about a thousand yards, on flat land dominated by a large wood. A Company, under Captain Cole, was in reserve on the northern edge of Mons. In fact, only two companies, C and D, were on the defensive against the six German battalions. Captain Byng of D Company had blocked the railway bridge with large drums of cable, wheeling them into position and turning them on their side, thereby forming a barricade.

Private A F Carter. D Company, 4th Middlesex.

Four 18 pdrs of 107 Battery of XXIII Brigade RFA had found positions close to the station at Mons from where they could support the two companies. At 8am all was still almost quiet, although movement could be heard in the woods on the other side of the canal.

To the left of the Royal Fusiliers was 1/RSF (Royal Scots Fusiliers), who had been brought by their commanding officer, Lieutenant Colonel Douglas Smith, to the eastern end of the Condé Canal on the 22nd. He marched them over the bridge at Jemappes, along the pavéd road across the flat, marshy land to Ghlin, two

Lieutenant Holt's bridge on the Rue des Bragnons. The lifting gear is on the Maisieres side.

German lancers watering their horses.

miles away. This was his allotted position, on the left of the Londoners, for the Corps advance.

However, long before nightfall, he was withdrawn to take up positions on a two thousand yard length of the canal, from Loch No. 1 on the right to the iron lifting bridge, Pont Richebe, at Jemappes on the Battalion's left flank. Several hundred yards east of that bridge was Lock No. 2, also bridged and 700 hundred yards again to the east was a lifting road bridge leading from Jemappes to Ghlin. Lieutenant Colonel Smith placed outposts over the canal near to the bridges. Captain Rose (B Company) and Captain Innes (C Company) shared the defence of the long length of canal on the right of the railway station, close to the southern bank. Captain Tullis (D Company) held the left flank at the Pont Richebe whilst Battalion Headquarters was in the village behind the church, where the reserve company, A, was also situated. The whole of the Battalion's position was amongst a small, heavily built-up area on the edge of the coal mining district.

As early as 6 am, just north of the bridge to Ghlin, the quietness of the morning was broken by B Company when its outpost was approached by a German cavalry patrol coming out of the mist. At 500 yards the Scots' machine gun hit the patrol, killing one and forcing the others to scatter. The fallen trooper was identified as being part of IXth Corps.

For the time being all was quiet, and soon the church bells sounded out. Many of the villagers (there was a population of about 6,000) appeared on the streets, either to go to mass or, so it seemed to the bemused soldiers, going to the station to board the holiday train that was already waiting there, to take them to their destination via Mons. They seemed quite oblivious to the imminence of fighting on their doorstep.

1/NF (Northumberland Fusiliers) were under the command of Lieutenant Colonel HS Ainslie. When they came close to the mining area near to Frameries, B and C Companies, under the Battalion's Second in Command, Major C Yatman, were detached and marched to the left and became the left flank troops of both the Brigade and the 3rd Division. They were positioned near Quaregnon, tasked with defending the lifting bridge at Mariette, a thousand yards to the left of 1/RSF. The remainder of the Battalion went into Cuesmes, some mile and a half south of Mons and a similar distance from the Condé Canal and Jemappes. Billets were found for Battalion Headquarters in the Curé's house on the village square. Just as in Jemappes, a remarkable holiday atmosphere prevailed.

Major Yatman's orders that evening had been to hold on as long as possible, so he knew that there would be no advance on the Sunday. The evening and night of the 22nd were spent in preparing the defence of the bridge, by A Company,

Swing bridge at Nimy, looking towards Mons.

British infantry preparing to meet the invaders. For a number of years the infantry had been training to fire fifteen aimed rounds a minute – the results were devastating against a massed infantry attack.

Mariette; a wooden one at Lock No. 3, barely a hundred yards to the left of the railway; and another lifting road bridge a thousand yards to the west of that. The Battalion's front was about 3,000 yards. D Company (Captain RGM Tulloch) would hold the railway bridge whilst C Company (Major P Hastings) was to guard the two to the left of it. These two forward companies were commanded by Major PM Buckle, the Second in Command. A and B Companies were in reserve in Hornu, two miles south.

The companies at the canal set about turning the buildings close to the canal into strong points, loopholing walls, erecting barbed wire barricades and digging trenches on the far bank. C Company had moved across because buildings on the north side obstructed their view beyond. The situation for the defenders was not helped by the ground round about consisting mainly of water meadows, useless for artillery.

Reports of the enemy by the Divisional Cyclists on the 22nd after their skirmish led to a decision to send men northwards to make contact with the enemy. At 5.30 am A Company (Captain GD Lister) received instructions to follow a cavalry patrol of 19/Hussars and the Cyclists over the canal and make a reconnaissance towards Tertre, two miles to the north; and to take up a position as far as the fork in the road on the southern edge of that village.

Shortly after 8 am the Company went over the canal and within half an hour had reached their objective. The men dug themselves in on either side of the road, about 400 yards from the village.

2/Duke of Wellington's was in support to 1/RWK and were billeted in and around the market square of Hornu. The Battalion had hardly settled in when Captain WM Ozanne, the machine-gun officer, was ordered to take his two guns forward to support 1/RWK at the railway embankment on the north side of the bridge. It was a dark night and no easy matter to drag the gun limbers over the tow path; however at 10.30 pm he met up with Captain HD Buchanan-Dunlop at Lock 3 and determined to stay with the Kents until daylight.

At 4 am on the Sunday morning some Belgian cyclists came through their position and said that they had seen large numbers of the enemy with field guns approaching the canal. The 2/Duke of Wellington's machine-gunners then went over the canal to the embankment; Captain Ozanne positioned one each side of the twenty foot high mound, the gun team on the right being commanded by Sergeant Smith. They were firmly in position by 7.30am.

The left flank battalion of 13 Brigade was 2/KOSB (King's Own Scottish Borderers), which had seven

and the canal bank to the right by C Company. The situation was somewhat complicated, for in reality there were two canals and therefore two bridges. The first was a short, twenty foot long bridge, that spanned the first narrow, but very deep, drainage canal and connected the south bank to the forty foot wide central tow path. Then came the lifting bridge (which lifted towards the far bank) over the sixty feet wide Condé Canal. On the north bank was the bridge keeper's house; Sergeant Panter with twelve men turned that into a small fort by loopholing the walls. The railway ran alongside the north bank, so the level crossing gates were jammed and a barbed wire barricade erected which connected the houses. A further obstacle was made on that side of the canal with some iron railings, virtually enclosing the Sergeant and his party, but leaving a small gap through which they could make their escape. The buildings on the central bank were demolished, but the ruins manned to provide support for the outpost beyond; whilst the main defence took up position in loopholed houses lining the south bank.

The men were still working on the defences when Major Yatman was summoned at about 7 am to the station in Quaregnon. There he spoke on the telephone to a man who spoke in perfect English; he was a British agent who told him that he was near the Bois de Badour, some four miles north of the canal, and that various German units were near him, which he identified. Suddenly the voice fell silent and Yatman never did discover either who the brave man was or his fate.

THE 5TH DIVISION

The first battalion of Sir Charles Fergusson's Division to arrive at the Condé Canal on the 22nd was 1/RWK (Queen's Own Royal West Kents). Lieutenant Colonel A Martyn's Battalion was to defend the three bridges at Saint Ghislain, 3,000 yards west of Quaregnon. There was a fixed iron railway bridge on the right, not quite 2,000 yards west of the Northumberland's bridge at hundred reservists in its ranks. It had arrived (under the command of Lieutenant Colonel CM Stephenson) at Boussu, two miles south of the Condé Canal and two miles west of Hornu, in the afternoon of the 22nd; after a short rest it marched north to the canal, to the left of 1/RWK, and stopped at the hamlet of Les Herbieres. The Battalion's task was to hold the iron road bridge of Les Herbieres at Lock No. 4 and the thousand yards plus of canal bank that lay between there and 1/RWK. 200 yards west of the Les Herbieres road bridge was a fixed railway bridge which was the responsibility of 1/E Surreys of 14 Brigade. As in 13 Brigade sector on their right, a deep drainage canal ran alongside the main one, separated by the wide tow path and beyond it the lifting bridge. On the north bank was a short row of houses.

B and D Companies of 2/KOSB under Majors ES D'Ewes Coke and Chandos Leigh were moved up to the canal and began digging trenches. They, too, were aware that there would be no advance. General Smith-Dorrien's orders to prepare a second line of defence had dispelled that idea. Opposite the short row of houses a tall white house on the south side of the bank was turned into a machine-gun post. Lieutenant JBW Pennyman, the machine-gun officer, used the top floor to give him good observation. Houses were knocked down or fortified and barricades built. Over the bridge, some 400 yards north, the road forked to the right, the road to Tertre, a village soon to be occupied by the Germans. By dawn on the 23rd, B Company (Major Coke) was in position half a mile north of Lock No. 4 to cover the approaches. The defence of the bridge and the bank lay in the hands of D Company. To the right A (Captain LD Spencer) and C (Captain EW Macdonald) Companies had their men stretched out toward the 1/RWK position. The machine guns of the supporting battalion, 2/KOYLI (King's Own Yorkshire Light Infantry), under the command of Lieutenant Pepys, had been brought up to cover these companies.

At 7.30 am things were quiet to their front, although sounds of battle could be heard to the right. It was not until midday that things began to happen on this part of the battlefield.

As the morning progressed Major Coke and some others continued to examine buildings for their defensive potential. They found in one the occupants who had remained despite the obvious preparations for a battle. They were made most welcome and fed omelettes and given coffee to drink. One of the ladies of the house suggested that all the visitors – and there were many by now – should write their names on the tablecloth. Four years later, in November 1918, Coke, who was by then a Brigadier General (he commanded 169 Brigade of the famous 56th (London) Division from its formation in France in February 1916 to the end of the war), found himself near Les Herbieres. He went to see if he could find the house once again. It was only a ruin, but on hearing his voice two ladies came out of the cellar. In minutes they were drinking coffee and he was answering questions about the officers the ladies remembered, such as Captains Smith and Spencer and they were telling him of their experience under German occupation. In due course they produced the tablecloth, safeguarded despite the vicissitudes of the war, and presented it to Coke; it is now the cherished possession of the Regiment's Officers' Mess.

The last battalion of 13 Brigade, 2/KOYLI, with the exception of its machine guns, were in support in Boussu; they would see no action until Sunday midday when enemy shells began to fall around the brewery where they were billeted and having their lunch.

In touch with 2/KOSB on the left were 1/E Surrey of 14 Brigade. Their commanding officer, Lieutenant Colonel Longley, had brought the Battalion over from Dublin via Kingston upon Thames, where 499 reservists were added to the strength. The Battalion reached the Condé Canal on the Saturday afternoon, having made an eighteen mile approach march. It was to defend the railway bridge at Les Herbieres, which carried the major Mons to Tournai line, and a lifting road bridge, the Pont d'Hautrage, almost a mile to the left of that. South of the canal the land was a vast water meadow and to the north, on either side of a five hundred yard long railway embankment, were small woods. Nearly two thousand yards away was the large and scattered village of Hautrage. A mile south of the canal flowed the narrow River Haine. Lieutenant Colonel Longley had also been told that there would not now be an advance over the canal, and so he placed his companies accordingly. C Company (Captain JP Benson) went over the canal and deployed either side of the embankment, taking with them the machine-gun section under Lieutenant TH Darwell. On the left flank was B Company (Captain EM Woulfe-Flanagan), at the road bridge; part of the company was put over the canal to guard the fork in the road to Hautrage, a couple of hundred yards beyond the north bank, with two platoons guarding the southern end of the bridge. Between these two was D Company (Captain MJ Minogue), spread out along the south bank, and nearby was Battalion Headquarters. A Company (Captain HP Torrens) was held in reserve about 500 yards to the rear of Headquarters, in a small wood. The Battalion Second in Command (Major HS Tew) took up post to the south of the railway bridge and held responsibility for that flank. The dressing station and transport lines with the reserve ammunition were well behind Major Tew, to the left of the railway line. The East Surreys had probably the best position of all the units in the 5th Division, with good fields of fire, and Lieutenant Colonel Longley had positioned his men very effectively.

At dawn on the 23rd a patrol under Captain Campbell went forward as far as the railway station at Hautrage (blissful, happy days, before the arrival of the Belgian Dr Beeching, when every settlement seems to have had a station) and found the railwaymen busily engaged getting steam up and removing the engines and carriages south over the canal and into the British lines.

Lieutenant Colonel Longley came forward and decided that he needed better fields of fire, which could be achieved by clearing the undergrowth. He sent A

Company forward to do this, and asked 2/Suffolk, the Brigade reserve, to lend him a company to help. Except for hard work in the hot and humid morning and the clank of pick and shovel, all was quiet and uneventful, at least until shortly after noon.

The left flank battalion of the whole of II Corps was 1/DCLI (Duke of Cornwall's Light Infantry). They had to guard over 3,000 yards of canal. The front extended from left of the Pont d'Hautrage to Lock No. 5, 2,000 yards away. Nearby, to the east, there was a lifting bridge which connected Thulin, two miles south of the canal, to Le Petit Crepin, five hundred yards on the north side and beyond that the large village of Pommeroeul. The frontage extended a further thousand yards to the west, but at least there were no more bridges or locks to defend along this stretch.

1/DCLI's commander, Lieutenant Colonel Martin Turner, was an extraordinary man. He was born in 1865 to middle class parents and left home at the age of 19 to enlist as a private. He was immediately bought out by his father, but left home again and this time joined the Gordon Highlanders, probably thinking that this would take him far enough away from his father this time. He served on the North West Frontier in India and was commissioned in due course into the DCLI. He went to Burma and fought in the war there and then saw service in 1897 in the Tirah campaign on the North West Frontier. He returned to Burma as Adjutant of the Burma Rifles and then returned to command the DCLI depot at Bodmin. In 1911 he took command of the 1st Battalion. He was severely wounded on the Aisne in September 1914 and ended his war as a Brigadier General, having been given command of a brigade in 1916.

Turner concentrated his Battalion along the road bridge and its approaches. The obvious line of attack would be down the long, wide and straight road from Ville Pommeroeul – the land on either side of it was water meadow.

He faced another potential problem if the enemy should breach the canal defences. Behind the canal, at its southernmost point perhaps a mile away, was the River Haine; not a particularly wide feature, but it could complicate matters if a retreat had to be made in haste, and certainly could affect the cohesion of the Battalion.

Most of the defences were put over the bridge, on the north side of the canal. B Company sent a platoon under Lieutenant Saville to take a position some four hundred yards forward on the road leading to the east side of Le Petit Crepin. He in turn sent three men, under Private Sambrook, a couple of hundred yards forward along this road. C Company took up a position over the bridge, whilst the remainder of B was concentrated at the southern bridgehead. A Company was deployed along the bank to connect with the troops to the right. D Company (Captain Woodham) were in reserve, but were spending their time preparing the defences of the bridge over the Haine, just north of Sardon. Lieutenant Colonel Turner, with his adjutant, Lieutenant AN Acland, made their advanced Headquarters in this hamlet, whilst the main Battalion Headquarters were in Thulin, several hundred yards further south – which was also the location of 5th Division Headquarters.

The two other battalions of 14 Brigade, 2/Suffolk and 2/Manchester, were deployed around Hainin, a couple of miles south of the canal; the Suffolks in support of the East Surreys and the Manchesters of the DCLI.

At 6 am on Sunday morning Private Sambrook and his two comrades were surprised to see riding slowly towards them a number of German cavalry. These men were from the 9th (Cavalry) Division, part of Marwitz's IInd (Cavalry) Corps. Von Kluck had continued to push his cavalry westwards, rather than concentrating them with his main army, as von Bülow wished. The dissipation of his cavalry force could well have had a crucial impact on the Retreat a few days later if they had been more readily available.

The cavalrymen were in no hurry, chatting as they rode, with no idea of the proximity of the British – or, indeed, the French. The three DCLI men held their fire, keeping well down in the ditch that ran alongside the road. The Germans came alongside them and one, an officer, glancing down, saw them. He fumbled for his revolver but he was too late and Private

Photograph taken by a British soldier at Mons. A canal boat turned into a bridge to facilitate a British withdrawal.

Sambrook shot him at close range. The patrol wheeled about and made off up the road, but one of the soldiers grabbed at the reins of the wounded officer's horse. He did not manage to stop it, but in all the excitement the officer's helmet fell off. In the meantime the other soldiers get up their fire, causing casualties, but the Germans got away. The three men of the outpost scrambled out of the ditch and back to Lieutenant Saville's position, carrying their helmet trophy with its bullet hole with them. It is now in the regimental museum in Bodmin.

Shortly before 7 am the Germans returned and looked for the Cornwall's outpost; not finding anyone there they continued their progress along the road towards the platoon's position. At less than a hundred yards Saville's men opened fire and once again the cavalry beat a hasty retreat, returning whence they came. Saville did not know how many he had hit, but there were a number of dead horses on the road and later in the morning villagers came in with various trophies such as swords, pistols, lances and items of uniform.

At 8 am one of the German Dragoons, badly wounded, was brought in by the villagers. He could stand, but was in abject fear, expecting to be shot. He was put on a stretcher and sent back to Battalion Headquarters. After he was examined the medical officer reported that all the man's stomach contained was oats; obviously he had been sharing the horse's rations.

The Germans had still not given up, and shortly after 8 am another cavalry patrol came up, this time along the Ville Pommeroeul road, probably oblivious of earlier events. This time the advance was taking the cavalry directly under Lieutenant Benn's machine guns, positioned at the bridge with several hundred yards of straight road along which to fire. Unfortunately, before they could be brought to bear a rifleman to the right of the bridge fired a shot, which was enough to send the cavalry back. Nevertheless, a dead horse could be seen lying in the road and shortly afterwards the wounded rider was brought in. He too was in fear of his life and begged for mercy. He was sent back to Headquarters at Thulin. The Germans were now well aware of the British left flank; but it was not until Sunday afternoon that any fighting returned to Lieutenant Colonel Turner's Battalion.

15 Brigade was put in reserve behind 13 and 14, towards the centre and west of the Condé Canal, in and around the villages of Boussu and Elouges.

The Royal Engineers had also been having a busy time. The CRE (Commander Royal Engineers) of 3rd Division was Lieutenant Colonel CS Wilson, who controlled the Division's two Field Companies, 56 and 57; the CRE of the 5th Division was Lieutenant Colonel JAS Tulloch, with his Field Companies, the 17th and 59th; they had been very industrious.

Gangs of Belgians had been recruited to assist with the construction of II Corps' second line of defence, and these needed to be supervised. However, the first priority was the bridges and their preparation for demolition.

Defending the rail bridge.

The sappers faced a real problem. There was a severe shortage of explosives – but more acute was the insufficient number of fuses. A short time before mobilisation the fuze instantaneous had been withdrawn (due to store changing). The speed of mobilisation meant that they had not been replaced. They would have to rely upon safety fuse and electrical firing, and these exploders were only issued on the basis of one per section. It would mean that to explode more than one charge simultaneously would require each length of fuse to be of the same length and all to be fired at the same time. As the iron girder bridges required multiple charges, much ingenuity would be required. There were eighteen bridges in total, more than there were officers to take charge, so much of the work fell upon junior NCOs.

At 2.30 am on the 23rd the sappers of the 3rd Division were told to prepare the bridges in their area for demolition but were further instructed at 8.53 am that nothing must be destroyed until the Division's retirement became necessary. The engineers of the 5th Division were busily engaged in preparing houses to be used as strong points; though the bridges had been reconnoitred, nothing as yet had been done about preparing them for destruction.

It took some time to get the men of the 56th and 57th on to the bridges, broadcast as they were on the task of preparing the second line. Nothing could be done until 6.30 am; Major NJ Hopkins of the 56th Fd Coy sent men into Mons in search of more explosives, but they returned empty handed. By 8 am the task had begun, but in the curve of the canal from the top near Nimy and down to Obourg firing had already commenced, so that it was impossible to work on these bridges.

8AM – MIDDAY:
BATTLES OF THE MONS SALIENT BEGINS

At about 8.30 am the attack by the 85th and 86th Fusiliers under the protection of a heavy bombardment began against the Middlesex on the right of the salient's tip at Mons. They were firing from across the canal and some of them got into houses on the hillside of Obourg and put strong pressure on D Company in the station. It was in this initial attack that Private Parr was killed.

On the left of the Battalion, opposite B Company, machine-gunners saw a German battery unlimbering their guns almost a mile away across the flat land below the hill; these were put under heavy fire and the gunners departed to seek an alternative site.

Gradually the German infantry attack spread further around the bend towards the bridge at Rue des Bragnons. At about this time, Major Hopkins was ready to send his engineers to demolish the bridges on 4/Middx front; two platoons of C Company of 2/RIrR (Royal Irish Regiment) went with the section to the bridge over the Canal du Centre at Obourg. However, when Captain Fitzgerald arrived it was already too late, the enemy were positioned on the far side of the bridge, making it impossible for the sappers to operate. The engineers also tried to get to the Rue des Bragnons bridge, but again the Germans had arrived first. The commander of the RE section, Lieutenant HW Holt, was killed when the Germans rushed his section; he has the dubious distinction of being the first Royal Engineer officer killed in the War. Sergeant Miles and the rest of the section were captured. Thus, all the bridges in front of 4/Middx were intact and available to the enemy.

The German infantry began to come towards the canal at about 10 am, advancing in solid blocks with rifles at the trail, firing from the hip. The intention was to storm by sheer impact of numbers. The rifle and machine-gun fire of 4/Middx tore great gaps in the compact ranks; but still they came on and, despite their awful losses, the sheer number of them forced the bridges and by 10.30 am they were over the canal.

At the railway station almost all of the defenders had been either killed or wounded, including the detachment's commander, Lieutenant ABW Allistone, wounded and captured. An unknown last man at the barricade on the station roof remained at his post; although wounded, he could still fire his rifle. By his actions he helped those who were physically able to make good their escape; in due course this nameless hero was killed.

Captain Glass was wounded by the time his D Company withdrew to the convent; whilst Major Davy was killed by the time that B Company was forced back to the railway cutting. At 11 am 4/Middx's line had not been broken, but it had been squeezed back so that it was well south of the canal and surrounding the group of buildings in front of the communal cemetery, including the convent and the hospital. Lieutenant Colonel Hull called on 2/RIrR (commanded by Lieutenant Colonel St. J Cox) to come up in support, which was done promptly.

4/RF stood to at daybreak after a gruelling night of digging and preparing their defences. They had heard the Germans moving about in the large wood on the far side of the canal. Shortly before 8 am a cavalry patrol was seen coming towards the opposite bank of the road bridge, which had been swung back. Galloping straight towards it, unaware of the proximity of the Fusiliers, the officer and six men were brought to an abrupt halt when the Londoners opened fire, killing four of them and wounding the officer, knocking him off his horse. The remaining two members of the patrol escaped, fleeing back into the wood. Quickly men dashed across the bridge and brought the officer in; he turned out to be Lieutenant von Arnim, the son of Sixt von Arnim, commander of IVth Corps, whose troops would soon be engaged against 14 Brigade. The Lieutenant was a member of the 'Death's Head' Hussars, and his notebook showed that he had been observing the British positions from the wood, yet had no idea of the scale of the force on the opposite side of the canal.

The Germans began their attack against 4/RF at about 10 am, led by the 84th Regiment in solid blocks, who advanced under a barrage of artillery fire. At a thousand yards the targets could not be missed and their leading sections of four abreast were destroyed, causing the whole regiment to retire back to the wood. After a heavy bombardment on the Fusiliers' trenches they came on again; the Royal Artillery could not reach them from the awkward firing positions that they had been able to find. Casualties began to mount, particularly amongst the officers. Lieutenant Mead was sent up from Nimy railway station to assist but was almost immediately wounded in the head. He returned to have it dressed and then went back without hesitation, whistling as he went, to be shot again through the head, this time fatally. By this time Captain Ashburner was wounded and Captain Fred Forster had been killed.

The Germans were still being held at bay, the two machine guns on the railway bridge in particular doing great execution, though suffering losses amongst their crews as well. By 11 am the machine-gun officer, Lieutenant Maurice Dease, had been wounded twice. Each time one of the guns stopped firing he went forward from his trench on the embankment some fifty yards back to find out why; and then returned once more with replacements or more ammunition.

C Company remained under constant bombardment; the road bridge was impassible because it had been swung back, but the valiant Germans still came forward to try and force a crossing over the railway bridge. Casualties amongst C Company continued to mount despite reinforcements; Captain Bowden Smith died of wounds and Lieutenant EC Smith was killed outright.

Major Howard had not given up all hope of destroying the railway and road bridges at Nimy. He sent one of his section commanders, Lieutenant AF Day to deal with them; but Day found that he had not got enough explosive to do both. In any case, the enemy fire was devastating and he could not get into suitable positions to lay charges. Nevertheless, he remained close to the railway bridge to await his opportunity. Further to the left things were altogether quieter, even though the men of 4/RF here did come under sporadic rifle and shell fire from across the canal. They had sunk the barges and other craft; and now they simply awaited their turn to be attacked. Corporal A Payne (later to become a Major) of 57 Fd Coy, with his six sappers, had laid his charges carefully at the road bridge to Ghlin and the nearby railway bridge. He did not have an electric exploder and so would have to set the charges off simultaneously with equal lengths of safety fuse. He waited the word of command to destroy the bridges.

Over to the left, before Jemappes, at the start of the Condé Canal, 1/RSF could hear the battle raging to their right but before them all was relatively quiet. At 10.30 am the artillery of IIIrd Corps opened fire on them, soon to be followed by the densely packed columns of infantry belonging to the 6th Division coming across the water meadows from the wood behind Ghlin. After being received with the accurate and rapid fire of the Scots, they spread out and came forward in rushes in small units. Some company commander had had the sense to abandon the suicidal formation used in most places that morning.

Lieutenant Colonel Smith had already withdrawn his posts north of the canal, and his Battalion's concentrated fire stopped the enemy not more than 200 yards from the Pont Richebe, in the built-up area to the left of the railway station. They would succeed in holding the 6th Division until early in the afternoon.

The sappers of 57 Fd Coy were here as well; Lieutenant PK Boulnois had left Corporal Jarvis and Sapper Neary to deal with the bridge over Lock No. 2, 800 yards east of Pont Richebe, when it was time so to do. Boulnois had with him four NCOs and four sappers on bicycles, with a forage cart loaded with explosives and a drum of cable. His responsibilities were the bridges from the right of Jemappes station to the lifting bridge at Mariette, the latter defended by 1/NF on 9 Brigade's left flank. The party was divided into pairs, one to each bridge; leaving explosives and cable at each, he arranged that he would return with his exploder and blow each in turn. Because the Mariette Bridge promised to be the most difficult, that was entrusted to his senior NCO, Sergeant Smith, and Sapper Dabell. The senior engineer officer at 9 Brigade's bridges was Captain Theodore Wright, the adjutant to 3 Division's CRE. He had a car and a roving commission from Mariette to the two bridges at Nimy. The morning for all these sappers was busy and dangerous, though they were constricted by the requirement to await orders before they could blow their bridges. Nevertheless, all the barges and boats, some of them homes, were sunk, to the misery of some of the owners who could only stand and watch it happening.

At midday, all the bridges in the 3rd and 5th divisional areas were still intact.

By 9 am Sergeant Panter, 1/NF, had seen nothing from his strongpoint in the bridge keeper's cottage north of the canal. Sergeant Johnson was with a small party in a coal shed on the central bank, equally alert. C Company were busy improving their trenches on either side of the road crossing the south bank of the canal; whilst B Company was engaged in similar activity at the road junction a hundred yards further south. Major Yatman

Much of the fighting at Mons took place in built up areas from which much of the civilian population had not had time to flee.

put his detachment's Headquarters 300 yards further down the road at the railway station. At mid-morning the sound of gunfire could be heard to the right; whilst two miles to the west, where 1/RWK held the canal at Saint Ghislain, a large battle was obviously taking place. Not a shell had fallen on Mariette before 10.30 am, almost as though the Germans had forgotten about the bridge here and were concentrating on those to the left and at Jemappes.

Sergeant Panter suddenly saw a column of German infantry entering the main street in front of them, four abreast, and proceeding as if unaware of the British presence. Within minutes the fire of him and his men had scattered the enemy, leaving many dead and wounded lying in the street. At 11 am Panter withdrew his small garrison back over the canal into C Company's trenches; as he did so the enemy artillery began to shell the northern bank where he had been. The fire lifted and the bombardment passed over the canal and also onto the central bank between the two canals, killing Sergeant Johnson. The three men who were with him were unable to make their escape due to the crossfire across the bridge. They took shelter in the cellar, where they remained until the battle had passed over them completely. They then emerged and managed to catch up with their battalion five days later when it had marched many miles to the south.

Massed German infantry attack.

1/Lincoln, the fourth battalion in 9/Brigade, was in reserve in Cuesmes, a mile and a half south west of Mons; on Sunday morning they were prepared to move to whatever part of the battlefield needed their assistance. At midday they were called upon to block the roads from the town at the south west corner, erecting four barricades. Whilst engaged in this they were not aware of how grateful 4/RF would be for their assistance an hour or so later.

'...in our first battle we had been badly beaten, and by the English – by the English we had so laughed at a few hours before.'

1/RWK (13 Brigade) found themselves engaged in fighting soon after 8 am. They had entrenched themselves and covered the three bridges in their sector. Did they but know it, they were only three miles from the concentration area of the German 5th Division. To the north of the canal was A Company, not far from Tertre, covering the approaches from Badour and waiting for the enemy which Cyclists had reported seeing in large numbers in and beyond the village. Meanwhile four 18 pdrs of 120 Battery had been brought forward to just south of the canal. At 8.15 am four of the Divisional Cyclists came down the road from Tertre at full speed and flung themselves down into the ditch where Lieutenant Gore's men were digging in. [Gore himself would be killed at Neuve Chapelle two months later.] They reported that the rest of the detachment had been blown to pieces by the enemy's artillery. Within minutes of this some hundreds of infantry began to come towards the Kents from the open land between the village and railway embankment on the right. As everywhere else, this was the first time 1/RWK had seen solid ranks of infantry steadily marching towards them; Captain Lister's men could not miss. These Germans were from 3 Battalion, 12th Brandenburg Grenadiers; their brave advance was brought to a halt with fearful casualties. The Germans then brought a battery of artillery into action and another body of infantry began to advance; in the meantime more of them, 1 Battalion, began to advance out of Tertre down the left hand side of the road through the wooded area.

(For an outstanding account of this battle from the German perspective, you should make every endeavour to get hold of a copy of The Advance from Mons by Captain Walter Bloem, who commanded B Company, 1 Battalion, 12th Brandenburg Grenadiers in the battle. It is a quite remarkable book; Bloem comments on this day's fighting:

> *'A bad defeat, there could be no gainsaying it; in our first battle we had been badly beaten, and by the English – by the English we had so laughed at a few hours before.'*

What is even more remarkable about this book is that it was published in Germany, by this well-established novelist, in 1916.)

Over on the railway embankment Captain Ozanne, commanding the two 2/Duke of Wellington's machine guns, had come across his first German. At 10 am, before he went into action against the Brandenburger's assaulting 1/RWK to his left, he had gone 200 yards in front of his emplacements and found a track that ran underneath the embankment; where he came face to face with a German cavalryman. Equally shocked, the German bolted off on his horse and Ozanne raced back the way he had come, neither having the presence of mind to draw a weapon. On returning to his guns he opened fire on more of the cavalry that had emerged from the wood, 500 yards to his left. Later in the day he would be wounded and have a remarkable escape from capture when, at 11 pm, he found a train about to leave a siding from Saint Ghislain station, arriving in Amiens some hours later.

A Company had now become so depleted that it was unable to withstand the pressure from the overwhelming number of Brandenburgers; shortly before noon the men retired, Major Beresford then brought B Company over to replace them, whilst the field guns got right up to the canal to support them. A Company had lost severely in the morning's fighting: one officer dead, two wounded and 93 other ranks killed, wounded or missing. During the withdrawal of A Company, Private Donovan of C Company saw Lieutenant Bell struggling to bring in a wounded man of A Company. He went forward to help, regardless of the lead mayhem around him; in due course he received the DCM for this action, the first won by the Battalion in the War.

'He went forward to help, regardless of the lead mayhem around him; in due course he received the DCM for this action, the first won by the Battalion in the War.'

The battle at Saint Ghislain continued throughout the afternoon, only ending at nightfall.

2/KOSB could only sit tight and listen – the men of von Kluck's army, his human scythe, did not reach their position until shortly after midday. 2/KOYLI were in the rear, but their lunchtime at the brewery in Boussu was to be rudely disturbed by enemy artillery. It was to be the last hot meal, disrupted or not, that the Battalion was to enjoy for some days to come. One man was hit and the rest bolted their food down. Lieutenant Pepys hurriedly returned to his machine-guns at the canal embankment; the rest of the Battalion would not see action (apart from being shelled) until 2.30 pm. 1/East Surrey also spent a quiet morning – nothing at all happened on their front; they could only listen and wonder as to what was taking place on their right. 1/DCLI also had a quiet morning, after the initial early morning flurry of excitement with Private Sambrook and German cavalry.

15 Brigade's four battalions were employed in digging defences two and three miles south of the canal, at Wasmes, Elouges and Paturages. Shells had not fallen far from them, but they would not see the real war until the following day.

MONS: AFTERNOON 23RD AUGUST
8 BRIGADE AND 4TH ROYAL FUSILIERS

The German infantry were now pouring across the Canal du Centre bridges in the Middlesex sector and were working their way round the right flank of D Company, moving out of Havre Wood, threatening to encircle the Company. On the northern, left, flank the Germans had reached the railway cutting where Major Davy, commanding B Company, had already been killed. Major Abell, taking A Company towards it, hoping to prevent the Battalion from being encircled, was also killed. The machine-gun officer, Lieutenant Sloane-Stanley, was wounded, but still there in the centre of the two front line companies, north east of the cemetery, with his surviving gun. In front of him he calculated that six enemy guns were in action. With six volunteers he intended to stay until overrun and captured. The German artillery had brought up more guns to the slopes on the far side of the canal and the whole of the sector east of Mons was being saturated with shell fire.

2/RIrR received the call for help from Lieutenant Colonel Hull whilst they were in the midst of their lunch, the last prepared one they would have for some time. They had heard the battle drawing closer and had been under shell fire since the middle of the morning. Lieutenant Colonel Cox sent A Company and two platoons from each of B and C, under the command of Major St Leger, at the double to the quarry above the cemetery. D Company under Captain Elliott moved to the cemetery, where C Company of 4/Middx were hanging on to their position. Two sections from A Company of 2/RIrR were put in the hollow at the western exit of the cemetery and at the major crossroads 200 yards beyond. Lieutenant FL Rushton, the Transport Officer, took the Irish machine guns well forward, close to the remaining one of 4/Middx, between A and C Companies.

The battlefield of 4/Middx gradually became that of 2/RIrR. Already the commander of A Company, Captain Mellor, had been killed by a shell burst as he went forward with Major St Leger. The whole Battalion, by 2 pm, was involved in an arc covering the crossroads at the Faubourg Barthelemy and the road to Binches and Harmignies. To the rear was the large Bois la Haut, the trees covering the hill which rose some five hundred feet high.

The battered remnants of 4/Middx who had survived the enemy onslaught thus far attempted to withdraw from in front of the cemetery. The Mental Hospital in front and to the right of the cemetery had caught fire, and hundreds of terrified inmates fled across the fields into the British defence lines, adding a macabre dimension to the confusion. Numbers were killed, whilst behind them came the advancing Germans, only a few hundred yards away and now dominating the battlefield; they were managing to infiltrate the Irish and Middlesex positions through the confusion of streets surrounding the cemetery. Captain Oliver withdrew with the remnants of C Company after the Middlesex machine gun was finally silenced and made for the large building which was the convent, a few hundred yards to the north of the cemetery. He wanted to get his horse out of the stables, but found that the Germans were already there. He took his men to the high wall at the back, but the gate was locked; one of his men blew it off, but injured himself in the process. Emerging from the gate on the Nimy Road, he and his men ran into crossfire; some fell, but the survivors crossed the road and went into the hollow where they found Lieutenant Ferguson with some men of the Irish A Company.

By 3.30 pm Lieutenant Colonel Hull's survivors had left the battlefield, though there remained some who were unable to move back with the rest and who were eventually overrun as they became isolated. Unfortunately the trials were not over for 4/Middx. They took the narrow road behind the west side of the hill and marched towards the tiny village of Hyon; the Germans were already there. They had managed to work their way from Nimy between the Middlesex and 4/RF. Here the Middlesex fought their last battle of the day and another sixty men became casualties. Eventually they reached Nouvelles, a few miles further south, and the roll call on that summer's evening showed that they only numbered 275. Fifteen officers were casualties, of whom five were killed and ten wounded and taken prisoner (including the Battalion Medical Officer, Captain Terry, who was himself wounded but opted to remain behind to look after the casualties). 453 other ranks were casualties, of whom ninety were killed; but a hundred of these reappeared over the next days as II Corps proceeded with the retreat. Still, given that the total British casualty count for the Battle of Mons was some 1,600, this was a very significant proportion of the total, well over 20 per cent.

By 1 pm the situation of Lieutenant Colonel McMahon's 4/RF was desperate. Although the railway bridge had still not been forced, C (also known as Y) Company had almost eighty casualties. Lieutenant Dease, twice wounded, had lost almost all of his machine-gun section and the left hand gun had been knocked out.

Round the corner at Lock No. 6 and the two bridges, the railway running under the Ghlin road bridge, Captain Byng and D (Z) Company had been under fire and direct frontal attack from the woods (about a mile away) and the open land in front for some hours. The defenders' fire had kept the (initially) massed ranks of Germans at bay, but by 1 pm the Germans had learnt their lesson and Byng had moved his men back to the canal. Corporal Payne of 57 Fd Coy had everything prepared to demolish the bridges as soon as the Fusiliers got across. The enemy artillery fire fell on the men of D Company as they ran back over the bridge, covered by Major Mallock's rearguard from A (W) Company. As the last man stumbled across, Corporal Payne and his men lit the six lengths of safety fuse and ran across the railway lines under the bridge. Because of the noise of bursting shells and the general sound of battle, Payne could not hear if his charges had exploded, but some evidently had as large pieces of the bridge came hurtling down behind him as he ran.

At 1.10 pm the Battalion received its first order to retire.

At Nimy, Dease realised that both his guns had ceased firing; he went forward once more and was hit for the third time, mortally wounded. There was no one left

'At Nimy, Dease realised that both his guns had ceased firing; he went forward once more and was hit for the third time, mortally wounded.'

Railway bridge at Nimy where Lieutenant Dease and Private Godley won their Victoria Crosses. This is not the original bridge – it was destroyed twice in the Second World War – however, the dimensions of the present-day bridge are the same as the original 1914 one.

The position of Private Godley's machine gun on the bridge.

alive at the guns, and only one in the machine-gun section. Only the right hand gun was fit to use, and that had bullet holes in its water jacket. Lieutenant Steele asked for volunteers who could use the gun, and Private Sidney Frank Godley of the machine-gun section, already wounded, said that he could. Moving forward he cleared out the position and set to work firing across the water into the enemy infantry. Lieutenant Day of 57 Fd Coy had remained close by the bridge in the hope of getting a chance to fix demolition charges, but the opportunity never came and during the morning he was wounded and, in due course, captured. With the sole machine gun still firing, Lieutenant Steele carried Dease back to the rear, where he died.

'Lieutenant Steele asked for volunteers who could use the gun, and Private Sidney Frank Godley of the machine-gun section, already wounded, said that he could.'

At 1.40 pm McMahon received the order to retire; with Godley remaining at his gun the survivors of the 4th Royal Fusiliers withdrew back into Mons.

A brave German, Musketier Oscar Niemeyer, went into the canal, swam over to the road bridge and operated the machinery to swing it back into position over the canal. He was shot and killed by the British in the process. But nothing could now stop the hordes of German infantry from pouring over the canal, especially as Godley had been wounded again and his gun had become too damaged to fire.

They harassed the Fusiliers as they fell back and set fire to the housing; they also herded a large number of civilians in front of them. This forced a number of Fusiliers, who were manning a barricade across the main street, to fall back into Mons, as they could not fire into that crowd. The four guns of 107 Battery also withdrew from Mons. The first battalion of Brigadier General Shaw's 9 Brigade to withdraw from Mons fell back through the winding and narrow streets towards the small village of Ciply, two miles away. Their retreat was covered by 1/Lincoln, who were dug in at the southern exits of Mons.

4/RF suffered more than 150 casualties. In the course of their fighting at Mons they had the honour to win the first two of the war, VCs, Dease and Godley. Maurice Dease's was gazetted first. Godley heard about his VC when he was recovering from his severe wounds as a prisoner; the news was given to him by the Commandant of the PoW camp.

At 10 am on 24 August 4th Royal Fusiliers withdrew from the Mons salient.

Private Sidney Frank Godley VC.

Now that all the bridges from Nimy to Obourg were available to the enemy, and with two battalions out of the fight, the full force of the enemy fell on 2/RIrR and 1/Gordons (Gordon Highlanders), commanded by Lieutenant Colonel FH Neish. In front of their curved perimeter line of only 800 yards radius from the major road junction at the Faubourg Barthelmy were the 85th (Bremen) and 35th Infantry Regiments; coming down through Mons, after 4/RF's withdrawal, was the 84th (Schleswig) Regiment. The Gordons had entrenched themselves along the main road to Harmignies in a position running south easterly from the road junction and on the forward slope of the hilly Bois la Haut. Their Headquarters were on the western slope in a large house. The whole area was thickly wooded. On top of the hill and at both ends were the three batteries of artillery from XL Field Brigade RA, the 6th, 23rd and 49th. A mile below the Gordons, and along the same road, was Lieutenant Colonel McMicking's 2/RS (Royal Scots). There were still three battalions of 8 Brigade to fend off the German attack on the Mons Salient.

Since 1.30pm, when the Middlesex had begun to withdraw, the machine guns of 2/RIrR had been out of action. Sergeant J Whittington recovered one and brought it back to the crossroads and got it into action. D Company, after their first advance to the quarry, had been so badly mauled that it was withdrawn back to Hyon, behind the hill, neither the Germans or the Middlesex having yet got there. When Quarter Master Sergeant Fitzpatrick saw this happening he collected about forty men from the Transport Lines – drivers, cooks, orderlies – and placed himself under the orders of Major Simpson. This officer commanded a company of Gordons at the crossroads and Fitzpatrick's men were put into a trench on the right hand side of the road, looking down the slope towards the right hand side of the mental hospital. Despite all that happened later in the day he remained in the position until 11 pm. When the position was invested by the enemy he scattered them with rapid fire and withdrew with eighteen survivors of his party. He was awarded the DCM.

'When the position was invested by the enemy he scattered them with rapid fire and withdrew with eighteen survivors of his party.'

Major St Leger brought his men back to the left hand fork of the crossroads in front of Gendebien Chateau. This building was being used by the medical officer (Major Long) as a first aid post; Red Cross flags hung from the windows and one was placed on the roof. Notwithstanding this it was hit by shells in the early afternoon and set on fire. All the casualties were evacuated into the surrounding woods, though the wounded commander of 49th Battery, Major JS Maidlow, and Private CH Jackson died in the ruins. Major Lyon, 6 Battery, was hit whilst galloping along the road towards his battery on the hill, and fell from his horse. Private Redmond of the Royal Irish and two gallant Gordons leapt out of their trench near to the crossroads, despite the shelling and heavy firing, and carried him to the makeshift hospital; he survived the subsequent fire.

A Company had by now lost all of its officers; Major St Leger, gathering all the men that he could, put them on the edge of the road looking down the slope of the ridge and across the shallow valley towards the cemetery a thousand yards away, and through which hundreds of Germans were pouring. Major Panter-Downes (commanding C Company) arrived and was directed to hold the position. The leading ranks of the enemy began swarming up the slope, firing from the hip as they came. Panter-Downes ordered his men (only about thirty of them) to fix bayonets and with Lieutenant Shine, who had previously been down in the valley, they charged at the Germans, who were now less than fifty yards away, and routed them. This had a cost, there were thirty or so casualties, including Shine, who was mortally wounded.

200 yards to the right Fitzpatrick's party, with the aid of the machine gun rescued by Sergeant Whittington on the right, was causing havoc in the valley. At about this time the Battalion's adjutant, Lieutenant REG Phillips, was severely wounded. Impossible to move him because of the extent of his injuries, he was taken prisoner in the evening.

There were some buildings on the eastern side of the road junction where some of the men had taken cover, firing from holes in the walls. At the road junction were two of the guns of 23 Battery, but the bombardment forced their withdrawal up the hill.

By the middle of the afternoon the Battalion had become scattered and depleted, so it was necessary to leave the crossroad position and retire behind the hill. Fitzpatrick remained, as did the Gordons, whose turn it now was to stop the Germans, helped considerably by the fire from 23 Battery on the hill; the advance of the enemy suddenly provided excellent targets. Between them the enemy was halted some 300 yards from the foot of the hill.

The land at the western side of the hill is flat and marshy, with a thin stream running through it. The Irish re-formed here; Lieutenant AMS Tandy and the survivors of A Company lined the road along each side of the narrow bridge and looked north towards Mons, as the last of 4/Middx came through en route for Hyon. B Company of the Irish had also come down the narrow road behind the hill and proceeded to climb up the very steep wooded slope in a fruitless search for the Gordons, who were mistakenly thought to be at the top. B Company returned down the hill, exhausted.

In Hyon it was becoming clear to Brigadier General Doran that he would have to move his Headquarters back. On the other hand he wanted to ensure that his Brigade was relatively safe, and he was desperate to make contact with the Gordons. Sometime before 5 pm he came up to 2/RIrR and led B and C Companies back up the narrow, cobbled lane at the foot of the hill. They could hear the battle going on to the left as the withdrawing 4/Middx ran into the Germans coming down from Mons. Within a couple of hundred yards of setting off along the lane they saw the Germans ahead of them. There was no room for manoeuvre, so the Irish had to return to the bottom of the hill and to the open land between it and the main road.

At 6 pm the Gordons were still holding their line on the main road, defying the enemy who seemed to have reverted to their tactics of pressing forward in massed, closed ranks. But the pressure was telling. The 18 pdrs on top of the hill had to be rescued; a platoon of Gordons under the command of Lieutenant IBN Hamilton was sent to extricate them, but these men did not realise that Hyon was in German hands.

The only way to extract the guns was down the back of the hill and along the narrow road, but as they moved along the lane they ran into a road block where a similar narrow lane crossed the bridge from Hyon to join the lane they were using. The leading horses were killed and the guns fell off the road into a ditch on the right. Nothing daunted, one group of Gordons chased off the Germans at the point of the bayonet, whilst another helped the gunners drag the horses and guns back up onto the road and then got away to join the Irish further along.

'The leading horses were killed and the guns fell off the road into a ditch on the right.'

To the right of the Gordons were 2/RS (Royal Scots). They had been in position all day some two miles down from the crossroads, spread out along the main road. Facing them was open and flat land, looking eastwards towards St Symphorien and Villers Ghislain. On their right were 1/IG (Irish Guards), of 4 (Guards) Brigade, 2nd Division, part of Haig's Ist Corps. They had an excellent field of fire, but except for the occasional shot at German cyclists, they had had a very quiet morning, in stark contrast to the raging sounds of battle coming from their left. Late in the afternoon, as the enemy attacked the Gordons to the north, a long line of German infantry came towards the forward companies, A and D, under the command of Major Tweedie. They were assisted in the defence by the Battalion machine guns under Lieutenant Laidley. The storm of defensive fire destroyed the German attack, bringing it to a halt 300 yards from the road in the flat and treeless fields. These soldiers from Bremen would wait until dusk before their next attempt.

With dark the Gordons withdrew, as did Fitzpatrick and his remnant; Major St Leger entrenched the survivors of the Irish along the track running from the bottom south east corner of the hill to the main road from Harmignies to Mons. This position was adopted to protect the guns of XL Field Brigade that were now gathered there, having escaped from their positions at Bois la Haut; and to stem any further German advances.

At 8 pm the Germans attacked the two Scottish battalions again, both from across the main road and from the flattish slopes coming down from the eastern edge of the hill. The attack from this latter point, especially as it was almost dark, was so sudden that four of the guns were temporarily lost, though a bayonet charge recovered them.

Shortly after this scrap the defenders could hear bugle calls. They were German, calling a halt to the fighting of the day. German losses had been tremendous; one estimate put them at more than 6,000 in Mons alone. The 75th (Bremen) regiment had lost six officers and 376 other ranks in one attack.

At 10 pm the British finally withdrew from these positions, bringing the guns with them, none of which had been lost during the day. The column passed on unhindered by the Germans and arrived at Nouvelles at 4.30 am on Monday 24 August. The Royal Irish had suffered 225 casualties, including five officers killed and five wounded. The Gordons (with 24 casualties) and the Royal Scots had got off very lightly. However, the battles in this part of Mons, involving five battalions and 1/Lincoln on the western fringes, had cost IInd Corps a thousand men. This was not a large number – indeed by comparison with later figures (even on 24 August) lost at Le Cateau, the Aisne and First Ypres, not to mention the vast battles later on in 1915 at Loos and the cataclysms on the Somme and in the Salient and the Hindenburg Line it is small – but the battle had been enormously significant for the well-being of the allied cause.

MONS: THE AFTERNOON FROM SAINT GHISLAIN TO LES HERBIERES AND THE ACTION OF 13 BRIGADE.

To the immediate right of 1/RWK were the 2/Duke of Wellington's. Captain Ozanne with his machine guns at the railway embankment had helped Lieutenant Colonel Martyn's men halt the attack of 12/Brandenburg; and for their efforts spent most of their time under shellfire. They could see the Germans sheltering behind corn stooks in the fields and fired on them intermittently; at 3 pm a shell burst in front of his emplacement, shattering his arm and wounding others.

He was able to make his way, along with the other wounded, back to the railway bridge and sheltered under it until nightfall. The bridge had already been prepared for demolition and nearby was Corporal Marsden of 17 Fd Coy ready to do the task. Whilst Ozanne was taking shelter there the Germans shelled the railway line and its bridge heavily, blowing off some of the gun cotton charges. The Corporal, despite the heavy bombardment, replaced them and the connecting leads. His work done, he returned to the south side, waiting for the exploder to arrive. Later on, whilst watching the action through a telescope, he was hit by shell fire and killed.

Lieutenant O'Kelly took a platoon of fifty-four men up to the canal on the right of the embankment at 1.30 pm. He came under fire from the direction of Mariette, where shortly the Northumberlands were to begin their retirement. Apart from some shelling, which generally went over their heads, these men came to no harm, but at 3pm O'Kelly saw a mass of infantry coming towards him across the open fields. Opening fire into the closed ranks, the enemy suffered fearful casualties, but 'as fast as they fell others came to take their place; each of my men must have fired hundreds of rounds'.

By 5pm they had come within 300 yards of O'Kelly's platoon and he ordered his men to fix bayonets. But then the Germans stopped and shortly afterwards the men heard the sound of bugles and the attackers started to melt away – for the moment at least, they had had enough. At 6pm he was ordered to retire, having suffered three killed and twelve wounded.

Captain RC Carter had taken B Company over the canal at about the same time as O'Kelly had gone forward. He put the men into buildings to the right of the road bridge near Lock No. 3. The Brandenburgers had slowed down since their battle with the Kents and Carter's orders were to fire at only good targets and not to give their position away in order to avoid artillery retaliation. Lieutenant-Colonel Gibbs had come up to examine the positions in the front line close to the canal; his orderly, Private Shellabear, was killed just a few yards from him at 3pm. At 4.30pm Brigadier-General Cuthbert sent an order to strengthen the right flank of his 13 Brigade, Major EN Townsend took A Company towards Mariette and told Captain EV Jenkins to stay with D Company in reserve on the square at St Ghislain. 2/Duke of Wellington's stayed where they were, the Brandenburgers having given up their attack for the day; the Battalion had only suffered three casualties amongst the officers thus far, all wounded.

'Opening fire into the closed ranks, the enemy suffered fearful casualties, but "as fast as they fell others came to take their place; each of my men must have fired hundreds of rounds."'

1/RWK and 2/Duke of Wellington's were responsible for four other bridges in 13 Brigade's sector. There was a lifting bridge at Lock No. 3, 200 yards to the left of the railway where Corporal Marsden was killed; a large lifting bridge carrying the main road from St Ghislain to Tertre, in the centre of 1/RWK's sector and where B Company of 2/Duke of Wellington's held the sheds on the north bank; only six feet to its left was a wooden bridge; and there was a lifting bridge 500 yards further on. Lieutenant Godsell was responsible for all of these bridges.

At 2pm Brigadier-General Cuthbert sent for him and said that he wanted them all demolished. The road bridge was a problem because it was constantly in use carrying orderlies, ammunition, wounded men and everything required by the infantry on the north side. The adjacent foot bridge could not deal with this sort of traffic, whilst to complicate matters it would be necessary to raise the road bridge in order to fix the charges.

Godsell made Corporal Gerachty and two men responsible for the Lock bridge; whilst Corporal Taylor was sent to the bridge west of the main one. Because of the heavy firing none of the bridges could be blown in the afternoon; in any case there was only one exploder and that would be used, as a priority, at the railway bridge. The road bridge and its small neighbour had to be blown at the same time, for fear of creating a mutual explosion; and they could not be destroyed until the men on the far bank had been withdrawn. Lieutenant Godsell had to wait.

2/KOSB had been waiting for their turn to get involved in the fighting all morning; they were not to be kept waiting overlong as the German IIIrd and IVth Corps moved around to swing against Smith-Dorrien's flank. Major AE Haig, the Second in Command, had his observation post alongside Lieutenant Pennyman's machine-guns at the top of the white house. At 1pm he saw Germans moving diagonally across his front. They were coming in a south westerly direction from Tertre, heading for the bridge; they were a party of Brandenburg Grenadiers, led by an officer who stood out because of his bandaged head. Haig could see that they were being cautious, but they also seemed to be unaware that there was anybody in front of them. They advanced in small groups over the water meadows, cutting the barbed wire fences as they came, Haig quickly informed Major Chandos Leigh's B Company on the far side of the canal as to what was happening; they brought the advance to a halt by their rifle fire. Haig reinforced their position, whilst the Germans commenced to bring their artillery to bear.

In the course of the bombardment the lock house and the cottage, whose occupants had welcomed the Borderers earlier, were hit; Haig saw the people, carrying a canary (strange what the memory recalls) disappear into the Battalion's lines.

Haig reinforced D Company with some of A Company; D Company moved forward to get clear of the houses now under heavy shellfire. This, unintentionally, became a counter-attack, and men began to fall as the Grenadiers opened up with machine-guns and the artillery showered them with shrapnel. In addition, the machine-guns in the white house which had been searching the woodlands from which the Germans had emerged with their fire, came under artillery fire; Pennyman was forced to take them out to a less obvious position.

At 3pm Major Haig ordered a retirement from the advanced positions to the canal; Major Leigh, who had won the DSO in South Africa, and had been wounded somewhere in the water meadows, could not be found and had to be left behind. He died shortly afterwards in German captivity. Other casualties included the Medical Officer, Captain Gibbon, and Captain Kennedy, both wounded; CSM Wilson was mortally wounded and Sergeants Adair and Murray were wounded – the latter would be killed on the Somme. Corporal Field was shot through the forehead but made a miraculous recovery in a German hospital; in all the Battalion suffered about a hundred casualties.

Lieutenant Pottinger of 17 Fd Coy had been waiting at No. 4 Lock bridge since the early afternoon, waiting for the infantry to retire and for permission from Lieutenant-Colonel Stephenson to blow it. This was not forthcoming until later in the evening and when the Germans were almost on the bridge. To Pottinger's dismay the charges would not go off; resourcefully, and using his skill as one of the army's best shots, he fired his revolver at the primer. The Germans were on the bridge and firing at him at this point; unfortunately the charges remained dead. He managed to make his escape, with his men, in the gathering gloom; in any case the enemy had stopped for the night and were not prepared to set off into the unknown in pursuit.

Lieutenant-Colonel Bond's KOYLI moved out of the brewery at Boussu after it had been hit by shell fire at midday and moved up towards the canal. The machine-gun officer, Lieutenant Pepys, was on the left of the St Ghislain road bridge, where he had been all day. The Battalion took up position 500 yards to the left of the road bridge and about a hundred yards south of the canal. At 2.30pm Captain Lowther took C Company up to the canal to strengthen the Borderers firing line; at about the same time Pepys was killed by a German sniper from the north bank and his place in charge of the machine-guns was taken by Lieutenant BN Denison.

The battalions of 13 Brigade were still at the canal at 6pm.

MONDAY, 24TH: THE LAST DAY

THE FIRST HOURS

The 3rd and 5th Divisions anticipated a long battle in their new positions in Smith-Dorrien's second line; Ist Corps also expected that it would be in a big battle on this day. Kluck had no intention of doing this, other than to engage them with enough strength to hold them; his opponents were to be swept into a trap by his manoeuvring right wing.

8 Brigade was on the right of Hamilton's 3rd Division; 4/Middx and 2/RIrR had suffered much the previous day, but they had hardly rested during the night, working instead at the trenches and defences of the new position. These men were the first beneficiaries of the new order, as Brigadier-General Doran's 8 Brigade moved south out of the salient, heading towards Bavai1.

To the right Haig's I Corps had a relatively easy time disengaging from its position. He too was cluttered with all his equipment up forward in hundreds of vehicles, carts and anything else that would carry the furnishings that go with an army on the advance. But he was able to start his move early in the morning and before the German artillery bombardment of the day had begun. He also set off towards Bavai, with 1st Division leading the way, followed two hours later by the 2nd. The route led them around the north of Maubeuge and down the very large – nine miles long by four miles wide – Mormal Forest. This feature was a major concern for all the senior commanders of the BEF, as it was inevitable that the two corps would have to pass either side of it, and they would therefore be forced apart for a significant period of time. This is not the sort of situation that forces in a withdrawing army appreciate.

German cavalry attempting to cross by pontoon bridge are caught by British artillery.

On top of this straight forward topographical fact, other difficulties were considerable. Road discipline was completely absent. The limited roads available – foot-destroying pavé – were congested with French troops heading south, pathetic hordes of refugees and French cavalry moving across the flow, heading for the BEF's west flank. There were problems at the few bridges across the wide River Sambre; there were some clashes with German cavalry patrols; it was very difficult to keep in contact with other elements of the BEF – but, in general, the retreat went smoothly enough in the circumstances.

The six brigades of IInd Corps were fortifying their new positions, confident of their ability after seeing the German infantry convincingly repulsed in their attempts to cross the canal the previous day. True, some had managed to make it across, but at a terrible cost and at a price that prevented them following through immediately. Now the British were in positions on hills with better fields of fire and with the likelihood of more effective artillery support. Besides their feverish work, many had their first food for eighteen hours.

Smith-Dorrien received the surprising, but not altogether unwelcome, order to retire his Corps at about 4 am. However, he had the major problem of withdrawing two divisions on very limited roads, already congested with refugees, and beside the infantry there would be transport, guns and the bulk of Allenby's cavalry.

He resolved that the 3rd Division should go first; it had taken the heaviest punishment on the first day, and his left flank was the more secure. The 5th Division should be able to follow afterwards, especially as he had some support in the form of 19 Brigade and the cavalry on his left, whilst Haking's fresh 5 Brigade was on his right.

Brigadier General Doran received his orders to retire at 4.30 am, just as the German IIIrd and IXth Corps artillery began their bombardment. Fortunately the infantry had learnt their lesson well, and was leaving it to the artillery to soften the British positions. Thus the Brigade was uninterrupted as, 4/Middx leading, it slipped away from the salient without further loss.

1st Northumberland Fusiliers had worked without ceasing during the night, erecting barricades at the crossroads in the village, having taken little food and even less sleep. During the hours of darkness, when the streets should have been empty of all but soldiers, a number of civilians were found wandering the place. Spy scares were at their height, and a number were arrested, despite some pleading to be allowed to go to Cuesmes to rescue British wounded who had been left in houses there.

In the same vicinity was Brigadier General Haking's 5 Brigade. 2/Worcesters were in Frameries; to their left and slightly forward, in front of Paturages, were 2/HLI and behind and to their left were 2/Ox & Bucks and 2/CR (Connaught Rangers). They had arrived at 1 am from the reserve area of the 2nd Division near Bougnies, three miles south east of Frameries. When 2/Worcesters reached the village, not knowing what they might encounter, they had bayonets fixed and the officers had drawn their revolvers. They found it unoccupied, as the men of 9 Brigade had not then reached it. The German shelling in the early hours of the morning caused them some casualties before they, unexpectedly, withdrew.

MONS: THE LAST HOURS OF THE BATTLE

1. THE BATTLES OF FRAMERIES AND CIPLY

The fight for the hilltop village of Frameries began with the enemy's bombardment of it which started soon after dawn. It fell on the centre of the village and 2/Worcesters's position. Within an hour it lifted and with an increased ferocity was put onto 1/NF's position, moving up towards the crossroads. The enemy infantry assault started at 7.30 am when the 24th (Brandenburg) Regiment advanced to the attack from the valley dividing the village from Flenu, a mile and a half to the north.

At this critical period when Major General Hamilton's 3rd Division came under attack as it was about to move out of the salient, 9 Brigade suddenly found that its neighbour, 5 Brigade, was withdrawing without warning. This was dismaying news for Smith-Dorrien and Hamilton, but it might have been expected as it was known that Haig's I Corps (2nd Division) were already on their way out of the salient. Nevertheless, it was a blow to their plans and would later cause 13 Brigade sever problems, but at this time it was 7 and 9 Brigades that were suffering; 8 Brigade had already moved off unscathed before the battle commenced.

At the crossroads in the centre of the village, where the street ran down steeply towards Cuesmes, was A Company manning three barricades. These blockaded the roads south, east and west and had been constructed during the night by the RE and were then being strengthened by 1/NF. At the foot of the hill, straddling the road to Cuesmes, were C and D Companies and in echelon on the right was 1/Lincoln. There were four guns from 109 Battery near the railway station on the south eastern edge of the village. The Germans may well

German 17th Division entering Boussu, 26 August 1914.

have thought that the village was empty, having seen some British troops pulling out earlier. They were to get a rude awakening when they approached the crossroads and the railway crossing at the northern edge of Frameries. Private Tebbut of 1/Lincoln later reported,

'I just kept firing my rifle until it got too hot to handle. At four hundred yards you could not miss and I never thought I would ever see so many dead men in such a small space.'

However, the Northumberlands and Lincolns casualties were also mounting up; both battalions slowly withdrew up the hill into the built up area. The Brandenburgers arrived at a point some hundred yards short of the barricade across the road to Cuesmes when Captain Sandilands witnessed an extraordinary incident. He was wounded, but still with his Company at the barricade, when an elderly lady approached in the midst of the mayhem. She insisted on going through the barricade to fetch a doctor to attend to the wounded who were being take into the hospital at the crossroads in the middle of the village. She could not be dissuaded, despite the bullets and flying shrapnel; she proceeded to go into a house beyond the barricade and soon reappeared with a little man carrying a black bag. No sooner had they emerged when a shell landed on the house opposite; they rushed back into the house. After a short while they came out once more, and ran back up the road to the barricade and on into the hospital.

Meanwhile the German effort had increased on the right; loud banging could be heard in the houses on the Cuesmes road as the enemy made passages through them to get at A Company.

At 8.45 am Major General Hamilton ordered Brigadier General Shaw to withdraw from the salient, increasingly concerned that otherwise his Brigade would be cut off on its left because of the withdrawal of 5 Brigade. The two battalions in Frameries began to disentangle themselves from the battle. On the left of A Company some Germans were seen attacking the western barricade fifty yards along the Paturages road. These were killed; and small rear parties kept the enemy at bay as the two battalions withdrew up the hill, en route to Eugies and Bavai. Their casualties had been considerable: 1/Lincoln had lost four officers and 134 other ranks, some of the wounded being taken prisoner in the convent hospital. Captain Ross, who was thought to have been killed, was later discovered to have been wounded and captured. 1/NF had suffered about fifty casualties, many of the wounded too badly hurt to move. A doctor, Captain M Leckie DSO, who was attached to the Northumberlands, died of his wounds in the hospital at Frameries on 28 August.

It was expected that Brigadier General McCracken's 7 Brigade at Ciply would have been able to withdraw before being attacked by the German 6th Division's attack began. Two battalions did – 2/RIRifles, which came down from the ridge a mile south of Mesvin and passed through 3/Worcesters; and the remnants of 4/RF.

2/South Lancs and 3/Worcesters in their positions on either side of main road into Cuesmes, five hundred yards south of the great, embanked railway system, had seen hundreds of Germans crossing their front since the early morning. The advance of the 24th Brandenburgers extended to this position and was met by equally effective rifle fire as they swarmed down the slope of Mount Eribus, a small hill between Ciply and Mons. The enemy was halted before they reached the triangle of railway lines and the station two hundred yards in front of 3/Worcesters' A Company.

On the left Lieutenant Colonel Wanliss' 2/South Lancs were equally under attack from the Brandenburgers; the Germans lined the railway embankment on the left, swarmed under the railway bridge and formed up behind the few houses that stood there. Facing them was D Company and Captain Travis-Cook with his machine-gun officer, Lieutenant Fulcher. They simply mowed down what they estimated to be two battalions armed with eight machine guns; they continued firing until ordered to retire. Travis-Cook, wounded seven times, finally fell with a bullet in his neck. Fulcher and his Sergeant, Harrison, shouldered the machine guns and took them away. However, a shell blew the guns off their backs and, it was feared, killed both of them. However, it was later learnt that Sergeant Harrison had not been killed but was badly wounded and taken prisoner. He was awarded the DCM and in due course served as RSM in the 5th Battalion. Fulcher was killed in November 1914 at Ypres.

Brigadier General McCracken became increasingly worried about his three battalions in the line – they should have retired long ago – and ordered them to get away as quickly as practicable and disengage from what was obviously an overwhelming force. 3/Worcesters were the first to move, covered by D Company (Captain de Salis) from a position at the railway, five hundred yards south of the sugar factory. The shell fire poured onto the escape route to the south, the Genly road, was so heavy that when it became D Company's turn the men had to retire in small sections to avoid destruction.

2/South Lancs acted as the rear guard, although 1/Wilts (Lieutenant Colonel Halstead), positioned at their road junction a mile south of Ciply and who had not been committed, would be the last to leave. As 2/South Lancs retired from the battlefield the enemy, with their machine guns on the railway embankment, raked the retreating columns of men. They had to move across the 2,000 yards of open land on either side of the Cuesmes road until they got into the shelter of the buildings on the east side of Frameries. The Battalion lost more than 300 men killed, wounded and missing – the great majority of the latter became prisoners. The RSM, Mr Robert, was found to be missing, but as happened in a large number of cases, he turned up – in this case five days and a major battle later. 3/Worcesters got off lightly with twenty-one casualties and 1/Wilts with thirty, amongst whom were Captain Dawes and Captain Rowan, the Adjutant. Halstead was fortunate to escape with only having his horse shot from under him.

The engagements at Frameries and Ciply in the four

hours since the bombardment commenced and the last man retired cost 7 and 9 Brigades almost 500 casualties; but the Germans had suffered far more. Colonel von Brandis stated that he had lost three company commanders, every second officer, every third man; Captain Liebenow of the 64th Regiment said that his Battalion had lost every fourth man and every lieutenant. The total German casualties were over a thousand, all dead or wounded; over half those of the British were prisoners, though many were wounded.

The Germans, crossing the Condé Canal at both its east and west ends, could now turn their attention to the left of the British line south of the canal. There seemed that there was still the prospect of driving Smith-Dorrien's IInd Corps into the trap of Maubeuge.

THE BATTLE AT WASMES

Essentially this battle involved 13 Brigade, with the addition of part of 1/Dorset from 14 Brigade. When the battalions were withdrawn in the very early hours of Monday morning, it was in the confident expectation that they were going into positions from where they could hold the enemy off for as long as need be. Their casualties thus far had not been heavy and they knew that they had inflicted a very heavy toll on the enemy in his attempts to cross the canal.

'I bayoneted a German, but before I could withdraw it I was clubbed on the head with a rifle.'

The village was packed with troops from the Brigade. 2/Duke of Wellington's were dug in on an arc a mile long around the northern edge, its peak at the crossroad a thousand yards to the north west of the village square at a point called La Justice. 500 yards east on the Binche road was an area known as Le Bosquet; 500 yards further to the east was D Company, at a large slag heap which marked the limit of the Battalion's right flank. On the left were three companies (A, B, C) of 1/Dorsets. They looked down the slope to Hornu, a thousand yards to the north; south of them, on the western perimeter of the Wasmes defences, was B Company (Major CG Pack-Beresford) of 1/RWK. Elements of all three battalions were inside the village perimeter, whilst the KOYLIs were in Paturages, to the south.

An artist impression of a British bayonet charge in process at Mons.

Until about 11 am the Germans contented themselves with bombarding Wasmes and the various positions of the infantry. Although Frameries had long since fallen, they were in no hurry to lose more men than they needed. They were content to hold the Brigade whilst the threatening sweep from the right developed.

Major General Fergusson gave the order for 14 Brigade to retire from the salient towards Bavai, to be followed by the 13th, which he knew would cover the former's withdrawal. They would be followed by 15 Brigade, which would cover the rear of the 5th Division. In turn, they would be followed by Allenby's cavalry and 19 Brigade. The salient was to be empty of British troops by the early afternoon. However, almost as soon as the order was given, Fergusson learnt that Allenby's cavalry had already gone, unable to find any signs of a great German advance, at 8 am. Drummond had withdrawn his 19 Brigade for the same reason. Smith-Dorrien's left flank was 'in the air'; the 5th Division had a long way to go before it could be clear.

To make matters worse, the Germans began to attack Wasmes in strength; and the 8th Division began to drive through Crespin to cut off the exodus of IInd Corps.

Fergusson asked Allenby to stop his withdrawal if he could and give some support to his left flank. He then formed a 'task force' from 15 Brigade to act as a left flank shield until he could extract 13 Brigade from the fighting at Wasmes; finally the 15th could move out – what was left of it, as 1/Dorset was fighting with 13 Brigade and 1/Bedfords with 14 Brigade, and these units would withdraw with them.

Before midday the German infantry had advanced against Wasmes in great strength. On the right flank was No. 12 Platoon of C Company, 2/Duke of Wellington's, who could see the enemy coming across a corn field carrying stooks as shields. Lieutenant LE Russel was down to twelve men (he had started with thirty). He ordered them to fix bayonets and to empty their magazines into the advancing Germans. They then stood up and charged into their foe, fighting a bitter hand to hand battle until all the Dukes had been killed. A platoon of D Company was near them; its commander, Sergeant Spence, ordered his men to fix bayonets and fight their way back into the village centre. A survivor, Corporal Williams, wrote;

'The bodies of Germans were piled up all

around. I bayoneted a German, but before I could withdraw it I was clubbed on the head with a rifle, knocked out and became a prisoner.'

Williams had been previously wounded in the foot. Lieutenant Colonel Gibbs, lying badly wounded and soon to be made prisoner, saw Sergeant Spence – also seriously wounded – gather his handful of men together and charge up the street near the church. They cleared the street, the Germans fleeing from the shouting, cursing men coming up the road at them, which enabled two platoons to retire. Spence earned a DCM for his actions, but was made prisoner.

At 4 pm the battle continued, but the village was invested by the enemy, with hand to hand fighting taking place amongst the winding narrow streets and the many slag heaps that were such a feature of the landscape here. On the left flank the battle had been no less intense. Major Pack Beresford, Captain Phillips and Lieutenant Broadwood of 1/RWK and many of their men were killed. The Dorsets gradually fell back south of the railway running through Wasmes. By 4.30 pm the Germans had removed any possibility of the men still in the village escaping capture. The casualties were high. 1/Dorsets lost three officers wounded and taken prisoner and 132 other ranks casualties; 1/RWK five oficers and twenty other ranks; but it was 2/Duke of Wellington's that suffered the most. The Adjutant, Major PB Stafford, Captain Denham-Jubb and Lieutenant Russel were killed; four other officers were wounded and captured, including the CO, whilst Lieutenant Thompson was to die of his wounds on 14 September. Captain Jenkins and Lieutenant Price were missing and 316 other ranks were casualties. The holding action at Wasmes had cost almost five hundred casualties.

The Royal Artillery had also suffered losses – including Major CS Holland, who commanded 120 Battery. For the most part, however, the guns were got out by midday and were able to play their vital part in the retreat.

The Belgians had helped as much as they could with the wounded. Captain Taylor (2/Duke of Wellington's) was wounded and was then taken into hiding by the Barbier family. In September he felt fit enough to make a run for home (it should be borne in mind that there was far from being anything resembling a solid line between the opposing armies at this stage in the war – that would not come to pass until November). Madam Barbier found him some clothes, money and provisions and also found a reliable man to act as his guide. The Captain set off, taking a large suitcase with him in which was his uniform, so that he could put it on if the situations arose and prove that he was not a spy. He alternately walked and hid through an area that was filled with Germans. He succeeded in making it to the small town of Peruwelz, fifteen miles to the north west of Wasmes and managed to catch the last train to Tournai and Ostend.

Captain Ellis and fifty men (also 2/Duke of Wellington's) were cut off in a wood; in the various encounters with the enemy the group was scattered until Ellis and Corporal Kerman were the only ones left. Still wearing their uniform, for twelve days they walked south at night and hid by day as they were amongst the advancing German army. Eventually a man found them and took them to a priest's house. The priest took them to a Belgian man who had worked in London to act as their guide. Armed with a card from the priest, asking all who could to help them, the two (now dressed in civilian clothes) with their guide set off. On the way they picked up two men from the Manchesters, and continuing their cat and mouse act with the Germans, they eventually made it through to Leuze, some thirty miles from where they had started. There they caught a train to Ostend and boarded a British destroyer, which took them to England, arriving there on 5 September. They returned to France in due course and rejoined their Battalion. The two officers from 2/DoW who escaped were to be killed on Hill 60, near Ypres, on 18 April 1915.

THE BATTLE AT AUDREGNIES: THE GLORIOUS LAST STAND OF THE 1ST CHESHIRE REGIMENT (22ND OF FOOT).

The left flank guard of the 5th Division consisted of 1/Norfolk (Lieutenant Colonel CR Ballard) and 1/Cheshires (Lieutenant Colonel DC Boger). With the two battalions was Major Alexander's 119 Field Battery and Brigadier General de Lisle's 2 (Cavalry) Brigade: 4/DG, 9/Lancers and 18/Hussars. The Dragoons and Lancers took up positions on the left flank, on the western side of the small hill top village of Audregnies and looking out to the north. Allenby also sent them Major Sclater Booth's L battery of the RHA (Royal Horse Artillery). Ballard, the senior officer, commanded the small force. They began to get into place at 11 am; facing them, not more than 3,000 yards away, were 5,000 German infantry approaching quickly from the left, from Quievrain, whilst at a similar distance 2,000 men were advancing from Thulin, to the north. Only 5,000 yards away there were nine batteries of artillery and a further fifteen battalions of infantry coming up behind this force. This was an overwhelming force, the sharp end of von Kluck's scythe that was to drive Smith-Dorrien's IInd Corps into Maubeuge. The British had a real fight on their hands.

The position at Audregnies was a good one. The German line of attack had to come across fairly level, low-lying and open ground to a ridge running north east from Audregnies towards Elouges, two miles away. The fields were scarred by coal mine workings, and the main railway line ran across them from the south east to the north west. There was a minor railway line that ran from a spoil heap in the middle of the German attack line and yet another main line from Mons ran through the south edge of Audregnies. On the left flank, coming out of Audregnies, a pavéd, narrow Roman road ran perfectly straight towards Quievrain and beyond. Some 2,000 yards along it was a sugar factory, a collection of

A rest period during the retreat from Mons.

brick buildings on either side of the road. From there two roads branched to the left, forming a letter V. Initially the 72nd Regiment would attack across and down either side of it.

The two batteries positioned themselves behind the ridge top road from Elouges to Angre, a village a mile and a half south west of Audregnies; Major Alexander's 119 Battery took the right flank, near the mineral railway and L Battery the left, in the low ground behind Audregnies. The two cavalry regiments that took part in the action were in the hollow behind Audregnies at the beginning of the Roman road – 9/Lancers on the right and 4/DG on the left. Their subsequent full-blooded charge would be the first such made by the British during the war. One other cavalry regiment would see significant action this day, when the Germans, frustrated by the flank guard, tried to get around it by coming through the hamlet of Marchipont. They were stopped by 5/DG [1 (Cavalry) Brigade] and D and E Batteries RHA.

At 11.30 am Lieutenant Colonel Ballard began to place his Battalion in position. They were spread out along a track that ran parallel to the main road from Elouges, 800 yards north of it and crossed the main railway line. Lieutenant Colonel Boger deployed in a similar fashion, dividing the line from the left flank of the Norfolks to Audregnies (about a mile) between his companies. They were behind the main road, with some of the platoons following the same track as the Norfolks, which came gradually closer to the main road until they joined two hundred yards north of the village. He put his two machine-guns in a deserted cottage on the bend at this road junction; they had an excellent view over the ground and the Roman road before them. The major landmarks to their north were a windmill a few hundred yards ahead and the sugar factory well beyond it.

The men had no time to dig trenches but made use of ditches and hollows, making them deeper if they could. Because the road undulated, no company could see another. At a few minutes after midday the German artillery began its bombardment; the British replied as the German infantry advanced on a 5,000 yard line.

Almost immediately the Cheshires suffered their first casualty. CSM Meachin (of Captain Shore's B Company) was struck in the head by a bullet as he went to his position on Farm House, some 200 yards down the road from the machine guns' position. Beyond C Company were, in order, A (Captain Dyer), C (Captain Dugmore) and out on the right, D (Captain Jones) – the extreme part of which was commanded by Captain Rich, whose men were spaced out at five pace intervals. Jones would be killed and Dyer and Dugmore wounded during the day's fighting. The Cheshires were taking casualties from the artillery (Lieutenant Bolton and Private Thorpe hit by shell splinters) before they had even fired a shot in reply.

Lieutenant Randall, commanding the machine-gun section, was the first to open fire; setting the guns range at 1,800 yards he opened up on German aircraft hovering over the British position. They were too high to be dealt with by such fire, and the Germans obviously registered their location, for all too quickly one of the guns was hit and put out of action.

The Norfolks received the same sort of treatment. A platoon that was perilously positioned forward of the spoil heap (marked 'collieries' on the map) between the railway line and the main road was in danger of being cut off. The Battalion soon lost two officers killed, Captain Cresswell followed by the Second in Command, Major JB Orr.

Boger then advanced some of his men further forward towards a sunken road that crossed the Roman road, so that they could get to a better range. Enemy shelling increased, now from a range of only 2,000 yards, and Captain Jackson was badly wounded (he was captured where he fell) and one of his sergeants, Walden, was killed.

Because of the lack of visual contact, Dugmore sent men to make contact with other companies and Battalion Headquarters in the village – none returned. The tremendous volume of fire falling on the road almost precluded movement. CQMS Pitt (D Company) saw a section of 119 Battery galloping furiously down the road to go into position behind the company, but it received the full force of a shell, piling men, horses, limber and 18 pdr into a broken mass on the road. With the Cheshires mules madly stampeding, the scene was of utter confusion and mayhem, to which was added flying shrapnel and bullets.

Fortunately the Germans chose to advance in the same reckless fashion so often employed in the battles in and around Mons – en masse and firing from the hip, with only an accidental chance of actually hitting someone. A captain of the Norfolks arrived with some reinforcements for D Company, but the shelling was so heavy that they had to take up position behind the railway embankment. Two German regiments, the 72nd and 26th, were now coming in close order behind the barrage, and were heading straight for the forward elements of the two battalions between the Roman road and the curving railway line.

It was now about 1 pm. Brigadier General de Lisle, seeing the serious situation facing the Cheshires, ordered his cavalry forward. There was to follow one of the bravest of cavalry charges, one of the epic moments of the war. Two squadrons of 9/Lancers, led by Lieutenant Colonel Campbell along with Captain Lucas Tooth and Captain FO Grenfall, charged up the right hand side of the Roman road, jumping the deeply sunken road crossing it a thousand yards ahead. Meanwhile two troops of 4/DG attacked up the left hand side of the road, led by Lieutenant Colonel Mullens and Major Tom Bridges; the latter had been involved in the first British cavalry charge of the war. Nothing then was more fear inspiring than 400 men mounted on horses, armed with lances and sabres, yelling and screaming in a mad charge towards you. A vague idea can be obtained by standing on the Mall in front of the Household Cavalry as they move to or from their public duties – one is more than happy to get out of the way as the sheer size of the force approaches.

Spearing or cutting down all who got in their way they raced closer to the sugar factory, scattering the terrified infantry, who had seen nothing like it, but losing men and horses all the time from the batteries of artillery, firing point blank at them, and from machine guns. The cavalry had met its historic fate with the advent of numerous machine guns, but it still had an important role to play in the war – there was no other land means of transport that could move so quickly and with such versatility during the whole of the conflict; whilst Flowerdew was to lead a full scale cavalry charge as late as spring 1918 against defended positions with vital consequences for a battle.

'On the left of the Roman road Major Bridges was one of the first to go down, his horse shot from under him.'

On the left of the Roman road Major Bridges was one of the first to go down, his horse shot from under him. Kicked in the face and unconscious, he was rescued by two RAMC men and taken to a cottage on the edge of Baisieux, 500 yards from where he had fallen. When he came round he looked through the window and saw lines of German infantry marching towards the village. He climbed through a window at the rear and found a wounded horse and made his way to Audregnies. He was deprived of speech by the blow in his face and was still disoriented and so sat down by the side of the road. Some time later he saw, to his complete disbelief, a blue and silver Rolls Royce being driven by an officer, 'having a look round'. The Major got aboard and was whisked away, thereby avoiding certain capture. He survived to become a lieutenant general, a knight and to have a chestful of decorations.

The Dragoons' charge was brought to a halt in front of the sugar factory – a charge whose cost was awful. 9/Lancers suffered similarly heavy casualties. On approaching the sugar factory they found that barbed wire divided the fields there, leaving them no alternative but to swerve to the right in front of the German guns massed in the area. The three officers (all wounded) with the survivors and riderless horses raced along the south edge of the railway embankment towards the spoil heap workings and main road, where the British infantry lines were. The Colonel and his few remaining men dismounted and fought with the Norfolks' platoon at the workings. Grenfell, still on his wounded horse, found shelter under the embankment. Campbell wanted to get fresh orders and so left Lucas Tooth in command and galloped across open ground and through the hail of steel to see de Lisle. Captain Lucas Tooth remained fighting with the infantry but eventually withdrew his men; his actions that day won him the DSO, but he was to be killed on the Aisne. The cavalry lost about 300 horses and 250 casualties in their day's fighting.

Captain Grenfell was not yet finished with the battle, however. He tried to return to his squadron, which was a mile away, on the other side of Audregnies. He came to Major Alexander's 119 Battery, which had been ordered to withdraw because of the proximity of the enemy. Only Major Alexander remained amongst the officers and some two dozen men, most of whom were wounded. There were no horses remaining. Grenfell walked his horse through the storm of steel to see where the guns had to be taken. On his return, on the track to Wiheries, he found a number of his officer comrades and returned with them. The total number at the battery was now forty and the four guns were manhandled over the fields until they reached the Elouges to Wiheries road, some 1400 yards away. Wounded again, Grenfell stayed with the battery until it was safely away from the action. Both he and Major Alexander were awarded the Victoria Cross and Sergeants Davids and Turner won the DCM. Grenfell was killed at Ypres nine months later; other members of his family killed in the war included his twin brother, and two of his cousins. His elder brother had been killed at Omdurman and another cousin in the Boer War. The military history and sacrifice of the Grenfall family is quite remarkable. Another member of the family was the outstanding comedienne, Joyce Grenfall.

The time was now about 4 pm. Boger's orders had been to hold on at all costs, and this is what he had achieved thus far. The Germans had got through his forward defences and were close to the road. He could see the Germans massing for a second assault on the left, coming out of Bois du Deduit, south of Quievrain. This was the 93rd Regiment whilst to the north, on his right flank, the 66th Regiment were fast approaching. Boger sent a cyclist to Lieutenant Colonel Ballard for his view

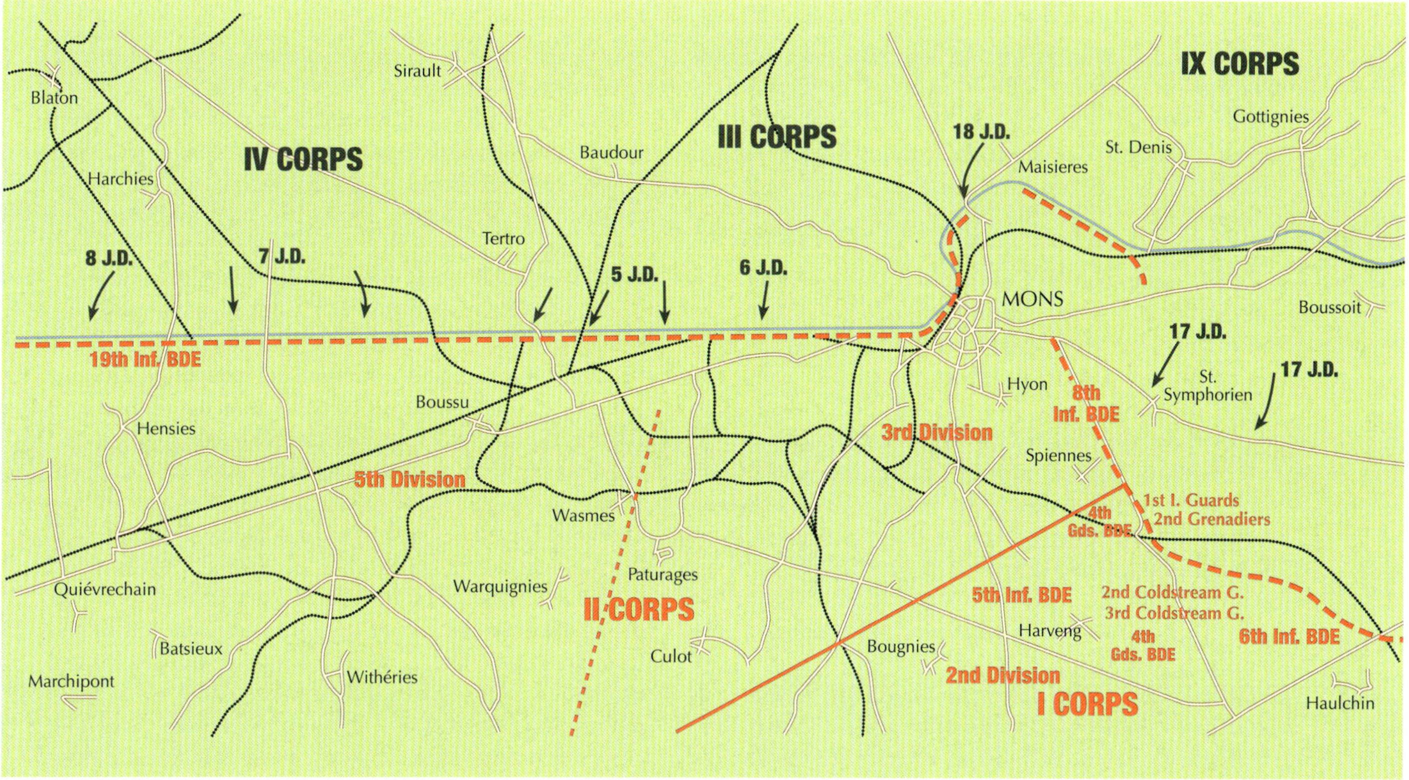

THE BATTLE OF MONS – 23 AUGUST 1914

of the situation – and then three more – but none of them returned. Similarly, Ballard had sent him three messages, informing the Cheshires that as the last of IInd Corps had withdrawn he was about to retire, and so should the Cheshires. None of these messages got through.

1/Norfolk retired. They had lost three officers killed, four wounded and 250 other ranks of whom a hundred had been left behind at Elouges, too badly wounded to be moved. Some of the Battalion was left behind with the Cheshires, near the spoil heap, as they had got detached from their own men and never received the order to pull out.

Boger's Battalion, did he but know it, was very much on its own. The cavalry had withdrawn after their fight at Marchipoint and L Battery had gone with them.

Both flanks of the Cheshires came under increasingly heavy pressure. Lieutenants Matterson (Scout Officer) and Campbell of B Company, who could see the pressure on A Company coming from the other side of the Roman road, took some reinforcements towards it; Campbell was killed almost instantly. The Battalion was now gradually being pushed in towards the village, with the enemy seemingly everywhere. Captain Dugmore, with eight men, retired to the small bridge at the light railway and put up their final resistance. Private Rich of B Company with some of his men and Sergeant Blackwell and a few Norfolks still at the colliery, fell back, with every man for himself.

A Company, on the track running north east of Audregnies towards the spoil heap, was about to retire when two machine guns began to fire on them. Captains Dyer, Joliffe and Massey, Lieutenant Matterson and about thirty men, with bayonets already fixed, charged them; in doing so they hoped to give the remaining men a chance to get away. They actually got more than 500 yards, the Germans melting away from them as they charged. Dyer, Massey and Joliffe were wounded and lay where they fell, with only some ten men surviving. Lieutenant Elliott of A Company rushed forward to pick

Wounded British cavalrymen in retreat.

up a wounded man, Private Miller, from the road, but was shot in both feet. Elliott managed to crawl to a deserted cottage and hid – in fact the occupants were hiding down a well. When the Germans found him and demanded his sword, he refused to surrender it; Leutnant Rogge (himself subsequently killed) of the 72nd Regiment told him to keep it.

Boger, seeing that his position was enveloped on both sides, ordered his men to retire to Audregnies Wood. At this time he was shot in the foot and in the right side.

Captain ER Jones saw some men of C Company pulling back from the main road; he gathered them to an embankment where there was better cover. They had to pull back still further, into the edge of the wood, soon after. He had about a dozen men with him, two of whom were young drummers. Coming across some Germans hiding behind corn stooks he opened fire with his revolver; both he and Drummer Hogan were killed instantly, and two others were mortally wounded. The long battle was nearly over.

Captain Shore (the only Captain left) with part of B Company were seen by a staff officer when they left the farm house they were holding because it was rapidly being destroyed. The staff officer gave orders that they were to go to the rear, where the two battalions were reforming. They kept going until they met up with the Norfolks; they were the only formed party of Cheshires to escape capture.

The time was now after 5 pm and the shelling ceased, because the German infantry had penetrated the Cheshires defensive perimeter almost everywhere and had got, in places, onto the main road. Lieutenant Colonel Boger lay in a field close to the road from Audregnies to Wiheries, unable to move. All about him were his dead and wounded men, but small parties were still fighting all over the battlefield and within the village and wood. At 6 pm all fighting had ceased and the surviving Cheshires rounded up as prisoners, though some hundreds of wounded were left where they had fallen and would have to stay there for some time before help came to them.

Some Germans came across the wounded Colonel and the group of wounded near him and took his revolver and binoculars and broke the men's rifles; but left them where they were. In the dark Boger heard a man calling faintly in the distance and crawled over to the spot, finding Sergeant Dowling, who had both his legs smashed. Some time later a German officer found Boger and had him carried into a cottage; and shortly afterwards he was joined there by Dowling and both men were treated by a doctor. Dowling died as a prisoner in 1917.

1/Cheshire had done more than could have been expected of them and had done more than anyone to defy the attempt of von Kluck's IVth Corps to surround the BEF; they had served to halt the great drive of the 7th and 8th Divisions to the south. The Germans found it difficult to believe that their tremendous casualties had been caused by a few riflemen and vigorously demanded to know where they had hidden the machine guns, as they were sure there must have been many deployed against them. The salient was at last quiet.

That night a roll call was taken in a valley at St Wast, three miles north of Bavai, of those who had got away. Out of 1,007 men and 27 officers who had taken part in the battle at Audregnies, only 192 men and 6 officers were able to answer their names. Lieutenant Colonel Boger's Battalion had been destroyed, but as with so many others during those first months of the war, was soon reformed and 1/Cheshire became once again a fighting force. Its new commander, Lieutenant Colonel Vandaleur, was himself seriously wounded near Bethune, captured, but then escaped back to England.

Field Marshal Sir John French's BEF had gone to Mons expecting to take part in an advance; instead they had been forced to fight a two day defensive battle. The German casualties, even when compared with some of the great battles of later in the war, were staggering. In the Battle of Mons proper, on 23 August, the British had lost over 1,600. On the second day, with the unexpected change in plans from a defensive stand to a hasty withdrawal, there were about a thousand casualties; except that on the left flank, the most vulnerable part of the operation, there were a further fifteen hundred from two battalions, some three squadrons of cavalry, a couple of batteries of artillery and some sappers. The grand total of 4,150 could be compared with the losses of, say, the 7th Division in First Ypres. In eighteen days this formation lost 356 officers and 9,644 other ranks, out of a total of 12,400 who had taken the field.

In the battle of the Mons salient six Victoria Crosses were won.

Then shrapnel is bursting 600 yards in our rear around the steeple of the village church. I distinctly heard the clock on the church tower chime the hour of nine. It was the last nine it ever chimed as it went 'bang' with the next salvo of shells.'

DIARY OF AN OLD CONTEMPTIBLE

There is no denying Edward Roe was a brave man by anybody's definition and yet he made no attempt to disguise the fears he felt at times. He was both shrewd and sympathetic in his analysis of people and events, and gifted with an observant mind and a story-teller's heart. His pleasant and easy sense of humour comes through in his writings and his descriptive gifts give the reader a vivid picture of events of the Great War.

By Peter Downham

Extracted from *Diary of an Old Contemptible* and reproduced by permission of Pen & Sword Books Ltd.

This was recognized by his peers and he became known as the 'Battalion diarist' as well as being in demand as a letter writer for the men to their families and sweethearts.

31 August: At midnight the Battalion halts in a village, the name of which I am told is St Sauveur. Outposts are posted on the right flank and in the rear of the village.

As we are preparing tea, kilometres of transport and Red Cross vans roll by. My Company, A are in supports to D Company. We lie down for a few hours sleep on the roadside and are in a constant state of alarm from 1.00 am onwards owing to repeated bursts of rifle fire on our left front.

At dawn we heard a tremendous burst of machine-gun fire and after a few minutes artillery chimed in. It lasted almost half an hour. We were told that L Battery RHA [Royal Horse Artillery] and the 5th Dragoon Guards were taken by surprise and cut up by a force of 2,000 Germans with a lot of machine guns and three batteries of artillery. The French cavalry regiment which held the ridge in front and acted as a screen withdrew during the night and did not think it worth their while to inform anybody, with the result that the Germans took possession peaceably and when dawn broke the Dragoons and artillery bivouacs were at their mercy.

Private Edward Roe, author of the diary.

Our outposts have opened fire, and so has somebody else to judge by the volume of sound. My platoon is ordered in the firing line to support D Company. We advance at the double under fire and form line on the edge of a mangel-wurzel field in rear of the village. We form a continuation of the line held by D Company. The German rifle fire is very erratic. We cannot locate the enemy as the country is heavily wooded and he has had the

1st Battalion East Lancashire Regiment, on parade at their camp in Harrow prior to their departure for France, 21 August 1914.

The Officers of the 1st Battalion, the East Lancashire Regiment on embarkation to France, August 1914.

advantage of taking up his position unobserved. By keeping up a brisk fire on the edge of a plantation on our right front, 500 yards away, we succeeded in reducing the enemy's fire somewhat.

They have brought some horse or field guns and also a couple of machine guns into action. Quite a number of men have been hit including Captain Seabroke. The inhabitants have evacuated the village in our rear, also the village on our left front. Their shrapnel is bursting 600 yards in our rear around the steeple of the village church. I distinctly heard the clock on the church tower chime the hour of nine. It was the last nine it ever chimed as it went 'bang' with the next salvo of shells. They are now shelling the village, which is about 180 yards in our rear.

My section are on the extreme left of the line so we swing back so as to form a flank facing the village on our left front in case the Germans might work their way into the village and enfilade or surround us. The German shells are bursting well in rear of our line and we suffer no losses from their shrapnel, although their rifle and machine gun fire is getting more accurate.

THE SPY

After we had formed a flank facing the village we distinctly saw a civilian standing on the road leading into the village. He was weighing our position up. He took two slow paces forward, halted and put his right hand above his head. He was signaling to the German observing officer that he was 200 yards over range.

We drew our platoon commander's attention to the civilian and explained his actions, but he would not

1st Battalion East Lancashire Regiment, in France, 24 August 1914. They are seen at a halt on their train journey to join the British Expeditionary Force. On detraining at Le Cateau they heard the news that 'There's the hell of a German army marching around our flank and were in CION there on 26 August.

allow us to open fire on him. We told Sergeant Hall that we were positive he was signaling to the German artillery and that there should be no civilians in in village as all had orders to clear out. It was no use; he would not let us fire on him.

The next salvo from the Jerries burst beautifully in front of our line, wounded six and killed two in my part or section of the line. The spy still stood on the middle of the road, gloating over his handiwork. He was 200 yards away so we determined to shoot him, permission or no permission. He turned around and commenced to run towards the village. Three of us opened rapid fire on him; he crumpled up on the middle of the roadway. We gave him another five rounds each to make certain, or in case he was playing 'possum'. Fancy his damned cheek! Standing on a roadway 300 yards away from a platoon of British infantry and deliberately signaling to the Jerry forward observing officer. Well, he will give no more 'tips' to an observing officer. The sergeant wanted to know what we were firing at. We told him we saw three or four Jerries in the village. It was a good job for us that they did not work their way into the village or they would have made our line untenable by enfilade fire.

RETIRE

They are giving us a pretty rough time. Their shrapnel is doing most of the damage as we have no cover and are lying in the open. Their machine-gun and rifle fire is not very accurate; nevertheless an odd bullet here and there finds a billet. We are fighting an uphill fight as we have no artillery support – not even a Maxim gun. I have not seen a German yet. Our volume of fire is decreasing owing to the practice of two men taking their equipment off and 'dumping' it in the firing line in order to carry one man out. Apart from the loss of fire effect, two lives are being risked, (as they offer a better target when walking) in order to bring one man to safety.

Captain Clayhills DSO [A Coy] dashes down to the firing line and orders us to get out of it as quickly as possible. He told us we should have retired over half an hour ago. The village, the houses rather, are built in one continuous line, one house adjoining the other. He warned us not to make for each end of the village; if we did the Jerries would mow us down with machine-gun fire. He advised us to force a way through the houses.

Platoons by now were just a little over the strength of sections. It was no use retiring by sections under covering fire, as the last two sections would remain there for 'keeps'.

Word is passed along to retire through the village and form up on the road on the Captain sounding a long blast on a wliistle. Meanwhile we redouble our fire on where we think the enemy is concealed.

The blast sounds and the line arose as one man and doubled back across the 'blasted' mangel-wurzel field to the gardens in rear of the village. The Germans redoubled their efforts to put a stop to our gallop. They did not meet much success as running targets are very hard to hit.

BARBED WIRE

A serious obstacle confronted us when we came to the orchards (or gardens). They were wired with a fence of barbed wire, five feet high and one foot between strands. Shrapnel and bullets flew all around us. We cannot get over the wire, we cannot get through it, as we have no wire cutters; therefore we must try and get under it.

The Germans have come into the open and are pursuing us. We can hear strange shouts of command and whistles blowing. A glance to the rear and there they are, advancing in line and firing from the hip as they advance.

'Dusty' Millar tries to wriggle through under the bottom strand of barbed wire and gets hopelessly entangled in the wire. He implores me to cut his pack off, which I do with my clasp knife. The Germans are getting closer as there is no covering fire from our side. In desperation I hurl myself body and soul beneath the bottom strand. I get hopelessly stuck. I undo my shoulder straps and belt and wriggle out of my equipment. I am one side of the barbed wire fence and my equipment is the other side. I shove my hand through, undo the flap of a pouch and transfer the remaining fifteen rounds to my pocket.

The Germans are about 100 yards away. They look pretty formidable in their picklehaubes and bearskin packs. I have got to leave my equipment and Millar his pack as to retrieve either means that we are either going to be shot or taken prisoners. In any case, we should have been shot thirty seconds ago if the Jerries could shoot. We dash through the orchard to the back doors of the houses. A shell bursts overhead and we are smothered in a shower of ripe apples, which fell off the trees owing to the concussion. We did not stoop to pick any up. The back doors are locked. I curse the back doors, the French and the barbed wire.

IN THE VILLAGE

Nothing for it but the butts of the rifles; we soon splinter the back door and dash into the house. We are gasping with thirst; a bottle and three glasses stand on a table – anything in the bottle? Yes! It is half full, I pour out a glass each. It is a white liquid and has a fiery taste. I called it white whisky. We made for the front door; it is locked. Smash a window then and get through to the road. I observed a canary in a cage and boxes of rabbits or hares in rear of the house. A girl of about ten years runs up to the house; she is breathless. She grabs the cage and makes off. Where did she come from? I hope she gets through.

I must get a set of equipment at all costs. There are some dead and wounded lying under cover of the houses, but their equipment has been dumped at the place where they got wounded. Who's this? 'Cockney' Williams. My God! the last time I saw him he was having a 'bust up' in Maxima Cafe in Cape Town. He got hit in the chin and the bullet ricocheted into his chest. He is well bandaged up and it does not seem likely that he will need equipment for some considerable time.

if at all. In any case, it will only fall into the hands of the Germans, so I annex it. We smashed up six of our rifles tliat we found lying up against the wall of the house.

We double up the road to the right as per instructions from the Captain, and join the Battalion, who are under cover of a hedge on the roadside facing the enemy's line of advance. We had to leave our wounded in the village. The Germans have ceased firing and everything is strangely quiet. We can see Germans on horseback in the distance scanning the country with glasses.

The Germans who chased us into the village are very quiet; probably they have no ammunition as they were very lavish in their expenditure upon us. The results did not justify the expenditure.

I am praying hard as I have left eight ounces of Gallagher's Plug (tobacco), three briar pipes, a butler and a Kropp razor, soap, towel and everything I possessed in my valise and haversack. I had no option of course. That scrap left me with an ounce of tobacco and a wheezy old pipe.

Dear reader, don't be under the impression that because I have used up quite 800 words in describing what happened from the time Captain Clayhills signaled the retire to the time I rejoined the Battalion on the road a mile away from the village that it took me two hours. Nothing of the kind, I did it in well under the half hour. The bullet is the finest incentive in the world for making men 'get a move on'.

I reflected on my boasting in Mr Pagan's smithy on 4 August, 'We'll swamp hell with German sausages etc. etc.' Well thank God neither Tom the Blacksmith or my fourteen neighbours who were assembled in the forge that morning could see Roe on the morning of 31 August running like Hell and the despised ferries' running after him. If they could see – well my cup of disappointment would overflow indeed.

GERMAN GUNS AT NERY

The Battalion waited for half an hour on the roadside in order to give stragglers time to come in as all were instructed in the firing line as to where to rendezvous. We form up on the roadside and act as rearguard in artillery formation. As we moved across the plain we came across eleven German guns out of action and abandoned. They are German and no mistake; the double-headed eagle and the manufacturers name engraved or emblazoned on the muzzles close to the breach. The remains of mangled horses and gunners are strewn around the guns, so this must be where the 'scrap' took place this morning at daybreak.

THE RETREAT CONTINUES

We carried on without incident until 5.00 pm in the evening, although at times during the day (or afternoon, I mean) we could see the enemys' cavalry well away on our left rear. Sometimes they seemed to be parallel to our line of retreat. At 5.00 pm a French force wedges itself in between pursuers and pursued and engages the enemy. We reach a small village [Rosieres], with a quaint old church built in the Norman style of architecture, and 'bed down' with the cows, calves and poultry until early next morning.

An elderly Frenchman, who could speak English, told us that an Uhlan patrol had been in the village one hour before the arrival of British troops and had abused (I

German Uhlans entering the French town of Doullens during the great German advance.

might as well call a spade a spade and say that they raped) two of the village maidens. They must have worked around our flanks.

The Middlesex or Essex. I am not quite sure which, are on outpost duty.

1 September: The Battalion moves off at 5.00 am, no sooner are we on the road than we are spotted by an enemy flying machine.

A French dragoon was picked up in the village and brought along by our transport. He cannot walk as his spinal column is injured. He told our interpreter that he got injured whilst charging with our cavalry against the Prussian horse. We think he has had a bad fall as his brass helmet is out of shape, badly bent and his sword badly buckled.

For two days we marched through an immense forest and strike open country on the third day. No sooner do we cross a bridge than French demolition parties demolish it.

French engineers, aided by the civilian population, are throwing up defensive works with feverish haste, and mounting guns. We ask ourselves the question, are we going to keep on retiring forever? When are we going to make a stand? We have had hardly any rest for the past seven days and are marched off our feet. We have daily passed groups of men of various units lying on the roadside thoroughly 'done up' and unable to march another yard. Generals and colonels have threatened and cajoled them in turn, but it was no use, they are 'dead beat'.

Brigadier General Sir Aylmer Hunter-Weston KCB, DSO.

In my own unit when we are a halt at night men drop where they stand. Others crawl into the wood and fall asleep. When we fall in again it is reported that six or maybe eight men are missing. We cannot stop to look for them. as we must keep moving. The Uhlans picked them up I suppose, immediately we moved off.

When we halt for an hour to make tea, we open the tin of bully (between two or three as usual) and get our biscuits out of our haversacks. Three or four of us may be lucky and be in possession of a loaf of bread each, which we 'scrounged' at some farmhouse. The camp kettles are boiling at last, the tea is about to become a reality, when the order is issued 'empty the camp kettles, pack up at once, the Uhlans are only three miles in the rear'. So we have to fall in and eat a dry breakfast as we march along. This scare occurs daily, the word Uhlan seems to be a form of terrorism. I suppose they are half starved like ourselves, and if they suddenly came upon us they would turn and bolt on sight.

The Brigadier (Hunter-Weston) is a pest. For the past two days he has been riding up and down on the flanks of the Battalion shouting *'Cover off, by the left, hold your heads up, swing your arms, Left, Right, Left, Right'.*

Everyone is grumbling and remarking, it's all right for you Hunter, you're on horseback, your feet are not sore, you have not averaged thirty-five mile per day for the last nine days in full pack and almost nothing to eat, if we had, we had no time to cook or eat it. If you cannot give us encouragement for Christ's sake don't bully us, we're bad enough.'

We marched past three generals today. They were sitting around a camp table, flagging maps. The expressions on their care-worn faces did not give us much encouragement. I enquired who the stout general in the centre was? I was told it was General Snow, the Divisional Commander.

As we march through the villages the inhabitants are the picture of despair. What a contrast; thirteen days previously we were hailed as the deliverers of France, *'Long live England, Vive-la-Angleterre'* Instead of defending France, we are retiring by forced marches in the direction of Paris. There is no enthusiasm now, no 'Vive-la-Angleterre' no Tipperary.' No! – nothing but black despair. The Prussian jackboot, Prussian soldiers and the Prussian cannon are going, so it seems, to repeat the performance of 1870. The oldest inhabitants of the villages, who remember that black page in France's history, ask us as we march through, *'Are the Prussians going to take Paris?'*

Our Adjutant, Lieutenant Belchier, wears a comical appearance. He attempted a much needed shave four days ago, but only succeeded in shaving one side of his face when he had to 'pack up', as the much dreaded Uhlans were only supposed to be half an hour in the rear. He has not had time since to finish the operation, with the result that there is a ten days growth on one side of his face and a four days growth on the other.

I shall never forget the unbounded hospitality of the French people on the retirement. the poorer the people the more generous. Had it not been for their generosity we would have to perform many a long march hungry and thirsty. At last we march under cover of the fortress of Lagny, one of the chain of fortifications defending Paris. Someone with a keen sense of humour spread the 'yarn' that we were going to take over the defence of Paris. He could not have perused the evolution of tactics or strategy, whoever he was, although tactics and strategy differ a hell of a lot. Yet a commander, to ensure success, has to combine both. In the field we can manoeuvre, in the first we are stationary objects.

Metz and Paris were two glaring examples of French strategy in 1870. We are told that German tactics forced Bazaine into Metz in 1870. Let us hope that 'Jacky French' wont be 'gulled' into slipping into Paris in 1914.

It is amazing the colossal ignorance of 90% of the

Battalion regarding military history. They never heard of Hadrian, Hannibal, Gustavus Adolplius, Wallenstein, Nero, Alexander the Great, the De Lacys, Macks and Dauns of Austria. Their knowledge of the Duke of Marlborough, one of the most brilliant soldiers of his age, is very remote. They will admit that the versatile Winston is a descendant of Marlborough. Mention Stonewall Jackson and the Valley Campaign, 'Oh! You mean him who plays full back for D Company at Hockey.' If you told them that the Hanoverians bore Gibraltar as a Battle Honour on their Colours and that they took part in the defence of Gibraltar, they would call you a damn liar.

Of course, the soldier is not to blame. As, for example, on numerous occasions on manoeuvres, I have been on outposts [and] group sentries were posted in a bad position by the sergeant. By simply moving a little forward, or to the right or left, they got better observation or a better field of view. They shifted accordingly, but when the sergeant came around again he, of course, noticed that the sentries had changed position.

> *'What the hell are you doing there? I did not post you there!'*
>
> *'No sergeant, but we thought we could get a better observation here.'*
>
> *'You're not supposed to think. As long as you have the necessary brains to execute your drill movements that is all that is required of you. I do the thinking my lads, I'm paid for thinking, so in future cut thinking out.'*

Of course it never entered the sergeants head that even a private's brain and intellect should be as highly trained as his own and that some day owing to casualties, as in the present case, privates have to take command of sections and platoons. The private is still under the impression that he is not allowed to think and naturally lacks initiative.

On entering the defence area, which is heavily wooded, a vast multitude of civilians of both sexes were engaged in felling trees in order to afford a better field of fire. The roads at frequent intervals were barricaded. The barricades were defended by 'mitraleuse' manned by much be-whiskered and rather ancient French soldiers. I believe the French invented the 'mitraleuse'. It was a type of machine gun, which had seven barrels and was manipulated by turning a wheel or crank. They were also armed with the chassepot rifle and bronze guns. The chassepot had a small bore and a longer range than the Prussian Needle gun. The French guns were inferior to the Germans as regards range, precision and weight of metal discharge.

ADVANCE TO THE MARNE

6 September: On the morning of the third day General French orders a 'general advance'. For the first two days nothing of importance happened, although depredations committed by the much-dreaded Uhlans were in evidence in the villages.

8 September: On the morning of the third day of our advance we were informed that the enemy were strongly posted and occupying the high ground around Chateau Thierry. On the evening of the same day, as we debouched from a wood into a plain the Middlesex were well in front, accompanied by their transport. The Germans had a battery of horse artillery concealed on some rising ground and opened fire on the Middlesex transport. What is left of the transport retires, carrying the wounded on their carts. The troops in front open out for attack, we lie clown on the roadside. Rifle fire has commenced. The German horse artillery limbered up and galloped like blazes over the crest of the rising ground, speeded on by our bursting shrapnel. The advance is resumed.

The French are heavily engaged on our left and their seventy-fives are making a tremendous row.

Our line of advance takes us into another wood. The Battalion wheels to the right and debouch from the wood by platoons and in the rear of three batteries of our field guns, who are shelling the Germans for all they are worth. The enemy does not reply.

It has begun to rain heavily and the Regiment gets a cheap bath. Wet through, we are marched to a large farmhouse and billeted for the night.

DEVASTATION IN LA FERTE-SOUS-JOUARRE

9 September: We rouse at 4.00 am next morning and deploy into line in a wood overlooking the village of La Ferte. The river Marne runs on the opposite side of the village. The Germans are wide-awake and rake the wood with machine-gun fire. The Royal Welch Fusiliers hold the village, as they drove the Germans across the river the previous evening.

The Battalion advances in Indian file down the slopes of the wood and into the village street. We advance under cover of a wall, which ran along a footpath in the village street. There were several wooden doors let into the walls to enable the villagers to gain access to their gardens. the thoughtful 'Jerries' had the doors marked and we had several casualties, as they kept up a continual rifle fire on the wooden doors from the heights beyond the river. One poor fellow, Private Roak, got hit in the left side as he dashed past a door. The bullet exploded his ammunition, blew his left side away, and set his clothing on fire.

We relieved the Royal Welch Fusiliers and commence erecting barricades. Houses, which overlook the German position, are taken possession of, loop holed, and windows barricaded. Bullets are flying in all directions.

The village presents a desperate and desolate appearance. It was the scene of a fierce struggle if appearances are anything to go by, with household property smashed up and strewn in the streets. The Germans could not hold the village, but Attila and his Huns could not teach the 'cultured Jerry' much in the art of devastation and destruction. Tables, chairs, mattresses, bric-a-brac, ornaments, chests of drawers, religious pictures, family photos and crockery were

British troops stop a German advance.

smashed into pieces and hurled through the windows into the streets. They smashed every pane of glass in the windows, relieved the wants of nature on bed sheets and rolled them up. Drank all the wine in the cellars. What they were unable to drink they destroyed or polluted. They commandeered all the coffee, sugar, flour and other commodities on worthless requisitions.

The footpaths are knee-deep in broken bottles and occasional dead 'Jerries' less picklehaubes but with bearskin packs. I never saw such wanton destruction, which served no useful military purpose. I came to the conclusion that they must have a corps of specialists for business like this. Sabotage is mild indeed in comparison to this.

British troops crossing the Aisne on 13 September.

The inhabitants stowed themselves away in their cellars when lighting commenced yesterday evening. We were over an hour in the village before they learned that the 'Jerries' had been chased out. The old men, women and 'kids' emerge from their cellars. 'Soldats Angleterre! Soldats Angleterre!' they shout from one house to another across the street.

They went wild with joy. In twenty minutes time they regale us with coffee. They tell us they are sorry they have not got bread, as the Allemands have taken it all. The Germans are raking the village from every conceivable angle with batteries of machine guns from the heights beyond the river. They cannot get us by direct fire, so they train their guns on the walls of the houses hoping to get some of us by the ricochet ofthe bullets. Our men are keeping up a heavy and sustained fire on them from the houses, which confront their position. Our artillery is making it hot for them. They do not appear to have any.

Brigadier General Hunter-Weston is running about like a madman in his shirtsleeves, giving advice and encouragement and finding targets for our artillery.

Our Colonel – Yes! If you want to find him, search where the bullets are falling thickest. It is a wonder he has not been 'seen off' hours ago. He has been engaged all morning seeking out positions where rifle fire can be used to the best advantage. He does not say to a section commander, get your section into that isolated house and make loopholes. You should get a good field of observation and fire from it. No! He goes himself first and reconnoitres the enemy's position and if he thinks it is too exposed and they could be enfiladed he will not send them. We never send a man where you would not go yourself is his maxim. He 'choked' off my platoon sergeant this morning over the barricade. We carried stones from a wall and, in a short time, erected a pretty formidable barricade across the street and then manned it. The Colonel came along and 'played up hell' with the sergeant for not utilizing all the mattresses that were strewn in the street, on the barricade. They would be a preventative against splinters from the stones in case the Germans re-crossed the river and opened fire on the barricade. We could have told the sergeant that hours previous, but we are not allowed to think or suggest.

Our casualties are gradually mounting up, as the Germans have spotted all positions occupied by our men in the houses, which face the river. The enemy rear guard is strongly entrenched on the heights beyond the Marne, and only natural to suppose he demolished the bridge in his retreat.

Lieutenant Colonel Louis Le Marchant, DSO. He was widely respected by all ranks of the battalion. Roe writes, 'He was ever where danger was most. We will never get another Colonel like him.' He was shot dead by a sniper on 9 September 1914 at La Ferté-sous-Jouarre during the Battle of the Marne. He is at La Perouse, some 5 miles south of La Ferté

DEATH OF LIEUTENANT COLONEL LE MARCHANT

We had the misfortune to lose our gallant Colonel. He got shot through the head by a German sniper as he was reconnoitring the German position from the upper storey window of a house on the rivers bank. As the stretcher-bearers bore him past our barricade, we asked, Who was that? They replied Private Jones' his body was covered with a blanket but we could see his left field boot and spur. Don't tell lies, it's the Colonel.' The stretcher-bearers admitted it was but they were told not to let the men know.

That's done it, what are we going to do now? He was ever where danger was most. We will never get another Colonel like him. They bore him into the chateau grounds; he passed from our vision forever. That familiar figure, beloved by all, will never lead the old 30th into action again. When I write 'lead' I mean 'lead' in the true sense of the word.

Well I suppose he died, as he would have wished, fighting for his beloved France on the soil of his forefathers. I am told he was a descendant of French Huguenots who were expelled from France by that perfidious Edict of Nantes.

TRIBUTE TO THE FALLEN WELSHMEN

Our artillery is subjecting the enemy's position to a heavy bombardment. At 4.00 pm we are ordered to evacuate the barricade and man a stone wall which runs along the road some 400 yards in the rear. Are the Germans going to counter-attack? We are told to prepare to receive one anyway.

On the opposite side of the road, to where we are in position, lie five privates and one officer of the Royal Welch Fusiliers. They had been killed the previous evening and their bodies are covered with their ground sheets. On our side of the road lie four Germans.

A procession of women reciting the Rosary and carrying wreaths start from the village and advance up the road. We are dumbfounded, as the bullets from the German machine guns are knocking sparks from the roadway. We crouch close against the wall for cover. Are they mad? They will all be killed. They advance slowly and form a circle around the fallen Welch Fusiliers, cover their bodies with wreaths and recite the rosary, on their knees, on the blood-soaked ground around the fallen Welshmen. During this simple and touching tribute the German machine gunners splattered the roadway and the wall behind which we were taking cover with a continuous stream of bullets. The British soldiers were under cover; the simple and pious women of La Ferte were kneeling in the open and praying for the souls of the departed British Tommies. The sight. I may say, of that touching ceremony, brought tears to our eyes. When they finished the Rosary they stood up and bowed to the dead and slowly filed away, with the German machine gunners still in attendance. 'Twas a miracle how they escaped.

Any of us who survive this war will always retain a warm corner in our hearts for the brave women of La Ferte, who amidst an inferno of German machine gun-fire paid their last tribute to the six British soldiers who paid the supreme sacrifice on the battlefields of France.

COUNTER-ATTACK AT LE GHEER

21 October: After a four-mile march we arrive in the village of Ploegsteert, or the Bois de Ploegsteert. We call it Plugstreet' for short. It is a sombre looking place. It boasts of an extensive and dense forest. Heavy rifle and machine gun fire is on our right flank and an occasional

British trenches at Ploegsteert. This photo was taken in November 1914 and shows the village of Le Gheer in the background. Note the rum jar and tin-cans littering the area.

shell bursts in the village. A German high explosive has blown the end out of the village church and the roadway is strewn with broken Saints. I am glad to meet St Patrick once again, although he is in decimal fractions. St Peters crozier reposes on Mary Magdalene's breast. John the Baptist and St Joseph are hopelessly mixed up. The Soldier Saint's sword is unbroken and Patrick Gates accepts it as a good omen. I carefully pick my steps over Saints legs, heads and arms.

We meet a crowd of Inniskillings coming down the road which leads alongside the wood. They have lost their trenches and are retiring. They inform us that the Germans have broken through in thousands. Not very encouraging as we are thoroughly done up and wet to the skin.

The East Lancs and Somersets open out for attack. Part of my Regiment are attacking through the wood in which the Germans had obtained a foothold. We can barely force our way through the dense undergrowth and have no field of view. Pheasants are numerous. My Company are in support; it is regular hell with bullets and shells. The Jerries have three machine guns in the houses at the crossroads, and are raking the wood. Mr Lewis took my platoon into the firing line. They have two machine guns trained on the edge of the wood and we lose heavily. The enemy held a well-concealed trench in a turnip field eighty yards from the edge of the wood.

When located they are charged by a platoon under Mr Hughes, who was shot through the head as he led the charge. The charge failed, and what was left of the platoon had to lie in the open under shrapnel and heavy rifle fire until two sections of the Somersets worked around their flank. The Germans then surrendered as they had run out of ammunition. One man refused to surrender; it took two of our men to put him out of mess. He was a brave man and we recognized him as

Lancashire soldiers in their winter dress. The goatskin coats were not popular with front-line troops, who christened them 'louse traps'.

such. He was a recipient of the Iron Cross.

At this stage we were slightly disorganized and fighting in isolated groups and were mixed up with the Somersets. We made a dash across a turnip field and rushed Le Gheer Convent with the bayonet. We bagged twenty Germans who were guarding a ration party, which they captured that morning when they were drawing rations. The Germans drank their rum; otherwise they treated them well and were in the act of making coffee for them when the tables were turned. The Convent was converted into a temporary hospital. It was full of German wounded when we captured it and the German Red Cross flag flew from the roof. It could plainly be seen from the German position, but the humane Germans turned their guns on the Convent. What a spectacle; British soldiers carrying German wounded out of the Convent at the risk of their lives in order to save them from their own artillery fire. The Convent is on fire. German wounded first, British last.

Le Gheer Convent just behind the front line and within 300 yards of the German trenches. The 1/East Lancs had two companies in the front line and one of these companies used the cellars of the convent as headquarters.

I witnessed another instance of misplaced chivalry at Houplines, when our stretcher-bearers had to carry in the German wounded on their stretchers. The Jerries had the comfort of a stretcher; our men were carried in on doors and planks. Would the Germans treat us in the same manner? We drove the enemy out of the line of trenches he captured that morning. We dash forward and line a hedge. A heavy fire is opened on us. We cannot locate the enemy as his uniform blends or harmonizes with the turnip and mangel-wurzel tops. Suddenly over forty of the enemy arise from the ground 100 yards in front, throw down their rifles, turn about, raise both arms above their heads and sprint for their own lines. They made a splendid target and the dear boys were also running in the wrong direction. We let them have it. A few got away with it, and the remainder did not. The Boer Commander-in-Chiefin the South African war at the Battle of the Tugela River would not, it has been said, allow his men to fire on a retiring foe for biblical reasons. There were no Jouberts amongst us; neither were we biblically minded. The enemy suffered heavily.

The troops against whom we were engaged were recognized as the 104th and 118th Regiments of Saxon Infantry. Why did we go to war with only two Maxims to each Battalion? Why, the Germans seem to have dozens of them. I'm sure they have five to our one at the very least.

BURIAL PARTY

I formed one of a party who were detailed for burial fatigue that evening. We buried twenty-one Saxons in two graves in a corner of Plugstreet wood. We had to search them and hand all their possessions over to Major Lambert before dumping them in the pits we had dug. One could open a first class jewellers shop with the contents of their pockets; gold watches, rings, bracelets, pendants and what not. Major Lambert retained all their papers, but made us bury all the jewellery with them.

'Heads were bobbing about and showing over their parapet in a most reckless way, and, as we looked, this phenomenon became more and more pronounced. A complete Boche figure suddenly appeared on the parapet, and looked about itself.'

BAIRNSFATHER'S CHRISTMAS TRUCE

Trench life was a great shock to Bairnsfather and he concealed his true feelings, as many officers did, under a puerile, public school approach to the war. It became a team game in which ritual patterns soon developed, so that preoccupation with routine dulled overt sensitivity to the horror all around.

By Tonie and Valmai Holt

Extracted from *In Search of the Better 'Ole* and reproduced by permission of Pen & Sword Books Ltd.

Christmas 1914 saw a lull in the 'game', and Bairnsfather took part in one of the most extraordinary episodes of the Great War, an episode that might have brought him a court martial. It started on Christmas Eve. He tells the story himself.

The day had been entirely free from shelling, and somehow we all felt that the Boches, too, wanted to be quiet. There was a kind of invisible, intangible feeling extending across the frozen swamp between the two lines, which said *'This is Christmas Eve for both of us – something in common.'*

About 10 pm I made my exit from the convivial dug-out on the left of our line and walked back to my own lair. On arriving at my own bit of trench I found several of the men standing about, and all very cheerful. There was a good bit of singing and talking going on, jokes and jibes on our curious Christmas Eve, as contrasted with any former one, were thick in the air. One of my men turned to me and said:

'You can 'ear 'em quite plain, sir!'

"Hear what?" I inquired.

'The Germans over there, sir; you can 'ear 'em singin' and playin' on a band or somethin'.

I listened; away out across the field, among the dark shadows beyond, I could hear the murmur of voices, and an occasional burst of some unintelligible song would come floating out on the frosty air. The singing seemed to be the loudest and most distinct a bit to our right. I popped into my dug-out and found the platoon commander.

'Do you hear the Boches kicking up that racket over there?' I said. *'Yes,'* he replied: *'they've been at it some time!' 'Come on,'* said I, *'let's go along the trench to the hedge there on the right – that's the nearest point to them, over there.'*

So we stumbled along our now hard, frosted ditch, and scrambling up on to the bank above, strode across the field to our next bit of trench on the right. Everyone was listening. An improvised Boche band was playing a precarious version of *Deutschland, Deutschland, über Alles*, at the conclusion of which, some of our mouth-organ experts retaliated with snatches of ragtime songs and imitations of the German tune. Suddenly we heard a confused shouting from the other side. We all stopped to listen. The shout came again. A voice in the darkness shouted in English, with a strong German accent, *'Come over here!'* A ripple of mirth swept along our trench, followed by a rude outburst of mouth organs and laughter. Presently, in a lull, one of our sergeants repeated the request, *'Come over here!'*

'You come half-way – I come half-way,' floated out of the darkness.

Bruce Bairnsfather.

Bainsfather captures the Christmas Truce in this cartoon.

Lieutenant Bainsfather on his way to the Christmas Truce, December 1914, St Yvon.

> *'Come on, then!'* shouted the sergeant. *'I'm coming along the hedge!'*
>
> *'Ah! but there are two of you,'* came back the voice from the other side.

Well, anyway, after much suspicious shouting and jocular derision from both sides, our sergeant went along the hedge which ran at right-angles to the two lines of trenches. He was quickly out of sight; but, as we all listened in breathless silence, we soon heard a spasmodic conversation taking place out there in the darkness.

Presently, the sergeant returned. He had with him a few German cigars and cigarettes which he had exchanged for a couple of Maconochie's and a tin of Capstan, which he had taken with him. The seance was over, but it had given just the requisite touch to our Christmas Eve – something a little human and out of the ordinary routine.

After months of vindictive sniping and shelling, this little episode came as an invigorating tonic, and a welcome relief to the daily monotony of antagonism. It did not lessen our ardour or determination; but just put a little human punctuation mark in our lives of cold and humid hate. Just on the right day too – Christmas Eve! But, as a curious episode, this was nothing in comparison to our experience on the following day.

On Christmas morning I awoke very early, and emerged from my dug-out in the trench. It was a perfect day. A beautiful, cloudless blue sky. The ground hard and white, fading off towards the wood in a thin low-lying mist. It was such a day as is invariably depicted by artists on Christmas cards – the ideal Christmas Day of fiction.

Walking about the trench a little later, discussing the

'Well, if you knows of a better 'ole, go to it'

curious affair of the night before, we suddenly became aware of the fact that we were seeing a lot of evidence of Germans. Heads were bobbing about and showing over their parapet in a most reckless way, and, as we looked, this phenomenon became more and more pronounced.

A complete Boche figure suddenly appeared on the parapet, and looked about itself. This complaint became infectious. It didn't take 'Our Bert' long to be up on the skyline (it is one long grind to ever keep him off it). This was the signal for more Boche anatomy to be disclosed, and this was replied to by all our Alf's and Bill's, until, in less time than it takes to tell, half a dozen or so of each of the belligerents were outside their trenches and were advancing towards each other in no-man's land.

A strange sight, truly!

I clambered up and over our parapet, and moved out across the field to look. Clad in the muddy suit of khaki and wearing a sheepskin coat and Balaclava helmet, I joined the throng about half-way across to the German trenches.

'I clambered up and over our parapet, and moved out across the field to look. Clad in the muddy suit of khaki and wearing a sheepskin coat and Balaclava helmet, I joined the throng about half-way across to the German trenches.'

It all felt most curious: here were these sausage-eating wretches, who had elected to start this infernal European fracas, and in so doing had brought us all into the same muddy pickle as themselves.

This was my first real sight of them at close quarters. Here they were – the actual, practical soldiers of the German army. There was not an atom of hate on either side that day; and yet, on our side, not for a moment was the will to war and the will to beat them relaxed. It was just like the interval between the rounds in a friendly boxing match. The difference in type between our men and theirs was very marked. There was no contrasting the spirit of the two parties. Our men, in their scratch costumes of dirty, muddy khaki, with their various assorted head-dresses of woollen helmets, mufflers and battered hats, were a light-hearted, open humorous collection as opposed to the sombre demeanour and stolid appearance of the Huns in their grey-green faded uniforms, top boots, and pork-pie hats.

The shortest effect I can give of the impression I had was that our men, superior, broadminded, more frank, and lovable beings, were regarding these faded, unimaginative products of

British and German soldiers nervous of the photographer in case of repercussions.

perverted culture as a set of objectionable but amusing lunatics whose heads had got to be eventually smacked.

'Look at that one over there, Bill,' our Bert would say, as he pointed out some particularly curious member of the party.

I strolled about amongst them all, and sucked in as many impressions as I could. Two or three of the Boches seemed to be particularly interested in me, and after they had walked round me once or twice with sullen curiosity stamped on their faces, one came up and said *'Offizier?'* I nodded my head, which means 'Yes' in most languages, and, besides, I can't talk German.

These devils, I could see, all wanted to be friendly; but none of them possessed the open, frank geniality of our men. However, everyone was talking and laughing, and souvenir hunting.

I spotted a German officer, some sort of lieutenant I should think, and being a bit of a collector, I intimated to him that I had taken a fancy to some of his buttons.

We both said things to each other which neither understood, and agreed to do a swap. I brought out my wire clippers and with a few deft snips, removed a couple of his buttons and put them in my pocket. I then gave him two of mine in exchange.

Whilst this was going on a babbling of guttural ejaculations emanating from one of the *laager-schifters*, told me that some idea had occurred to someone.

Suddenly, one of the Boches ran back to his trench and presently reappeared with a large camera. I posed in a mixed group for several photographs, and have ever since wished I had fixed up some arrangement for getting a copy. No doubt framed editions of this photograph are reposing on some Hun mantelpieces, showing clearly and unmistakably to admiring strafers how a group of perfidious English surrendered

On the edge of Ploegsteert Wood at Le Gheer. It was on ruined buildings in this area that Bruce Bairnsfather began his cartooning.

Bairnsfather with time on his hands in the winter of 1914 .

Bairnsfather at work – one of his own cartoons.

Young inquisitive replacement: "Who made that 'ole?" Fed-up old soldier: "Mice!" The Germans felt the need to explain this when they used it in a manual on humour. 'It was not mice. It was a shell.'

unconditionally on Christmas Day to the brave Deutschers.

Slowly the meeting began to disperse; a sort of feeling that the authorities on both sides were not very enthusiastic about this fraternizing seemed to creep across the gathering. We parted, but there was a distinct and friendly understanding that Christmas Day would be left to finish in tranquillity. The last I saw of this little affair was a vision of one of my machine-gunners, who was a bit of an amateur hairdresser in civil life, cutting the unnaturally long hair of a docile Boche, who was patiently kneeling on the ground whilst the automatic clippers crept up the back of his neck.

The Commander of the BEF, General Sir John French, heard about the Christmas Truce, as it became known, and although in retrospect his attitude mellowed, at the time he reacted firmly:

> *'I issued immediate orders to prevent any recurrence of such conduct and called the local commanders to strict account...'*